CW00798044

CONJURE
CODEX
V

A COMPENDIUM OF

INVOCATION
EVOCATION

&

CONJURATION

Conjure Codex: A Compendium of Invocation, Evocation & Conjuration
Content Editor: Jake Stratton-Kent
Art Editor: Dis Albion
Editor in Chief: Erzebet Barthold
Assistant Editor: Brian Johnson
Volume 1, Issue 5
Copyright ©2022 Hadean Press
Cover Art 'The Death of Death' © Michael Tsouras
All interior artwork © the original creators.
ISBN 978-1-914166-31-0
All Rights Reserved Worldwide.

No portion of this book may be reproduced by any means, physical or electronic or otherwise, without the written consent of the publisher.

'The Book of the Archangels by Moses the Prophet' © J. P. F & L. K..
'The Magic of the Psalms' © Patrick M. Dey
'It's All Down in Black and White: Thai Lanna Buddhist Occult Tattoos of Magickal Power' © Sheer Zed
'Sleeping with One Eye Open' © Fredrik Eytzinger
'Τά έσχατα παύείν: To suffer the fate of death' © Humberto Maggi
'Wheels of Divine Influence: The Iynx and the Strophalos' © H. Feist
'Mother, Daimones and goêteia: ecstasy and civilization' © Simone Baldacci
'Isis of the Magicians: the Faces of Isis in the Greek Magical Papyri' © Kim Huggens
'Every Nekuomanteia is a Katabasis: Ancient Insights for Contemporary Goetic Practice' © Kadmus
'Corvid Codex' © David Rankine
'A Sable Passage: Black Light and the Magic of the Starry Road' © J.M. Hamade
'Lodged Among the Graves: Towards A Practical Syllabus of Early Modern Necromancy' © Alexander Cummins

HADEAN PRESS
WWW.HADEANPRESS.COM

Conjure Codex

Edited by Jake Stratton-Kent
Dis Albion & Erzebet Barthold

Illustrations

TABLE OF CONTENTS

WELCOME TO THE
CONJURE CODEX

CONJURE CODEX V IS DEDICATED TO JAKE STRATTON-KENT,
WITHOUT WHOSE VISION THIS SERIES WOULD NOT EXIST.

This *Conjure Codex* brings to a close the first volume of the series; it was never our intention to theme the issues by colour, but that is what happened and so it is fitting that our final number is the black of moonless midnight. Jake Stratton-Kent was not only the driving force behind the *Conjure Codex*, but he has also been a pioneer in changing our perception of what used to be known as *black magic*—the magic of spirit conjuration, of speaking to the dead, of pact-forming and offering, of demons. His work with the *True Grimoire* and his seminal *Geosophia: The Argo of Magic* forever altered the landscape of contemporary goetic practice. With Jake at the helm, *Conjure Codex* began in 2011 as a means of facing and overcoming misconceptions surrounding spirit practice, and has since fulfilled its brief of breaking new ground in presenting inter-related material from a range of traditions. *Conjure Codex* V showcases that new ground with essays by some of the leading scholars and practitioners working today. It is our great privilege to bring to you this black issue, and we thank all of you for carrying the work forward.

the editors

The Book of the Archangels by Moses the Prophet
A Greek Byzantine magical text

Introduced & edited by J. P. F.
Translated by L.K.

Introduction

THE BOOK OF THE ARCHANGELS, or 'Archangelic hymn', is a Greek Christian magical text, possibly traceable to the early Medieval period, but likely originating in late antique Byzantium. This work was hitherto only published in its original Greek form, by R. Reitzenstein,[1] and is here translated for the first time into English. The book consists of a protective/exorcistic invocation against several demonic forces from Greek and Byzantine lore. Its title resembles those of two earlier works that are mentioned in late antique literature. One is referred to in the Gnostic text 'On the origin of the World' as the source of the names of the planetary archons (spiritual rulers) and their uses:

> These are the seven forces of the seven heavens of chaos. And they were born androgynous, consistent with the immortal pattern that existed before them, according to the wish of Pistis: so that the likeness of what had existed since the beginning might reign to the end. You will find the effect of these names and the force of the male entities in the Archangelic (Book) of the Prophet Moses, and the names of the female entities in the first Book of Noraia.[2]

The other similarly titled work is the 'Archangelic…[Teaching?]', also attributed to Moses, and quoted in the 'Eighth Book of Moses' (PGM XIII), an important fourth-century magical papyrus, where it is said to be the source of a series of holy names:

> And as Moses says in the Archangelic [Teaching]: 'ALDAZAŌ BATHAM MAKHŌR', or 'BA ADAM MAKHŌR RIZXAĒ ŌKEŌN PNED MEŌUPS PSUKH PHRŌKH PHER PHRŌ IAOTHKHŌ'.[3]

---

1 Richard Reitzenstein, *Poimandres: Studien zur griechisch-ägyptischen und frühchristlichen Literatur* (1904), pp. 292–302.

2 J. Robinson, *The Nag Hammadi Library in English* (Brill 1996), p. 174.

3 Hans D. Betz, *The Greek Magical Papyri in Translation, Including the Demotic Spells* (Chicago University Press, 1996), p. 193.

The similar subject matter may indicate a connection between all these works, but this cannot be proven before other corroborating sources are found. Strong parallels to our text are also found in the *Testament of Solomon*, which lists demons and formulas to thwart their influence. Solomon himself is mentioned in the text, in his legendary role as the magician who shut evil spirits in sealed vessels.

The text itself is a variegated series of invocations to be collectively written as a phylactery or talisman, and especially designed to combat demonic powers and evil magic. Many angels are invoked against demons, the personified evil eye (*Baskhania*), and various dangers and calamities. It also shows parallels with material from the contemporary Coptic magical papyri, notably the magical use of the names of the twenty-four Elders of Revelation,[4] and the liturgical style of the invocations, though unlike the Coptic material, the *Book of Archangels* is devoid of Gnostic elements. Some parts of the text include demons and evil powers themselves speaking, and revealing their names and powers, just as in the *Testament of Solomon*. There are also short historiolae found here and there.

The section on the 'Prayers of Gregory', which lists angels and their virtues, has several parallels in Jewish magic.[5]

The *Book of Archangels* is attributed to Moses (as typical of many other magical texts), and said to have been given to him by God on Mount Sinai, but besides this brief mention it makes no other reference to the biblical figure. The text ends with an instruction to write the names of the seven youths of Ephesus (a group of martyrs honoured by the Orthodox Church) on olive leaves.

The *Book of Archangels* is chaotically ordered and corrupt in certain parts, but its condition is relatively decent otherwise. The pagination is that of Reitzenstein's text.

I have done my best to edit and polish the text, properly transcribe the Greek names, and clarify obscure passages. I have not had a chance to experiment with this text, but my impression is that it is an amalgam of different (but related) rites, which can be individually used. The wording can even be adapted, and as an alternative to a phylactery the invocations are likely effective when combined with a standard Conjure spell (e.g., one idea I have considered is to use the first invocation in modified form in one's home, burning asafoetida or another pungent herb in a censer between three tealights, as a means of banishing evil spirits from the house, or guarding it against them).

Many thanks to L.K. who did the lion's share of the work, and sent me his draft translation for editing and analysis.

J. P. F.

---

4 Marvin Meyer, *Ancient Christian Magic: Coptic texts of ritual power* (Princeton 1999), pp. 118, 267, 268.

5 Similar lists are found in the *Sword of Moses* and the *Berit Menuhah*.

THE BOOK OF THE ARCHANGELS

Pages 292–294.

Phylactery for the servant of God (NN), which shields and guards thy servant (NN), the archangelic hymn, given unto Moses by God at mount Sinai, when He said unto him 'take this hymn and wear it and thou shalt fear no demonic phantasm (or illusion)'. Let he who bears this phylactery kiss it and read it, in the name of the Father and of the Son and of the Holy Spirit. **BELÔN THABÔR AKANTHA NAMELA LAMBALA ARIMISAI BISAASMA ANALOUM SELEEM DIAKH BARAKHATHÔN BIBATHA KHAKHOUL ABABOUBAR ADONAE**, Lord—and invoke the name of great God and say, 'I bind you, every wicked spirit and every sign, flee from the servant of God (NN) the bearer of this phylactery, from his house and from his children, whatsoever demon may be, either female or male, either coming from wind or one that walks on water. By that name (of God) I bind ye, wicked and unclean spirits, by Him who beholds the earth and makes it shake, **ADONAE, THÔDONAÊL, ALAETH**, the terrible **SABAÔTH, BARAÊTH, ADEÊTH, EMANOUÊL** and the holy angels, whose (294) names are **GABRIÊL MIKHAÊL OURIÊL RAPHAÊL SAMISAÊL HIERAMOUÊL ABRASON XENAÊL ARKAPHAÊL AKHAÊL SAPHOUÊL ABRISÊL EMOUÊL ARMON ZÊKHAÊL METHODÊM BRUZAÊL** and the name of the great God, the living one, the former and enduring one, unto the vast and unending ages, so that they may not harm or enact iniquities or draw nigh the servant of God (NN), the bearer of this phylactery or his house or his vineyards or his land or his beasts, but let them flee to wild mountains and retreat thereat, in the name of the Father and of the Son and of the Holy Spirit, the triune Godhead. I bind ye, the unclean and wicked spirits, who dwell where two and three roads meet, whether (spirits) of the noon or of the night, by the great God, I bind ye, and by His own Son, who was crucified for our sake under Pontius Pilate; He who gave orders to Noah lest mankind should perish. I abjure ye by the great and exalted God, before whom stand countless angels and unto whom the Cherubim, Principalities, Authorities, Thrones, Dominions, six-winged and many eyed (Cherubim), and Powers sing in constant praise, exclaiming 'Holy Holy Holy'.

Footnote to pp. 294: For when the unclean spirit leaves man, it goes to a land without water, seeking rest that shall not be found.

Should any drugs (*pharmaka*) be deposited and incantations bound and left in the foundations of a house, its entrance or exit, or threshold, or in a cavity, or a room, or in dirt or water, or where two or three roads meet, on mountains, in grottoes, tombs or desolate places, or wherever drugs (incantations) are found, or wheresoever they are deposited; so let every wicked spirit, and any encounter with them, be gone and flee from the servant of God (NN) from every entry or exit in this hour, and tread upon the heads of those that sent you or conspired with you, whether he be a stranger or the same, a neighbour or passerby, a sorcerer or a witch.

I bind you myriads of spirits of 990 names of the Church of Evil, who are sworn unto king Solomon, that whithersoever you hear the name of the Lord **SABAÔTH**, ye leave hence. Solomon, who received wisdom from God and shut them in bronze vessels, sealing them in the name of God, with the aid of the archangel Gabriel, he who wields power over Baskhania (the Evil Eye), who stagnates the springs and holds back the waters, who besets souls with hardships and deadly anger; and the archangel of the all-powerful God bound her thus:

I bind thee *Baskhania*, by the great God whom the heavens fear, before whom the land is made barren and stirs, stars fall, the sun hides from his terrible wrath. Tremble and be thou bound wicked Baskhania, along with all the evil spirits under thee, from the servant of God (NN) the bearer of this phylactery and from his house and from his children, remove from him every throe and pain in the forehead or the eyes, from the mouth, from the neck, the shoulders, the hands and chest, and any bite, from the loins and from the belly, from bowels, any inflammation from the knees and legs, from the feet and from the brain and the 365 joints, and from the 25 vertebrae. Do thou flee hence to the wild mountains and settle in the house of mine enemies, shutting and muzzling their mouths that they may be unable to speak against me, in the name of God.

Phylactery for a man and his house: Phylactery of the servant of God (NN), (protection) from everything evil. Lord aid thy servant (NN) the bearer of this phylactery from wicked tongues or falsehood or aspersion, sorcery or slander and from any hostility towards the servant of God (NN). Let them be rendered powerless and motionless like the dead, that they may not pry or speak, or act or slander or taunt, that they may not work aught deadly against me or my servants, and that my lords or satraps may not utter, or do anything guileful against me.

I bind ye, wicked and unclean spirits, by Him who restrained the lions in the pit of Daniel, and preserved him unscathed, that ye obey what I say unto you, and may no longer hold sway over the servant of God (NN) or over his house and over the children of him who bears this phylactery. Thus I bind ye by the archangels of Lord **SABAÔTH** the all powerful, by the supreme angel **MIKHAÊL**, he who governs the human spirit, by

Gabriêl who rules merriment, by **Ouriêl** who has power over health, and by **Raphaêl** who has power over healing. † **Mikhaêl** over judgment, **Louêl** over sleep, **Sikhaêl** over shivering and fever, † **Raphaêl** over pain and suffering, **Melkhoidon** over water and springs, **Raphaêl** over rivers, **Sarazaêl** over mountains, **Samousaêl** over the wooden abode, and to **Emanouêl**, the son and word of our God, who will judge the living and the dead, and to all of the archangels, who stand before the throne of God, **Mikhaêl**, **Gabriêl**, **Ouriêl** and **Raphaêl**, **Enopriêl**, **Barnabaêl**, **Iouêl**, **Tathêêl**, **Melôn**, **Exankanthá Astenaêl**, and by every single one over the hosts, to perform as ye were commanded (to the evil spirits). Let all of God's holy angels, and ministers of his majesty, aid the servant of God (NN) the bearer of this phylactery. Repel all evil from him and from his house and from his children, and grant unto him victory over enemies seen and unseen, yea Lord Jesus Christ, the Lord our God, begotten of thy holy mother, and all of thy saints. Amen.

Page 297.
Prayers of Saint Gregory the Theologian: **Nasaêl** who rules over mountains; **Samaêl** of the river; **Aphemeêl**, of the house (of God?); **Sukhaêl** of the shivering fever; **Iôêl**, of sleep; **Ragouêl** of the oxen, sheep and goats; **Mekhisedek** of the river and of wells; **Agathoêl**, of triumph (victory) and of merriment; **Phlogothoêl**, he of the thunderclap and hail; **Pharmakhaêl** of the bed (or bedchamber); **Sarisaêl**, of peace, day

and night; **Saêl** of afflictions and of those who suffer; they who coabide before God the All Ruling, **Mikhaêl**, **Gabriêl**, **Ouriêl** and **Raphaêl**, by the prayer of Saint John the Theologian and of Gregory and by the seal of fate, coming to judge the living and the dead, our Lord Jesus Christ, and the angels of great God, **Mikhaêl** in the spirit of man, **Gabriêl** of joy, **Ouriêl** of health, **Raphaêl** of pain and sickness, **Samouêl** of precipitation and hail, **Samizaêl** of wood, **Iôêl** of sleep, † **Ouriêl** of vigil, **Sukhaêl** of shivering and of fever, **Aphamaêl** of love, † **Ouriêl** of peace, **Samouêl** of thunder, **Amoikhiêl** of lightning, **Krítimos** of judgment, these aforementioned angels and archangels are the ones found before God. I invoke ye in the name of **Mikhaêl** the archangel, that you give answer concerning the sorcery and inquire about it, whence she cometh and whither she goeth.

And she answered: 'I go forth to cut off the seven sources of water, to burn fields, and to spread dust.

Page 298.
Nerves and bones I crush, empty minds, cut off the youth, separate men and women, disrupt the spleens of children, deceive the eyes, and defile virgins and ruin their beauty, and every sickness I inflict upon man', she said. **Mikhaêl** the archangel, may he exorcise (it) by the Omniregent God, and by the seven-mouthed pit of Hell.

Fear thou O Baskhania, the great name of God; shouldst thou disobey these mine commands, Lord Sabaôth shall dispatch an angel to torment and restrain thee in the Furnace of Burning Fire; I exorcise thee, **STRAGGALIA** ('she who strangles'), multiform one, she who approaches small children, who has iron hands which drag away children and steal them and kill them.

These are the names of the holy angels and archangels who nullify Geloun and any unclean spirit male and female, in the Hebrew tongue: **MIKHAÊL, GABRIÊL, OURIÊL and RAPHAÊL, MANOUSAMOUÊL, ABESABEK, SIKHAEL, ERÊREÊL, IABOUÊL SABAÔTH ADONAÊL, ELIAR, ARAKHÊM MAROUÊL KHÊZA IAZAKHAÊL MISAÊL,** (expelling the breath with strength), avaunt every unclean spirit! As the archangel **MIKHAÊL** descended from heaven, he came upon an unclean spirit who was hairy up to her legs, having burning eyes, and the archangel **MIKHAÊL** said unto her 'whence comest thou, and whither goest thou?'

The filthy one answered, saying to him: 'I enter the house as a snake, as a dragon, as a serpent, four legged beasts (cattle). I wreak destruction wheresoever I enter (or when I leave). I inflict wounds on women, making their hearts ache, causing their milk to dry, the hair of the householder to fall from fear, and again I make them grow (?) and then I slay them. My name is **PAXAREA** and thus I am called. When holy Mary bore the Word of Truth, I betook myself to her, caused her to falter, wonder, and be deceived.' And the archangel **MIKHAÊL**, having seized her by her right braid, and said unto her the archangel **MIKHAÊL**, 'give me

Page 299.

thy twelve names', and she said, 'the first name is **GELOU**, the second **MORPHOUS**, the third **KARANIKHOS**, the fourth **AMIXOUS**, the fifth **AMIDAZOU**, the sixth **MARMALAT**, the seventh **KARANÊ**, the eighth **SELÊNOUS**, the ninth **ABIZÁ**, the tenth **ARIANÊ**, the eleventh **MARÁN**, the twelfth † **MARMALAT** (repeated). Thus are my twelve names, and thy name, Archangel **MIKHAÊL**, and thy name **SISINIE**, and **SINODÔRE**, that I may not enter the house of the servant of God, (NN), in the name of the Father, Son, and Holy Ghost, forever and ever, unto the eternal aeons.

Page 301. _(Page 300 merely has German commentary)._

<Thou> conceived from Spirit, do thou repel all wickedness from thy servant (NN), Thou who wert begotten of a Virgin, Thou who wast brought by the angel, do Thou repel all evil from thy servant (NN). He who hath said 'hearken and pray', He who opened the eyes of the blind from birth, who raised Lazarus from the grave, the immaculate lamb, (by) the names of the twenty-four elders which are: **ENÔÊL, ARNEÊL, APHAÊL, ROKHTHIÊL, BRIX, TRIPHAÊL, BRÍGMATOS, ÊMITHRIÊL, PHTORÔRÔI, SUMÔRAS, NAPHAÊL, ERÊREÊL, ANÊL, † TRIPHEÊL, ZÔXÔBRAÊL, TARXIÊL, ANIÊL, XIPHIÊL, ABNIÊL, APHEDEEÊL, ZAMIÊL, KHALALAÊL, AZAZÔÊ, MAMÔNA,** here then are the names of the

seven ministers: **NAKENAÊL**, **KHIÊL**, and **IÊL**, † manifest, **RAPSANAÊL**, **ATHANESTÁN**, † **Analiptikôn**.[6]

In the name of the Father and of the Son and of the Holy Ghost, as our Lord Jesus Christ walked unto the village of Gethsemane with John, He heard a great and terrible sound arising from the earth and John said, 'Lord what is this rumbling and tumult upon the earth?' But Jesus left John, and spake into his right ear: 'leave the child, leave the child thou daemon who attacks children, from the house of the servant of God (NN). Be still, and stand in awe. Amen.'

Page 302.

… : I, having a holy spirit residing within, hurled her into the burning fire, and not having suffered one ill from her, retired to sleep: I adjure ye, who are half of the generations of the beasts that crawl upon the earth, &c.

Furthermore, write the names of the seven saintly youths of Ephesus (**IAMBLIKHOS**, **EXAKOUSTODIANÓS**, **MARTINOS**, **ANTÔNIOS**, **IÔANNÊS**, **MAXIMILIANOS**, **DIONUSIOS**), upon olive leaves.

BIBLIOGRAPHY

Betz, Hans D., *The Greek Magical Papyri in Translation, Including the Demotic Spells* (Chicago University Press, 1996)

Meyer, Marvin, *Ancient Christian Magic: Coptic texts of ritual power* (Princeton, 1999)

Reitzenstein, Richard, *Poimandres: Studien zur griechisch-ägyptischen und frühchristlichen Literatur* (1904)

Robinson, J., *The Nag Hammadi Library in English* (Brill, 1996)

---

6 A Greek word which implies 'transcendence', it also refers to stimulants and revitalizing drugs, such as tonics.

THE MAGIC OF THE PSALMS

PATRICK M. DEY

The which Psalms, are nothing else, but a means unto the seat and Majesty of God: whereby you gather with yourselves due power, to apply your natures to the holy Angels. —The Archangel Uriel to Dr. John Dee, March 10th, 1582[1]

THE BOOK OF PSALMS constitutes the largest book in the entire Bible. It is a massive collection of prayers, thanksgivings, and benedictions; there truly is nothing else like this book in the entire Bible. Throughout history, the Psalms have been celebrated, prayed, and used in a variety of ways by numerous cultures. They have long been viewed as more than mere words to be recited, but rather to truly hold power in and of themselves. They are, after all, prayers and petitions to God, and they were written by powerful and holy patriarchs. By this reasoning, why should they not hold power?

Consider for a moment the Lord's Prayer. It is a short prayer that many of us know, and have probably known since childhood, and for most of us, it is just something we recite when called to do so. We do not usually give this prayer much thought, nor do we consider it to possess any kind of power. But it is a prayer, a petition to God. Does God not hear prayers? Are prayers empty recitation with no efficacy? If one is a materialist, no, prayers do not hold any power. But if one is a person of spirit, aiming for connection with the Divine, then yes, prayers have efficacy, and God and the angels and other spirits do hear them, and even respond. Further, the Lord's Prayer was given to us by Jesus himself. Does that not give this prayer some power? Jesus was a very powerful exorcist, if not the most powerful, and he had a peculiar connection to the Divine: he was the Son of God, gifted with the Holy Spirit, and spoke for God on earth. So would a prayer composed by Jesus himself lack any potency? Again, the materialist would say a prayer, no matter who wrote it, carries no actual power, but a spiritual person would say yes, emphatically.

---

1 John Dee, *John Dee's Five Books of Mystery*, ed. by Joseph H. Peterson (Red Wheel/Weiser, 2002).

Indeed, it is a powerful prayer. To quote Morton Smith, it is an 'all purpose'[2] prayer that is part invocation ('Our Father…'), part praise ('hallowed be thy name…'), part petition ('give us this day our daily bread… deliver us from [the] evil [one]'[3]), a request for forgiveness ('forgive us of our trespasses…'), et cetera. Given all of this, should we not consider the Lord's Prayer to be an immensely powerful prayer? Why then should the Psalms be treated any differently? They are a collection of potent prayers that were written by great holy men—e.g. Asaph, Solomon, David, Ethan, Moses, et cetera—and for thousands of years have been held in great regard as special prayers that God hears and answers in particular.

For our purposes here, it would be best to understand how the Psalms have been used throughout history by various mystics for magical ends, from the most traditional and orthodox to the most extreme and rather 'ungodly'. We will explore the Psalms in magic from Jewish Kabbalah to Christian grimoires to Voodoo. We will be looking at selections of Psalms in the grimoires, comparing their different uses, and the perceptions thereof according to various mystical traditions.

As we explore these it will become apparent that some mystics have borrowed their uses of the Psalms from older sources. For instance, in *Le Livre d'Or* (*The Book of Gold*, a seventeenth-century Christian grimoire), Psalm 1 is used to protect a pregnant woman, and uses the holy name *El HH.AD*,[4] which is clearly derived from the *Sefer Shimmush Tehillim* (*The Book of Magical Uses of the Psalms*), where this Psalm is used for the same purpose, with the holy name אל חד *El Chad* taken from certain words in the Psalm.[5] Clearly, *El HH.AD* is a corruption of *El Chad*.

In another example, the *Sefer Shimmush Tehillim* uses Psalm 5 to obtain favor with authorities, and in Anna Riva's *Powers of the Psalms* it is used to obtain special favors.[6] We see some similar uses of the Psalms, most likely derivative of the *Sefer Shimmush Tehillim*, in Part 2 of *A Treatise of Mixed Cabalah* (Wellcome MS 4669).[7]

Given the eclectic uses of the Psalms in various occult practices, it could be surmised that their magical use began as a folk practice, and over centuries was steadily adopted into more formal magical rites—as is probably the case for the vast majority

---

2 Morton Smith, *Jesus the Magician* (Harper & Row, Publishers, 1978), p. 132.

3 The original Koine Greek reads: του πονηρου, and literally translates as ‹the evil one›. See also Jeffery Burton Russel, *Satan: The Early Christian Tradition* (Cornell University Press, 1981), p. 39, n. 21.

4 David Rankine and Paul Harry Barron, *The Book of Gold: A 17th Century Magical Grimoire of Amulets, Charms, Prayers, Sigils and Spells Using the Biblical Psalms of King David* (Avalonia, 2010), p. 22.

5 Selig, Godfrey, 'Sepher Shimmush Tehillim', in *Sixth and Seventh Books of Moses*, ed. by Joseph H. Peterson (Ibis Press, 2008), p. 173.

6 Compare Selig's *Tehillim* with Anna Riva's *Powers of the Psalms* (International Imports, 1999), p. 11. It should be noted that Anna Riva (Dorothy Spencer) was very familiar with the *Sepher Shimmush Tehillim*, as well as the *Sixth and Seventh Books of Moses*, as she cites this text and its seals many times in her *Golden Secrets of Mystic Oils* (International Imports, 1990) in reference to Abra Melin, Chango Macho, Gris Gris, and various other oils.

7 *A Collection of Magical Secrets and A Treatise of Mixed Cabalah*, trans. Paul Harry Barron, Avalonia. 2009, pp. 110–122.

of magical practices. It is my conjecture that the folk magical uses of the Psalms were a means to circumvent certain prohibitions on magic in the Torah—who is going to protest praying the Psalms? How could that be forbidden? These powerful prayers must have been found to be useful, and thus we begin to see the Psalms being incorporated into magical practices, whether reciting entire prayers or using specific verses from them as necessary.

Of course, the Psalms have some traditional uses in various religious observances and liturgical rites. For instance, Psalms 120 through 134—otherwise known as the Songs of Ascents, because they begin with the phrase 'a Psalm of ascent'[8]—have elicited several theories as to their use, namely for ascending the road to Jerusalem[9] or the steps to the Temple.[10] Anyone who has ever been present when last rites are given by a Catholic priest will know that Psalm 50 is recited after the Lord's Prayer; or if the person has been ill for a long time, and it is uncertain when they may pass but death is imminent, additional Psalms are recited (Ps. 50, 70, and 143). Then there are the Psalms

8 These phrases are usually removed from the King James and nearly all other English translations.

9 Frank-Lothar Jossfeld and Erich Zenger, *Psalms 3: A Commentary on Psalms 101–150* (Fortress Press, 2011), pp. 293–294.

10 Leon Liebreich, 'The Songs of Ascents and the Priestly Blessing', *Journal of Biblical Literature* 74(1), 1955, 33–34.

recited as part of a ritual confession, commonly called the Penitential Psalms or Psalms of Repentance: Psalms 6, 31, 37, 50, 101, 129, and 142. These Penitential Psalms are significant in the Abramelin rite. Thus, specific uses of the Psalms have long had a place in religious and spiritual practices.

The first aspect we should explore in Psalm magic is when to recite them. Traditionally the Psalms are meant to be recited regularly and frequently. This is such a crucial practice in Judaism that the *Tehillim* of Ohel Yosef Yitzchak[11] (OYY) divides the Psalms as they should be recited either according to the seven-day week program or the thirty-day month program. That is, the *Tehillim* OYY encourages certain Psalms to be recited on certain days of the week, so that one will recite all the Psalms in a week,[12] or, if that is too extensive, recite certain Psalms on each calendar day of each month so that one will have recited all the Psalms in a month.[13] However, the *Book of Abramelin* takes this further by requiring the magician to recite all the Psalms at least twice a week, claiming that the great power these verses possess will give the ritual greater efficacy.[14]

The Abramelin rite is extensive and extreme. If one follows Mathers's translation of this grimoire, the rite takes about six months to complete, whereas other manuscripts of this ritual take eighteen months. The point being, the Abramelin rite is a trial of purity and endurance. One has to be very committed to pull it off. The 2016 film *A Dark Song*, while not an accurate representation of the ritual itself, does illustrate just how extreme and difficult this ritual of calling one's Holy Guardian Angel can be. Thus, having to recite all the Psalms twice a week is just par for the course when it comes to the Abramelin procedure. Further, one who is conducting the Abramelin ritual has a lot of free time. It is a rite that calls for extremely long periods of fasting, celibacy, and general isolation, and so the rite calls for the magician to study, meditate, and prepare things for other parts of the ritual. It stands to reason that with so much free time the magician would have enough time to recite all the Psalms twice a week.

Other grimoires are not so extreme, and most have limited, if any, requirements of when to recite or write the Psalms. One notable example is *The Book of Gold*, in which a number of the Psalms' magical uses must be conducted when the moon is

---

11 A Jewish center for the Chabad-Lubavitch movement.

12 Sunday, Ps. 1–29; Monday, Ps. 30–51; Tuesday, Ps. 52–72; Wednesday, Ps. 73–89; Thursday, Ps. 90–106; Friday, Ps. 107–119; Sabbath, Ps. 120–150.

13 Day 1, 1–10; day 2, 11–18; day 3, 19–22; day 4, 23–28; day 5, 29–34; day 6, 35–38; day 7, 39–43; day 8, 44–48; day 9, 49–54; day 10, 55–59; day 11, 60–65; day 12, 66–68; day 13, 69–71; day 14, 72–76; day 15, 77–78; day 16, 79–82; day 17, 83–87; day 18, 88–89; day 19, 90–96; day 20, 97–103; day 21, 104–105; day 22, 106–107; day 23, 108–112; day 24, 113–118; day 25, 119:1–96; day 26, 119:97–176; day 27, 120–134; day 28, 135–139; day 29, 140–144; day 30, 145–150. In months that only have twenty-eight days, the Psalms for the 29th and 30th days should be recited on the 28th day; for those months with only twenty-nine days, the Psalms for the 30th day should be recited on the 29th day as well; and in months with thirty-one days, the 31st day is a day of rest.

14 Guth and Dehn indicate that it is the Penitential Psalms that are recited twice a week, though the text itself appears to imply that it is all the Psalms. (Abraham von Worms, *The Book of Abramelin*, trans. Steven Guth, ed. Georg Dehn, revised and expanded edition, Ibis Press, 2015, p. 167, n. 47).

in a certain zodiac sign and during a certain planetary hour. For instance, Psalm 61 (60 in the Vulgate Latin Bible) is used for reconciling a husband and wife, and is to be employed when "the moon is in Sagittarius, hour of Jupiter."[15]

For *The Book of Gold*, there is no explicit statement that the planetary hour must also be observed on that planet's day, but traditionally it has been deemed good practice to do certain magical operations on the day and hour of whichever planet may rule over the operation in question.

On the other hand, as has been recently discussed by Adley Nichols, the planetary hours need not be dependent on the day. In his essay 'Disregard the Day and Hour Combo (Elucidarium)', Nichols explores how the different names of the hours throughout the day, plus their angel name and appropriate sigil, indicate that the hours are to be observed, but give little to no regard to respecting day and hour simultaneously.[16] Indeed, *The Book of Gold* seems to observe the same importance of only the hour itself, rather than day and hour together. In fact, this text does not even mention the planetary rulership of the day, but only the hour. Further, it would prove difficult to try to match the planetary day to the moon's position in the heavens. The moon typically spends two and a third days in each zodiac sign, so if one was trying to align the planetary days to the moon's placement, it could take months to get a proper alignment. This may be why the moon's placement is used, as it gives one a month to plan an operation, and then calculate the hour for any portion of the two-plus days the moon is in that sign.

The Book of Gold is not exactly the greatest book on astrological timing as it pertains to the use of the Psalms; that is, there appear to be some errors. For instance, the operation for Psalm 1 states that it should be done with "the Moon being in ♂ or in Pisces, hour of Jupiter."[17] Obviously the Moon cannot be in another planet, and it is doubtful the text intends that the Moon should be conjunct with Mars. According to Rankine and Barron, ♂ should be one of the zodiac signs ruled by Mars, i.e. Aries and Scorpio, or it should be the sign that looks like Mars's symbol, Sagittarius.[18] In this instance, Sagittarius is probably what was intended, as Jupiter is the hour to be observed, and Jupiter rules over Pisces and Sagittarius. However, there are other instances in the text where it is less clear what was intended, such as Psalm 11 (10 in the Vulgate Latin Bible), in which "the Moon being in ♂ or in Virgo, hour of Jupiter or of Venus."[19] Looking at these planets and zodiac signs and their correspondences of dignity, detriment, exaltation, and fall, there is no discernable pattern to give us a viable clue as to what was intended.

---

15 Rankine and Barron, *The Book of Gold*, p. 124.

16 Adley Nichols, 'Disregard Day and Hour Combo (Elucidarium)', *Adley's Magical Art*, 21 December 2020, <https://adleysmagic.com/disregard-the-day-and-hour-combo-elucidarium> [accessed 28 December, 2020].

17 *The Book of Gold* uses the astrological symbols, but for clarity I have written them out with the exception of the symbol of Mars.

18 Rankine and Barron, *The Book of Gold*, pp. 22–23. The original manuscript only uses the astrological symbols for planets and zodiac signs, and they are only being spelled out here for clarity.

19 Ibid., p. 44.

Next, we should consider how the Psalms should be recited. The term 'psalm' implies that these prayers were meant to be sung and were probably put to music. Even though the Hebrew name for the Psalms is תהלים *tehillim* or 'praises', the Greek name used is ψαλμοί (*psalmoi*) or 'instrumental music'. This is indicative of the fact that many Psalms begin with the phrase 'for the conductor' (e.g. Ps. 4, 5, 6, 8, et al.), referring to the musical conductor. Further, several Psalms indicate the instrument to be played, such as the *nechilot* (e.g. Ps. 5), the eight-stringed harp (e.g. Ps. 6, 12), and the *gittit* (e.g. Ps. 8, 81, 84). Some Psalms are explicit in the direction to sing and play instruments, such as Psalm 33:2: "Praise the Lord with harp: sing unto him with the psaltery and an instrument of ten strings" (KJV). And again, Psalm 92:1–3: "It is good to give thanks unto the Lord, and to sing praises unto thy Name, O Most High... upon an instrument of ten strings, and upon the psaltery; upon the harp with a solemn sound" (KJV). Paul considered singing, even singing of the Psalms, to be a divine form of communication: "Speaking to yourselves [with each other] in psalms and hymns and spiritual songs, singing and making melody in your heart to the Lord" (Ephesians 5:19, KJV).

With these examples, it is clear that the Psalms are intended to be sung with instruments. Attempts have been made to reconstruct the music of the Psalms, such as the work of Suzanne Haïk-Vantoura, though many of these reconstructions have been contested and are still debated. Then there are the countless number of composers who have incorporated the Psalms into their compositions or who have composed their own artistic settings for the Psalms, but these assume a great amount of leeway with artistic license rather than academic or archaeological rigor.

There is no instruction given in any grimoire (that I am aware of) or other magical writings that direct the magician to sing the Psalms. However, Adam J. Pearson has written on the subject of bells, trumpets, and other instruments to be used in Solomonic magic, and illustrates the rich traditions of incorporating music into occult practices.[20] Thus, it stands to reason that singing would augment the power of one's occult practices relative to Psalm magic. It has been my experience that greater efficacy is indeed given to the spell or ritual when I sing the Psalms when called to recite them, rather than just mindlessly repeating them like Freemasons do with Psalm 133 at the opening of the Lodge.[21] Something very different happens, not just psychologically, but also atmospherically when the Psalms are sung. The intonations and resonances of the vocal cords enhance the psychological state of the practitioner, but singing also alters the conditions of the space one is working in. I do not know what it is, but certainly other

---

20 Adam J., Pearson 'The Bells and Trumpets of Solomon: Resounding Instruments of the Solomonic Grimoires', *Light in Extension: A Magical Journal*, 5 June, 2018, <https://lightinextension. wordpress.com/2018/06/05/the-bells-and-trumpets-of-solomon-resounding-instruments-of-the-solomonic-grimoires/> [accessed 17 September, 2020]. See also 'Solomonic Bells, Wands & Consecrations (Oh My!) with Frater S.C.F.V.', *Glitch Bottle*, ep. 033, 20 January, 2019.

21 I must confess, when I have attended Masonic lodges outside the State of Colorado, it has traditionally been the Chaplain or the Worshipful Master alone who recites Psalm 133, and it is weak and feels hollow as it is mindlessly uttered. However, in Colorado it is common for all the members of the Lodge to recite this Psalm together, and the great chorus of many voices simultaneously chanting it provides a certain power to its intonation.

practitioners have observed that something different happens when one adds music, musical instruments, and song to their occult practices, as Pearson discusses in his 'The Bells and Trumpets of Solomon'.

The singing of the Psalms does not have to be on par with Bach's cantatas, or even follow a reconstruction such as those by Haïk-Vantoura. It does not even have to be that good. It can be as bad as that guy at your local Catholic church who does the singing of the Psalms, but really just sounds like he is reciting them in a vaguely song-like tone. I personally would suggest at least trying to make the singing of the Psalms aesthetically pleasing—find your voice and give a good sincere attempt at singing something of which we have no idea how it was originally sung.

However, one does not necessarily have to sing. Some may find it uncomfortable or even inappropriate. One could and probably should at the very least alter the tone of their voice to give a more sincere, solemn, and deliberate intonation when reciting the Psalms. The *Sefer Shimmush Tehillim* iterates several times in the various parts of Psalm 119 that the selected verses should be recited "in a low and conjuring voice."[22] While a grimoire purist may believe this only needs to be done for these few portions of this Psalm, it is my experience that the best practice is to always do so, though I still feel that singing the Psalms is the most powerful. It should be borne in mind that the Psalms are prayers, and prayers are not meant to be mindless utterances, but spoken with sincerity and reverence.

As an aside, but important nonetheless, is the term סלה *selah*.[23] There are a total of seventy-four times this word is used in the Tanakh, and seventy-one of those are in the Psalms, thus it is very important that we understand this word. It does not have a literal meaning, nor is it precisely translatable. It is similar to the word *amen*, though amen usually ends a prayer, whereas *selah* may be found in the middle of a prayer, as well as at the end, but always at the end of a sentence. If it does end a prayer—many examples of which may be found in the *Sefer Shimmush Tehillim*—it precedes amen. *Selah* is a call to pause and reflect upon what was just said. If the Psalms are being sung, it is a pleasant musical rest, a moment to enjoy the last few notes, and builds anticipation for the next. So remember, when you are reciting the Psalms and come across *selah*, take a significant pause at that moment and briefly reflect; do not just say Selah and then immediately continue on reciting the rest of the Psalm without a break.

The next mystic aspect of the Psalms to explore is the holy names of God that are derived from them. In Judaism, from the most austere and orthodox to the super-duper mystical, it is believed that within the Psalms are holy names. In the *Tehillim* OYY there is a prayer one should recite before beginning the weekly recitation of the Psalms. In this prayer is the following: "May the merit of the verses of Tehillim and the merit of their words, letters, vowels, and cantillations, as well as the Divine Names formed by [acronyms of] the initial and final letters…".[24] And something very similar is said when

---

22 Namely for כ Caph (v. 81–88), מ Mem (v. 97–107), ק Koph (v. 145–152), ר Resh (v. 153–160), and ש Schin (v. 161–168). Selig, *Tehillim* (= *Sixth and Seventh Books*, Peterson, pp. 205–206).

23 My wife's name is Sélah, so I take this word very seriously in my own practices and devotions.

24 *Tehillim Ohel Yosef Yitzchak* (Kehot Publication Society, 2002), p. vi.

one completes their recitation of one of the books[25] of the Psalms.[26] Thus, certain words in certain Psalms are believed to be significant, and a letter is taken from each of these words to compose a holy name of God.

Let us look at an example of how one of these names is formed. According to the *Sefer Shimmush Tehillim*, Psalm 18's holy name of God is אל יה *El Jah*. According to the text, this name means 'mighty, all-merciful and compassionate God'.[27] The name is composed from letters found in the following words in this Psalm: אשר *Asher*, verse 1; שאול *Scheol*,[28] verse 1; תמים *Tamim*, verse 33,[29] and האל *Haöl*, verse 47.[30] Thus, we get א *alef* from אשר *'aser*, ל *lamed* from שאול *saul*, י *yod* from תמים *tamim*, and ה *he* from האל *ha'el*.

אל יה

El Jah

אשר שאול תמים האל

'Aser sauL tamIm Ha'el

One may even be tempted to construct some kind of meaning from these words that form the holy name, and it does not seem that far-fetched to consider such. In this example, אשר שאול תמים האל (*'aser saul tamim ha'el*) translates literally as: "who | of Saul | perfect | [it is] God". It almost seems to mean something. We could tinker with its interpretation, looking for contextual clues or comparing it with such a phrase from elsewhere in the Torah and Tanakh, as well as the vast collections of rabbinical writings; or we could explore gematria to find deeper meanings in the numeric value of these words and phrases, but this goes beyond the scope of this essay. Suffice to say that I have found no deeper significance of these words, why they are selected to form the holy name, or if there is further meaning in the words themselves.

The *Sefer Shimmush Tehillim* instructs the practitioner to meditate on the holy name while reciting the Psalm (if there is a holy name associated with that Psalm). I myself have found greater efficacy in these operations by replacing the words 'Lord' and 'God' with the associated holy name, or saying the holy name after each instance of 'Lord' and 'God'.[31] This is not essential or even necessary, but if you have not previously

---

25 The Psalms are divided into five books, like the five books of the Torah: Book 1, Psalms 1–41; Book 2, 42–72; Book 3, 73–89; Book 4, 90–106; and Book 5, 107–150.

26 *Tehillim Ohel Yosef Yitzchak*, pp. 180–182.

27 Selig, 'Tehillim', p. 183.

28 Refers to Saul, and is not to be confused with *sheol*, the Hebrew underworld, though the two are spelled the same with minor differences in inflection.

29 KJV: verse 32.

30 Selig, 'Tehillim', p. 183.

31 There are instances in which I do not do this. For example, I will not say 'El Jah Sabaoth' instead of 'Lord of Hosts' (i.e. אדני צבאות *Adonai Tzevaot*), since this is already a holy name unto itself, and contextually awkward to change it as such. Another instance would be 'God of Israel', which is more of an epithet than an actual invocation of God.

memorized the Psalm, it is a bit difficult—at least for me—to recite the Psalm and meditate on the name simultaneously. Thus, I opted to add it into the recitation of the Psalm, which met with great success. For those Psalms that I have memorized and am able to sing and meditate upon simultaneously, I have noticed no difference from saying the name when appropriate.

Let us look at another example of forming holy names, one that stands out as the most peculiar of any of the magical uses of the Psalms in the *Sefer Shimmush Tehillim*: Psalm 91. This Psalm has some standard uses, and even one that is commonly used today amongst practitioners in performing exorcisms, even if they are not aware that this Psalm historically is associated with casting out evil spirits. It has two typical holy names, El and Shaddai, of which only *El* is derived from two words in the text. But there is another use: "Kabbalists ascribe to this Psalm… the most wonderful virtue."[32] It will remove all distresses, danger, suffering, and the like. This Psalm should be recited ninety-one times "according to the number of the two holiest names of God, יהוה אדני Jehovah Adonay." In other words, add up the values of the letters in *Jehovah* and *Adonai*, which is $(10+5+6+5) + (1+4+50+10) = 91$. And after each recitation, the devotee will say a rather long prayer.

Further, Psalm 91 can be used to protect the devotee from pestilence and plague by reciting it seven times each day. The devotee will meditate on a mental amulet representing the menorah, which is composed of forty-one holy words and names, thusly:

וני	אעו	יכע	ויכ	יבע	בשי	אלם	ואא
Veaa	Alm	Bichi	Iba	Wich	Ika	Aau	Veni
בכה	ימי	מהב	ילו	כתצ	ואל	תמל	מיי
Mii	Tmol	Veal	Ktaz	Ilu	Mehob	Imi	Becha
מבי	מיצ	ימא	ומא	ליר	בתו	רתכ	אימ
Aim	Retak	Betu	Lir	Uma	Ima	Miz	Mebi
עשמ	לתא	רול	יבכ	מול'	לכד	עכי	
Aki	Lakad	Mil	Ibak	Rul	Leta	Ascham	
פתכ	רעש	ותת	כוכ	בחו	אכי	שיו	עאב
Aab	Shiu	Aki	Bechu	Kuck	Vetat	Raash	Petash
אוא	יאוב						
Iaub	Aua						
ויל'	אמו	אהע	הוש	הוי	עתו	יהל	אבל
Awal	Jahel	Ito	Hui	Husch	Aha	Amo	Vil
וזפ	הלא	פעב	ביב	באמ	ובה	והו	נשחסלז
Vehu	Uba	Bam	Bib	Peb[33]	Halo	Vesop	Nischaszlas

---

32 Selig, 'Tehillim', p. 196.

33 Selig renders פ P as a Z, i.e. Zeb, which Peterson puts (?) next to (ibid., p. 199).

These holy words are created from the first letter of each word in this Psalm, along with the words in Exodus 12:23 and 28, plus נשחסלו Nischaszlas. It should be noted that this image of the menorah is only composed of the letters derived from Psalm 91, and does not include the letters from Exodus or the name Nischaszlas. Further, the menorah as drawn in the *Sefer Shimmush Tehillim*, or at least the version found in Joseph Peterson's *Sixth and Seventh Books of Moses*, is actually missing two names: מהב *Mehob* and ילו *Ilu*. The version depicted here moves two names (בשי *Bichi* and אלם *Alm*) from the left-most branch over to the right, and adds the missing names into their place on the left. This actually provides a beautiful numeric arrangement, as the outer-most branches have seven names, the next inner set of branches have five names, and the innermost two branches have three.

This formulation of these holy names is reminiscent of the manner of creating the seventy-two names of the Shem ha-Mephorash—i.e. writing the Hebrew text of Exodus 14:19–21 in a boustrophedon manner (verse 19 written right to left, verse 20 from left to right, and verse 21 from right to left), and taking these seventy-two columns to form new three-letter names. We will return to the Shem ha-Mephorash momentarily.

Godfrey Selig comments on the bizarre nature of these words and their incomprehensibility outside the Hebrew language: "The extraordinary powers ascribed to the 91st Psalm may all be right and proper enough, but it is to be regretted that the reader cannot avail himself of its benefits, especially in the last experiment, because all the recorded holy names consist of the first letter of all the words of the 91st Psalm, and likewise of the 23rd and 28th verses of Exodus, chapter xii… It is, therefore, impossible to pronounce this name properly, neither can it be translated into English or into any other language. And how shall we then memorize the first letters of each word of the Psalm together with the points or vowels belonging to them? If anyone, notwithstanding the difficulties attending the use of this Psalm, should desire to avail himself of its virtues, then he must undertake the burdensome task of learning the Hebrew language, or he must write it, and wear it upon his heart as an amulet."[34]

---

34 Selig, 'Tehillim', p. 199.

In many ways, these strings of mysterious words that are untranslatable and appear to be lingual gibberish are reminiscent of the *voces magicae* or barbarous names of the *Papyri Graecae Magicae* (PGM). It is entirely possible that there are barbarous names in the PGM that could have been composed in the manner explained above: taking a prayer and making new words out of the words in that prayer, with the original prayer lost to us and only the seemingly barbarous names surviving. This is beyond the scope of this essay, but it is curious to contemplate such a possibility.

The fact that there are secrets buried in the Psalms based on the Hebrew alphabet is not unusual to consider. There are six Psalms that notoriously stand out for using the alphabet in their composition, namely that each verse corresponds to a letter of the Hebrew alphabet in successive order. Psalm 25 does just this, with the exception of verse 5, which uses ה *he* and ו *vav* together, and verses 19 and 22, which do not correspond to a sequential letter of the alphabet. Psalms 34 and 145 do the same thing without skipping letters. Psalms 111 and 112 do this as well, but a little differently. Each verse will start with one letter, and somewhere in the middle of the verse will be found the next letter, and so forth. Only verse 10 has three letters assigned in this way.

The most notorious example is the longest Psalm, a Psalm so long that the *Tehillim* OYY dedicates two whole days to reciting it: Psalm 119. In this Psalm, each letter of the alphabet is dedicated to eight verses—that is, the first eight verses all begin with the letter א *alef*, and the next eight verses begin with ב *bet*, et cetera. Thus, each of the twenty-two letters of the Hebrew alphabet begins eight verses in sequence, for a total of 176 verses. In the *Sefer Shimmush Tehillim*, each set of eight verses has its own unique magical use,[35] and Anna Riva follows the same format in *Powers of the Psalms*.[36]

Apart from the manner in which the *Sefer Shimmush Tehillim*, *The Book of Gold*, and Anna Riva make specific magical uses of the Psalms, the Psalms and their verses have variously been used in connection with other magical rituals and the making of amulets and phylacteries. There are examples found in the PGM that appear to be derived from some of the Psalms, though these examples are debatable. Two grimoires in particular stand out in making extensive use of the Psalms in their rituals: *The Book of Abramelin* and *The Key of Solomon*.

The French manuscript from which Mathers translated *The Book of Abramelin the Mage* lacked a fourth part commonly found in the German manuscripts. This additional section, Book 2, contains a plethora of simple magical spells one can perform that are irrelevant to the Abramelin ritual. These are spells that Abraham von Worms believed were useful and good, and were not illusions or trickery of the devil. They usually involve writing or saying verses from the Tanakh, and a fair portion of them are Psalms. Since the Psalms were largely written by David fleeing from enemies and desiring to conquer his foes, a large number of the magical uses of the Psalms in the *Abramelin* concern war and defeating enemies.

For instance, and picking at random, there is a spell 'to bring misfortune to your enemy', in which the magician will write on seven wax tablets Psalm 68:2: "As smoke is

---

35 Ibid., pp. 204–206.

36 Riva, *Psalms*, pp. 90–97.

driven away, so drive them away: as wax melteth before the fire, so let the wicked perish at the presence of God." Then they will place the tablets on seven burning coals with some incense. As the wax burns and melts, the magician will recite Psalm 18:40 seven times: "Rise up, Adonai, and let your enemies be scattered; and let them that hate me flee before you." After the incense has burned up, he or she will extinguish the coals with water "that has not been exposed to sunlight",[37] and then bury the ashes at the doorstep or camp of their enemy, who will then experience great misfortune.[38] Such is but one example.

Such examples are common in the traditions ranging across the grimoires, even the spurious *Grimoire of Pope Honorius*.[39] But no grimoire makes a more extensive use of the Psalms than the *Key of Solomon*. In nearly every aspect of preparing for the ritual to conjure a spirit, the magician will recite an array of biblical verses, most commonly the Psalms. Just in taking the ritual bath, the magician will recite numerous Psalms. For instance, while disrobing to get into the bath, the magician will recite Psalms 14 (or 53), 27, 54, 81, and 105. While bathing, the magician should recite Psalm 51:7, "Purge me, O Lord, with hyssop, and I shall be clean; wash me, and I shall be whiter than snow." While putting on clothes again, the magician will recite Psalms 102, 51, 4, 30, 119, 114, 126, and 139—and that is just to purify oneself enough to make exorcised water to bathe in. After this, the magician will then say a prayer over some salt and recite Psalm 103, then cast the salt into the bath, disrobe, and bathe again, this time reciting Psalms 104 and 81 while bathing.[40] All of that is just to take a bath. Numerous Psalms are recited while exorcising water and preparing the aspergillum, constructing the magic circle, creating the quill and reed, the iron instruments, consecrating wax and clay, making the shoes and other garments, et cetera. It truly must be exhausting to even prepare for the ritual of the *Key of Solomon*, much less perform the ritual itself.

Then there are all the Psalms used on the various planetary pentacles. For instance, the seventh pentacle of Jupiter has Psalm 113:7 written in Hebrew around its circumference, and this pentacle is used by the magician to protect them against poverty, as well as to drive away spirits that guard buried treasure and to uncover that treasure. This is indicative of the contents of Psalm 113:7, "Lifting up the poor out of the mire, and raising the needy from the dunghill, that he may set him with princes, even with the princes of his people."[41]

---

37 Water that has not been touched by rays of the sun was a common source of curse water, as it had not been blessed by the light of the sun. The *Sefer Shimmush Tehillim* uses well water (straight from the ground and easily collected at night) or water not otherwise exposed to the sun in the operation of Psalm 7 for making an enemy humble before you, or Psalm 15 and 29 for exorcising a demon, or Psalm 67 for release from prison or curing a fever, et cetera.

38 Abraham von Worms, *The Book of Abramelin*, trans. by Steven Guth, ed. by Georg Dehn, revised and expanded edition (Ibis Press, 2015), p. 63.

39 See for instance *The Complete Grimoire of Pope Honorius*, ed. by David Rankine, trans. by Paul Harry Barron (Avalonia, 2013), p. 104.

40 *Key of Solomon*, II.5, trans. Samuel Liddell MacGregor Mathers (Weiser, 1974), pp. 90–91.

41 Ibid., pp. 70–71.

Finding buried treasure seems cliché, but it was a common concern and hobby in the Middle Ages and Renaissance. It was not uncommon for soldiers to bury their wealth before going to war, and if they died in war, then their treasure was up for grabs if it could be discovered. It was not uncommon to believe spirits guarded these buried treasures, as treasure was usually composed of precious minerals and metals, and spirits are attracted to these substances. Numerous magical spells and even whole grimoires are dedicated to using magic to find these treasures and drive away the spirits that guard them.

Wealth and treasure are, of course, Jovial in nature, i.e. they are ruled by the spirits of Jupiter. So not only is the Psalm and verse appropriate, but also the pentacle's corresponding planet. However, there are unusual examples in which the same Psalm is used in the pentacles of two completely different planets. In the *Veritable Key of Solomon*, Psalm 13:3 is written in the Vulgate Latin (where it is Psalm 12) for the first pentacle of Jupiter, and 13:4 for the eighth pentacle of Saturn. The former is used for gambling, while the latter is used to protect against sudden death and accidents. Thus, we have two very different uses for the same Psalm, and this indicates the richness of the Psalms and their magical uses.

In many ways, we may think of these verses or versicles as words of power that are inscribed around a sigil or magical image. They could be protective words that ward the image in the center of the pentacle, similar to the way that holy names of God are written around the magic circle which protects the magician from spirits during the ritual, as we see in the *Key of Solomon*, *Heptameron*, *Goetia*, et cetera. It is believed that spirits will not cross over divine names when written, thus providing a great deal of protection for the magician during a magical operation.

We can also consider the versicles around the pentacles as containing or constraining the power of the sigils, much like we see in the Triangle of the Art in the *Goetia* of the *Lesser Key of Solomon* (or *Lemegeton*)—the purpose of which is to contain the spirit in the triangle—where three holy names are written along each edge and one more holy name written within the triangle to help restrain the spirit. This is also a method of 'binding', that is, containing the spirit that responds to that pentacle's sigil. We can see examples of this in Voodoo, in which someone or something may be bound by the verses of a Psalm. For instance, Anna Riva instructs that the practitioner should select a verse from Psalm 109 that corresponds to an offense someone has committed against them, and then to write that verse around the offender's name in dragon's blood ink on a piece of parchment. This will return the evil upon the offender,[42] thus binding them to their own wrongdoings. Riva also instructs that to have God forgive you of a particular sin, that sin should be written down, and Psalm 136:1 be written around the written confession, thus binding the sin to be forgiven by God.[43]

These verses of the Psalms written around the pentacles in the *Key of Solomon* have a similar use in the *Goetia of Dr. Rudd*. This is a version of the *Lesser Key of Solomon* that was reportedly written by Thomas Rudd, an English engineer and mathematician, and purportedly an occultist and hermeticist. This grimoire has unique additions and

---

42 Riva, *Psalms*, p. 85.
43 Ibid., pp. 104-105.

modification, supposedly of Rudd's own devising. What is of interest to us here is the addition of Psalms on the back of the seals for each of the seventy-two spirits in the *Goetia*.

Like in the *Key of Solomon*, the magician will make a seal or pentacle out of the appropriate metal according to the spirit's corresponding planet. This seal is to be worn as a lamen or held by the magician and is used to command the spirit and gain its obedience. The seals in the *Goetia* bear unique sigils for each of the seventy-two demons, as opposed to the sigils in the *Key of Solomon*, which are not listed for specific spirits, but appear to be for a class or genre of planetary spirits. Other versions of the *Goetia* (e.g. Sloane MS 2731, 3648, 3825, etc.) have the sigil inscribed on one side of the lamen and nothing else, but the *Goetia of Dr. Rudd* includes a verse of a Psalm on the back of each lamen.

The purpose of the spirit sigil and the Psalm on the back is similar to a relation we see in the *Testament of Solomon*, in which each demon is coerced or commanded by an angel. In the *Testament of Solomon* each demon tells Solomon that they are 'frustrated' or 'thwarted' by a specific angel, and this angel must be called upon to command the demon.[44] Similarly, the demons called upon to assist the magician in the *Goetia* are commanded by one of seventy-two angels of the Shem ha-Mephorash.

The names of the Shem ha-Mephorash may be 4, 12, 22, 42, or 72 letters; in magical practices it is usually seventy-two letters, as is the case in the *Goetia*. In some manuscripts of the *Lemegeton* one will find the *Goetia* starts with the word Shemhamphorash, as one sees in Mathers's translation.[45] Putting the word 'Shemhamphorash' at the beginning of the *Goetia* is probably a scribal tradition. Some scribe somewhere saw a correspondence between the seventy-two demons and the Shem ha-Mephorash angels, wrote Shemhamphorash to indicate as much, and then it continued to be copied by successive scribes.[46] Not all manuscripts of the *Goetia* include this word,[47] and only the *Goetia of Dr. Rudd* includes the delineation of which demon is commanded by which angel. This is what makes this grimoire very unique. As Dr. Skinner explains, "Anyone who thinks they can order around demons, just on their own say so, without the reinforcement and support of a higher authority, is just kidding themselves."[48] Indeed, this is why many names of God, angels, saints, and other deities are called upon in various magical traditions. One cannot command the spirits without the support of divine authority.

Each demon is indicated by its sigil and its name in Hebrew at the top of the circular lamen, and its name in Latin letters at the bottom. The same is done for the angel on the back of the lamen, its name in Hebrew at the top and in Latin letters at the

---

44 F. C. Conybeare, 'Testament of Solomon', *The Jewish Quarterly Review* 11.1 (1898), 1–45.

45 *The Goetia: The Lesser Key of Solomon the King*, trans. Samuel Liddell MacGregor Mathers, ed. Aleister Crowley, second ed. (Weiser Books, 1997), p. 27.

46 See also 'Entering the House of Solomon with Dr. Al Cummins', *Glitch Bottle*, ep. 029, 20 January, 2019.

47 See for instance Joseph H. Peterson's *Lemegeton Clavicula Salomonis: The Lesser Key of Solomon*, (Weiser Books, 2001).

48 Stephen Skinner and David Rankine, 'Evocation Methods', in *The Goetia of Dr. Rudd* (Golden Hoard Press, 2019), p. 71.

bottom, with a verse of a Psalm in the center. Like the sigil of the demon surrounded by its own name, so too does each Shem ha-Mephorash angel have its own Psalm passage with its name surrounding it.

Why these passages of Psalms are associated with the Shem ha-Mephorash angels is not certain. The fact that these Psalm verses are treated like a spirit's sigil in calling upon the angels to command control over infernal spirits only enhances the power attributed to the Psalms, even if it is not entirely understood why.

Of course, the Psalms can be used in their own right. One need not peruse the multitude of grimoires and magical psalters for the complicated magical uses of the Psalms in order to petition God for something. As demonstrated in the examples above, many of the magical uses of the Psalms are derived from the content of the verses themselves, though some seem odd, like Psalm 1 being used to protect a pregnant woman in the *Sefer Shimmush Tehillim* and the *Book of Gold*. However, one may simply read the Psalms themselves, take them at face value and recite them appropriately to one's needs. The *Tehillim* OYY even gives brief explanations of each Psalm, and occasionally suggests when a devotee may want to recite them. Further, at the very end of this edition of the Psalms there is a prayer and series of Psalms to recite to heal a sick person.[49]

Lastly, always give thanks to the Lord when your petitions with the Psalms have been answered. Just like one may make offerings to the spirits or saints one works with as a gesture of gratitude, one should offer a Psalm of gratitude to the Lord—"Offer unto God thanksgiving; and pay thy vows unto the most High" (Ps. 50:14, KJV). Psalm 100 might be the most perfect Psalm to do this and is the one I use most often. This, of course, is not out of line in occult practices of the Psalms. Anna Riva lists Psalm 65 as a Psalm to sing when the Lord has granted the devotee benevolence, and Psalm 66 when the Lord has delivered the devotee from troubles,[50] as well as several others. There are numerous Psalms of thanksgiving, as well as individual verses that can be recited on their own. It is important to thank the Lord in such as manner, as not only does the Lord appreciate it, but it will strengthen the practitioner's connection with the God Most High. God is more likely to grant your petitions through the Psalms in the future if one offers thanks.

Thus, we can clearly see that the Psalms have a long, variegated history and development, not just in religious devotions, but also magical practices. These practices range from prescriptions for when to recite the Psalms, to specific verses to bind a spirit via its sigil, to cursing an enemy. And why should they not hold power? They are powerful prayers and petitions written by holy men and patriarchs of antiquity. The contents of the Psalms have been believed to comprise divine names that can be extracted through Kabbalistic exercises in the Hebrew alphabet, and these divine names possess great power that enhances the uses of the Psalms. Their magical and mystical history and use have proven to be one of the most versatile and complicated traditions, not just in a religious context, but also in enhancing magical operations or being used on their own as a magical operation unto themselves. There is truly nothing else quite like the Book

49 *Tehillim Ohel Yosef Yitzchak*, pp. 183–185.

50 Riva, *Psalms*, pp. 52–53.

of Psalms in the entire Bible, and certainly these texts are a hallmark in the various western magical practices. It is difficult for any spiritual person to doubt the power the Psalms possess, especially in reviewing their multitude of uses over thousands of years.

BIBLIOGRAPHY

'Entering the House of Solomon with Dr. Al Cummins', Glitch Bottle, ep. 029, 20 January 2019

Tehillim Ohel Yosef Yitzchak (Kehot Publication Society, 2002)

The Goetia: The Lesser Key of Solomon the King, trans. by Samuel Liddell MacGregor Mathers, ed. by Aleister Crowley, second edition, (Weiser Books, 1997)

Conybeare, F. C., 'Testament of Solomon, *The Jewish Quarterly Review* 11.1 (1898)

de Abano, Peter, Cornelius Agrippa, et. al., *A Collection of Magical Secrets and A Treatise of Mixed Cabalah*, ed. by Stephen Skinner and David Rankine, trans. by Paul Harry Barron, (Avalonia, 2009)

Dee, John, *John Dee's Five Books of Mystery*, ed. by Joseph H. Peterson (Red Wheel/Weiser, 2002)

Jossfeld, Frank-Lothar and Erich Zenger, *Psalms 3: A Commentary on Psalms 101–150* (Fortress Press, 2011)

Liebreich, Leon, 'The Songs of Ascents and the Priestly Blessing, *Journal of Biblical Literature* 74.1 (1955)

Nichols, Adley, 'Disregard Day and Hour Combo (Elucidarium)', *Adley's Magical Art*, 21 December 2020, <https://adleysmagic.com/disregard-the-day-and-hour-combo-elucidarium>

Pearson, Adam J., 'The Bells and Trumpets of Solomon: Resounding Instruments of the Solomonic Grimoires', *Light in Extension: A Magical Journal*, 5 June 2018, <https://lightinextension.wordpress.com/2018/06/05/the-bells-and-trumpets-of-solomon-resounding-instruments-of-the-solomonic-grimoires/>

Peterson, Joseph H., *Lemegeton Clavicula Salomonis: The Lesser Key of Solomon* (Weiser Books, 2001)

Rankine, David, and Paul Harry Barron, *The Book of Gold: A 17th Century Magical Grimoire of Amulets, Charms, Prayers, Sigils and Spells* (Avalonia, 2010)

Rankine, David, and Paul Harry Barron, *The Complete Grimoire of Pope Honorius* (Avalonia, 2013)

Riva, Anna, *Power of the Psalms* (International Imports   , 1999)

Russel, Jeffery Burton, *Satan: The Early Christian Tradition* (Cornell University Press, 1981)

Selig, Godfrey, 'Sepher Shimmush Tehillim', in *Sixth and Seventh Books of Moses*, ed. by Joseph H. Peterson (Ibis Press, 2008)

Skinner, Stephen and David Rankine, *The Goetia of Dr. Rudd: The Angels & Demons of Liber Malorum Spirituum Seu Goetia Lemegeton Clavicula Salomonis* (Golden Hoard Press, 2019)

Smith, Morton, *Jesus the Magician* (Harper & Row, 1978)

von Worms, Abraham, *The Book of Abramelin*, trans. by Steven Guth, ed. by Georg Dehn, revised and expanded edition (Ibis Press, 2015)

It's All Down in Black and White

Thai Lanna Buddhist Occult Tattoos of Magical Power

Sheer Zed

"In Borneo, the Philippines and Indonesia, several tribes maintain traditions of spiritual tattoos. '*A man without tattoos is invisible to the gods.*' says an Iban proverb in Borneo." – *Sacred Tattoos of Thailand: Exploring the Magic, Masters and Mystery of Sak Yant* by Joe Cummings and Dan White (2012)

"Once the Yant is complete, the tattoo must be consecrated. During the consecration ceremony the master recites a magical sequence of syllables and evokes the spirit of the Yantra, asking it to enter and possess the characters of the tattoo. This spirit may belong to a Ruesi, a god, a hero, a monk or to a deceased master." – *Thai Magic Tattoos: The Art and Influence of Sak Yant* by Isabel Azevedo Drouyer and René Drouyer (2013)

"Both sexes print their bodies, Tattow as it is called in their language. This is done by inlaying the colour of Black under their skins in such a manner as to be indelible." – *Journal During his First Voyage: 1768-71* by Captain James Cook

PAIN IS A GATEWAY to another dimension. As a practicing shaman, pain has featured naturally throughout my life. Emotional and physical pain is something that we all experience. However, it is how we cope with and endure pain that separates us. Some people are totally detached and can take the needle easily, while others scream long before it has gone into the flesh. By willingly and humbly entering into pain to receive its teaching, we don't just transcend that pain but acquire access to higher realms wherein spirit dwells. The mark left by a tattoo, much like the scars from life events upon your mind, can be of great assistance when traversing new and unfamiliar territory. Tattoos and their application have always been a sacred and ancient ordeal of sacrificial courage, rite of passage, and initiation.

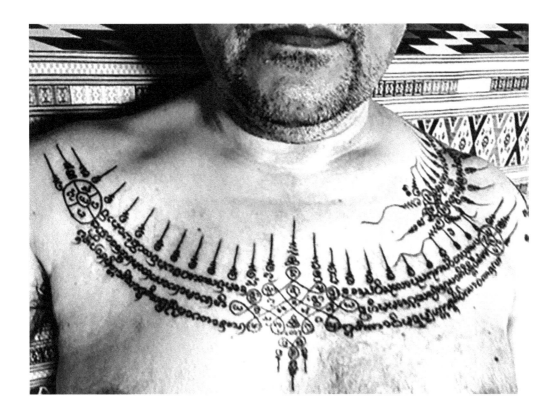

The Thai word *sak* (originally loaned from the Khmer word meaning 'tattoo') means 'to tap', while the word *yant*, derived from the Sanskrit word Yantra, means literally 'machine' or 'contraption', a divine mystical diagram rich with occult meanings. *Sak yoan* is the Khmer term for 'yantra tattoo'. References to sacred tattoos date back to second century Chinese records of the Cambodian Funan kingdom located around the Mekong Delta from first to seventh centuries. It is accepted however that the Cambodian tattoo tradition can be traced from Northern Thailand. In the fourth century CE Chinese records refer to the tattooed P'u people on their southern borders as wearing 'skin garments'. Sak Yant can use Kham Meuang, Dua Tham, Tai Yai, Burmese, Khmer or Khom script to write Buddhist Sutras and other sublime hybrid spells using the Pali Sanskrit alphabet. Some consider Khmer to be the most powerful, though this is completely dependent on the practitioner and their skill. Only the Ajarn themselves knows where the true power of the Sak Yant is hidden. An *Ajarn* is a Thai language term, which translates as 'professor' or 'teacher'. It is derived from the Pali word *ācariya*, and is a term of respect, similar in meaning to the Japanese *sensei*. Ajarn is a term that I personally recognize as meaning 'magician'. Sak Yant have the power to create defence against sickness, possession, injury, sorcery, and magical attack, and are often called 'medicine'. Sometimes letters are inserted into squares and can be read in various directions; sometimes syllables are omitted, at other times they are added. Each Ajarn has the capacity and ability of encrypting their Sak Yant designs to work on many hidden levels. A Sak Yant like a sigil is a spell hidden in plain sight. In Tantric Buddhism, the human body, through a series of ritual practices, is re-imagined as a mandala. Body mandala is a form of tantric technology. Sak Yant tattoos are visible tantric magical technology providing a physical map of one's mastery, magical ability, and supernatural protection.

In ancient Thai Buddhist society extensive *Sak Yant* from at least waist to knee was customary among soldiers, the layering of which would create a magical barrier through which evil spirits could not penetrate. Being tattooed gives a certain status, depending on the extent and pain endured during the application of the tattoos. Those without Sak Yant were labelled 'unripe' or 'not cooked'. I have so far in total experienced eight separate rituals pertaining to Sak Yant. Sak Yant is a tattoo of profound magical power and can only be applied by a fully realized and recognized master of the art.

It is quite simply impossible to receive Sak Yant from a regular uninitiated tattoo artist who has not received the transmission of wisdom, techniques, and training of an authentic Sak Yant master. The training can take anywhere from seven years to a lifetime for more specific *wicha*, the knowledge of the magical practices from a specific and unbroken lineage of masters. The wicha is the tattoo's source of power, which can encompass a myriad of designs, sacred spells, types of ink, the ingredients of the ink, techniques of application (time, location, and precise astrological positionings), verses chanted to control spirits, and the supernatural powers summoned at the beginning, during, and at the end of application of the tattoo. Anyone attempting to receive Sak Yant from an uninitiated master or copyist is acquiring a hollow, empty, and completely pointless set of tattooed ink drawings that are devoid of any meaning, magical functionality, supernatural power, or transmitted spiritual divine essence. The lights are on but nobody and absolutely nothing is at home. Generally tattoos are remarkable and sublime art forms of body modification. They convey countless incredible visions, meanings, and associations. However, when it comes to Sak Yant and these very highly specific forms of tattooing, there can be absolutely no substitute whatsoever for an authentic and bona fide master giving and bestowing the power and magic contained within these remarkable multidimensional sigils.

Since the mid 1980s, with my interest with the Beat Poets and their love of Zen Buddhism, I have been on an inexorable pathway. One day my mother brought home a sculpture from her class. It was Buddha. I was fascinated by the shape, not just the shape of the statue she'd sculpted but also the shapeless shape of the philosophy surrounding it. In the early 1990s I became interested in Nichiren Buddhism, which is a branch of Mahayana Buddhism based on the teachings of the thirteenth century Japanese Buddhist priest Nichiren and is one of the Kamakura Buddhism schools. After five years I moved away from this branch, going further into textual studies of Tibetan Buddhism. Chanting mantras has been the core focus throughout my life (with the odd class studying the art and techniques of Tibetan over-toning). During my childhood I experienced numerous instances of leaving my body. It has taken me a very long time to assimilate, process, and learn to work with this. I came out of the shamanic closet so to speak roughly a few years ago. Throughout my life of fifty-five years there have been countless inexplicable, and one could say esoteric experiences relating to otherness that have led me up to this point in time. I work and commune with over thirty to forty spirit entities and guides which a medium and various clairvoyants have helped me to identify over the years. My ongoing personal relationship with katas (mantras), amulets, rituals, practices, and deities are deeply satisfying and in a constant state of evolutionary development.

I move through different realms and states of consciousness without the aid of drugs, though I have in my life absorbed considerable amounts of various organic and non-organic forms. As a friend once said to me, "Once you open the doors of perception there's no closing them, they're just flapping in the wind." However, such pursuits are now pretty much an anathema to me due to a life-changing event that occurred in Thailand.

My first visit to meet Peter Jenx, author and photographer of The Thai Occult book series in Thailand, was in late September 2017. Peter offered to me a Phuang Malai, the traditional Thai flower garland which is often given as an offering to visitors as a visual symbol of honouring, love, and generosity which was both humbling and touching. I had come to know Peter in the Coil Facebook group as we both share a love and admiration of the group Coil and the artists associated with it. He had recreated some Coil badges that were sourced by the same producer that Peter Christopherson (Uncle Sleazy) had used. Peter was a close friend and business associate of Uncle Sleazy and a Psychic TV tour manager, which was initially unbeknownst to me. I bought both editions of these rather lovely sets of badges and still treasure them to this day. (I collect badges. It's a fetish thing with me.) Then Peter produced a set of two very beautiful small Thai Buddhist statuette items, a Paladkik Monkey amulet and a Garuda or Phra Khrut Pha, meaning 'Garuda, the vehicle (of Vishnu)' as they are known as in Thailand, that were originally earmarked for an earlier release from Uncle Sleazy but sadly never materialized. My animist sensibilities had been piqued by Peter's creative and inventive manifestations and his thoughtful and praiseworthy collectibles. Peter friended me on

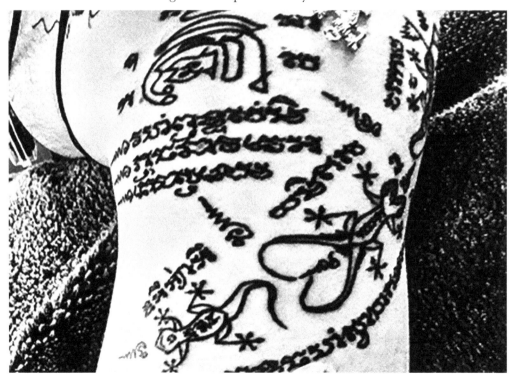

Facebook, and later on I joined his Thai Occult Book page. To say the least, I am not the same man that stepped off the plane in Bangkok airport.

On the 22nd of September 2017, after a hair-raising and extremely challenging journey via bus and then pillion on a motorbike alongside Peter Jenx through flooded villages, motorways, and rampant Thai countryside, fifty miles outside of Bangkok I visited the magnificent Wat Sanomlao, the last temple founded by Luang Phor Pina (1st March 1913 – 13th November 2002) a recognised Buddhist *arhant*.

I clearly remember during this eventful ride seeing a baby seated happily in a basket on the front of a motorbike riding along with its mother who was coming down the access road of a motorway the wrong way. Such is the casual and everyday constant chaos of Thailand. An arhant (Sanskrit: 'one who is worthy'), or Pali arahant, in Buddhism is a perfected person, one who has gained insight into the true nature of existence and has achieved spiritual enlightenment. The arhant, having freed themselves from the bonds of desire, will not be reborn. While at Luang Phor Pina's temple a very strange and bizarre occurrence happened. After I had made obeisance (bowing on the floor three times), I decided to purchase one of his famous amulets, the remarkable Dao Star, which is said to bring good fortune and realign the fate of the person wearing it. While outside taking a break for some water it happened. The voice spoke. I looked around. There was myself, my guide Peter and nobody else. The voice said very clearly and pointedly inside my head: *"You have led a dissolute life but now it will be better."*

The true impact of this statement from whom I believe to be Luang Phor Pina himself only made its full force known when I was back in Bangkok. At night in my Ari district hotel room, I suddenly became indignant and upset, my ego fighting long and hard against the words I'd heard in my head. I then decided to try to understand what exactly 'dissolute' meant, since I wished to be one hundred percent certain of its full meaning. One by one I slowly checked off the definitions online as I found out the word 'dissolute' is in fact an umbrella term, which means many things. No, that's not me. No, that's not me. Oh, this one though. Hmmm. No, that's not me…oh, this one though, that's me. There were indeed terms within 'dissolute' that did apply to me. Luang Phor Pina was right. I felt ashamed and then concurred and decided to change my life there and then. It was in Chiang Mai however that crisis point was reached and my ego and my strong resistance to change were challenged and fully confronted. I received my very first Sak Yant from Ajarn Nanting in September 2017. Ajarn Nanting has had twenty-eight masters pass on their profound magical knowledge to him. Using the traditional Sak Yant rod, Ajarn Nanting applied an invisible tattoo made up of secret herbs and oils to my upper back, dedicated to the magnificent Thai and Burmese deity Mae Surasatee, the deva that rides a swan. She is the deity of Buddhist scriptures, knowledge, and music.

The experience was a painful, electric, intense, and an extremely powerful encounter. The design was tattooed or indeed tapped with the rod onto my upper back over a period of twenty minutes, but time seemed to slip and my mind, as in all extreme rituals, went into another realm, another place. Afterwards the extraordinary Ajarn Nanting, sorcerer and undertaker par excellence said, *"This Sak Yant will help you to feel lifted."*

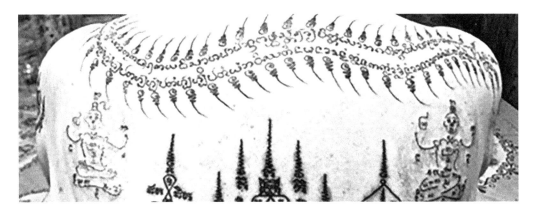

Lifted? My entire being was elevated. I soared high as a kite. My whole core had been subjected to a feeling that is akin to being placed directly into the mainframe of a central electric generator. I was flowing with infinite vibrations, holding the bliss of knowing that my dreams, which were requested by Ajarn Nanting to be held in my mind during the ritual, were to be made real during my lifetime. Three gold leaves were then placed upon the Sak Yant during the final blessing ceremony. In January 2020 Ajarn Nanting gave me two permanent ink Mae Surasatee Sak Yants on my left and right shoulders in solid black ink. These two exactly similar ancient designs reflect numerous qualities that work together in tandem as a pair. The application of these two ancient Sak Yants in front of his shrine was then finished off with a blessing which took place underneath a sacred deep red cloth rich with diagrams, symbols, and delicate images dedicated to Mae Surasatee. Then a skull hat was placed on top of this cloth upon my head. It was a rather ornate and beautifully red initiation skull hat that resembled dragon's scales. Red sequins and gold trimmed lining threaded this one-of-a-kind headwear. It had the vague look of a Tibetan Lama Buddhist headwear, though it was much shorter and far more highly decorated.

The first two Sak Yants bestowed to me from the mighty Ajarn Daeng occurred in September 2018. Ajarn Daeng became a temple boy aged twelve and then became a novice monk for nearly ten years. His superb and almost laser-guided services are very highly sought after by practitioners, temples, and students alike. He has spent his entire life absorbing and learning Sak Yant spells and incantations from numerous masters. My first Sak Yant from this great master was the Yant Phra Lak Na Thong which is a modern version of the Golden Face Phra Laks design. It uses the Heart Kata of Lersi in its face invoking great charm, popularity, protection, and wisdom. Phra Lak is a major character in the Ramakien, literally 'Glory of Rama', one of Thailand's epics from its literary canon, deriving from the Buddhist Dasaratha Jataka. His name derives from the Sanskrit 'Lakshmana', meaning 'he who has the signs of fortune or auspiciousness'. Lakshmana, who is described as the incarnation of Shesha, is the thousand-headed Naga upon whom rests Lord Vishnu in the primordial ocean of milk (Kshirasagara), a powerful warrior or The Perfect Man as personified by Rama. The sporadic use of the colour red in the Yant Phra Lak Na Thong symbolizes the consistent ability to regenerate in any given situation.

The second Sak Yant was the animist-inspired Yant Takaab or 'Centipede of Luck', which refers to the local belief that centipedes bring luck, protection, and good fortune. The centipede can also bring authority to the bearer. If you think a centipede is of little consequence, you haven't seen one in Thailand. Vietnamese Centipedes (Scolopendra subspinipes), Chinese Red Headed Centipedes, and Asian Forest Centipedes can often grow to ten to twelve inches long with a bite which is said to be excruciatingly painful and worse than a snake's. Some people suffer more adverse effects such as breathing difficulties and a rapid heartbeat. As for Yant Takaab itself, the two tentacles have been said to represent appreciation, the two tails to represent patience, the two pincers to represent conscience, and the two eyes to represent gratefulness. I very clearly remember the day I acquired these first two solid ink Sak Yants from Ajarn Daeng almost as if it was only just yesterday. An unbreakable bond of timelessness is created when the devotee and master form a union through the ritual of Sak Yant. The Buddhist teaching that is transmitted is a lesson for life and countless lifetimes thereafter, beyond the flesh and into divine realms of holy emptiness.

During September 2018 I travelled several hundred miles within Thailand to meet the powerful and remarkable Ajarn Apichai. I first met Ajarn Apichai in September 2017 when he performed two life-changing rituals for me: The Kasin Fai (a fireball is directed by the Ajarn towards the devotee while they are underneath a sheet to remove evil spirits) and the Na Naa Thong Ritual or 'gold face blessing' (all unhappiness and ill-fortune is removed by having gold leaf slammed into different areas around the body).

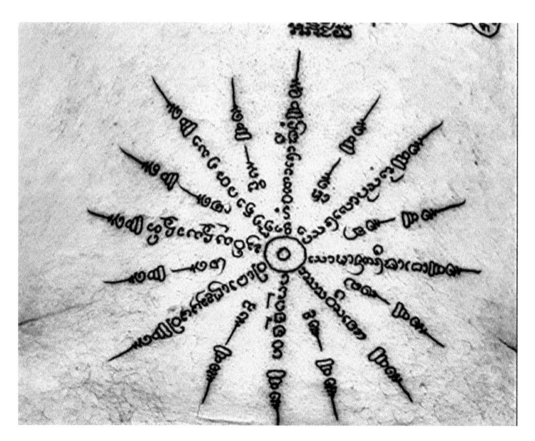

Sak Yant tattoos can offer the bearer powerful magickal protection along with many other sublime benefits. Countless instances of this form have been recorded throughout Southeast Asia, Indonesia, and the Philippines. Over the course of many centuries Sak Yant tattoos have emerged from Cambodia, Laos, Thailand, and parts of Myanmar. The tradition has however originated from indigenous tribal animism which has many examples throughout global history. Solomon Islanders have punctured out their face tattoos with the claw of a flying fox. Florida Islanders used the bone from a bat's wing, while Maoris utilized sharks' teeth. Egyptian mummies were sometimes tattooed for various magical and social functionality. It is said that Burmese women tattooed a triangular love charm on lips, tongue, or between the eyes using the 'drug of tenderness', this being vermillion, herbs, and the skin from a spotted lizard. Southeast Asian tattoos became tied to the Hindu-Buddhist concepts of yantra, or mystical geometric patterns used during meditation, when this philosophy became assimilated into their culture. In Cambodia and central Thailand, the Old Khmer script of the Khmer Empire is used, while in northern Thailand yantra tattoos may use Shan, Northern Thai, or Tai Lu scripts, and in Laos the Lao Tham script is employed. Some designs have been adapted from pre-Buddhist shamanism and the belief in animal spirits. People from many walks of life have Sak Yant tattoos: military personnel, police, taxi drivers, fighters, gangsters, and others in what are perceived to be dangerous professions.

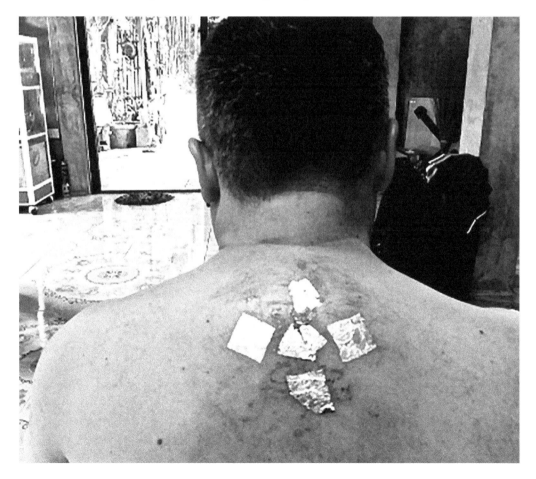

The most recent Sak Yant I've received at this point in time from Ajarn Apichai was during January 2020. Ajarn Apichai is widely accepted as an Accomplished Grandmaster of Wicha and Saiyasart (occult knowledge and science of influencing life through unnatural and supernatural forces). Situated at his samnak in Chiang Mai, Northern Thailand, I received the Khun Paen Khrong Muang Yant (*Khun Paen* Rules the Land and City *Yant)*, which comes from the knowledge of Luang Pu Suk, one of Thailand's most legendary ancient guru monks.

Khun Paen (c. 1491–1529) was a legendary Thai magician and warrior. The Gan Suam Yant and Gan Kom Yant, which were applied either side of the Khun Paen Khrong Muang Yant, both wield incredible magical weight and power. The numerical value of the number three appears throughout designs of Sak Yant tattoos. This represents The Three Jewels of Refuge, Buddha, Dharma (the teachings), and Sangha (the Buddhist community), along with the Three Higher trainings of morality, concentration, and wisdom. These last three sak yants Ajarn Apichai insisted that he give to me specifically because they were his Yant Kru, which means that they are his master yants or central controlling trademark yants. This is regarded as a powerful Sak Yant and will protect you in many unseen ways. By having an Ajarn's Yant Kru you show respect to the master, and you become a disciple of that master. I collect and work with numerous Thai Lanna Buddhist occult amulets, enchanted beeswax, and charms from Ajarn Apichai. My admiration and respect for him is without measure, as with all the Ajarns that have been my privilege and honour to meet.

Before I left Chiang Mai in Northern Thailand during the early days of January 2020 and before the Covid 19 virus ran rampant upon this earth, I acquired two final Sak Yants from Ajarn Daeng, one of which was recommended by Ajarn Suea. Ajarn Suea, through meditational visionary insight, saw that I needed a very specific Sak Yant called Yant Soi Sangwan. This Sak Yant is applied across the upper chest. I agreed to his advice without question. Any advice an Ajarn gives to you is to be acted upon. They are supreme teachers and can help devotees immeasurably; half-measures are not an option when consulting with a realised master. Yant Soi Sangwan represents the power of invincibility. The lines of script that make up this Sak Yant can go from two to as many as eight. The word itself means 'necklace' and is a Sak Yant from ancient times that was popular among warriors. Many Thai boxers have this Sak Yant since it protects the bearer from danger and harm. It is believed that no weapon could hurt the body of the bearer of Yant Soi Sangwan. The day Ajarn Daeng gave me the Yant Soi Sangwan was after an incredible Wolf Moon. The resonance and astrological significance of this event was an undeniable and powerful foundation underpinning the ritual, during which I was transported into new realms of being, breaking through profound new thresholds of pain. Ajarn Daeng's samnak is on a main road. While under the tattoo gun (Ajarn Daeng employs both rod and gun and is extremely gifted at both) traffic thundered by. At one particular point of intense pain (the breastbone) a very large truck powering past had its horn blowing which morphed into a kind of psychedelic dub drone whilst the needle hammered out the yantra. My drone album Unalome is dedicated and focused on this singular ritual <https://sheerzed.bandcamp.com/album/unalome>.

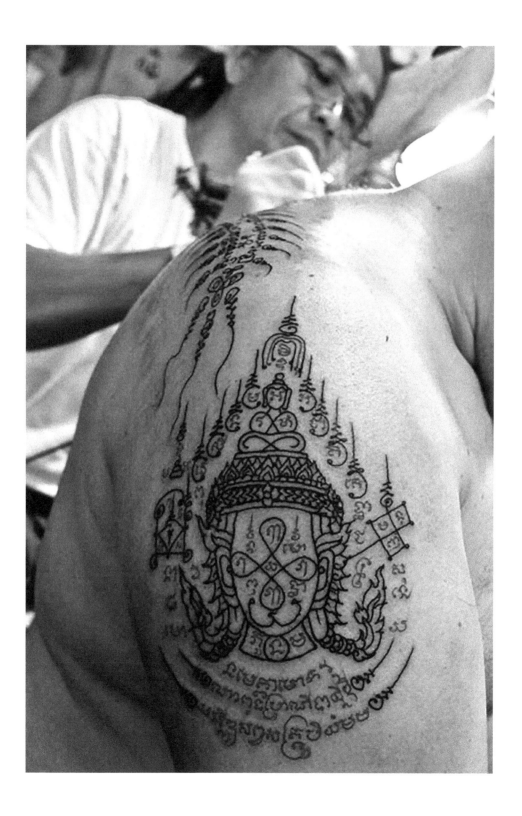

In this most surreal and cosmic of moments I knew there and then that this ritual would be a visceral and profound cornerstone in my spirit body for many years to come. The last Sak Yant I received from Ajarn Daeng was Yant Ittipiso Paed Tidt or the eight directions of the universe. This beautiful multi-directional Sak Yant, of which there are many variations, removes danger from all directions. Like a form of chaos star, it sends out raw magical vibrations of protection while bestowing the attributes of Metta (loving-kindness and compassion for the self and others) and Serm Duang (the attribute of realigning the fate of the bearer to be of greater benefit). There are nine mantras, or as they say in Thai, *kata*, that can be chanted for each specific direction that you may travel in to ward off any evil spirits or ghosts that may dwell on the pathway of your journey.

Ajarn Daeng, Ajarn Suea, Ajarn Apichai, Ajarn Nanting, Ajarn Tui, Ajarn A Klongkarn, and Ajarn Perm Rung are all profound masters who have altered the course of my life. Thai Lanna Buddhism is a highly unique and I would say absorbing and fascinating philosophy. It is a very beautiful, deep, and iridescent diamond hybrid philosophy of shamanism, divination, necromancy, herbalism, astrology, numerology, animism, deity worship, sak yants, chanting, spells, candle magic, ceremonial magic, amulets, buchas (sacred statues with active spiritual ingredients), rituals, dreams, and temples all in the framework of Buddhism, Hinduism, Daoism, and Brahmanism. Sak Yant are truly incredible sources of occult and supernatural power that any serious seeker of spiritual and magical truth would be highly advised to seek out, investigate, and engage with irrespective of their proclivities or personal leanings.

I am no longer the being that stepped out of the aircraft at Bangkok airport in September 2017. In an unpublished interview with Peter Jenx, the artist, author, and animist Charlotte Rodgers stated, "A magical premise that people don't talk about enough is the transformation of people...knowing yourself and changing, and confronting taboos, people don't look at it enough and I think that they need to be reminded because you get so focussed on the practice and the verbiage, and the discipline, and the hierarchy." I sincerely believe that I have been magically transformed from both the inside and out by my experiences and the rituals I participated in on the three pilgrimages I undertook. I notice changes both large, small, and subtle that are reflected in numerous parts of my life. Whether this falls in line with hardcore Buddhist doctrine is of little interest to me because I live and function within the end results of this transformational process and continue to follow the five precepts handed down to me from the Ajarns.

In the paper *The Role of the Magic in Buddhism, with Special Reference to Ch'an (Zen)* by Dr Stewart McFarlane he states, "If we accept the implications of the third viewpoint, that a magical worldview is an integral part of traditional Buddhism, then there is no difficulty in accepting the concepts of higher-knowledge (abhinna/abhijna) and powers (iddhi/siddhi), and their manifestations as magical abilities acquired as a result of advanced level samadhi and jhana practice." Displaying these powers in front of laity however can be a questionable and problematic act. Finding a conveniently located phone booth will always be an ongoing issue if this is the case.

Over the course of three years and three pilgrimages I underwent a series of intense, extreme, all-encompassing, and extraordinary personal transformations and rituals that I am still processing and evaluating to this day. I do not see or feel that my encounters were some form of overt, banal, or grandstanding spiritual tourism or, as some less cognizant and limited commentors have weighed in on, my experiences are a type of exoticisation. Indeed, some people may feel that my practice is possibly a touch monochromatic for their own personal tastes. The term monochrome comes from the Ancient Greek meaning 'having one colour'. Monochromatic practices, while seemingly of one colour, can ultimately be the most colourful and difficult to master, as they include all colours while at the very same time exclude all, allowing the true, naked, and full spectrum of your own personal colours to come out. My initial calling and experiences have a direct and fundamental link to deeply personal meaningfulness, a myriad of feelings, highly intuitive cosmic compassing, and the guidance of spirits. Before I undertook my first pilgrimage in 2017, during a session with a local medium, two monks and a Goddess form transpired around me. The medium shuddered while witnessing this particular apparition during this darkened-room séance. It could be said that my Sak Yant tattoos were inevitable and guided by supernatural forces. I see my collection of Sak Yant so far as the pages of a magickal flesh-bound living grimoire. Occasionally on sacred days they are opened up and exposed in the fecund rawness of full unadulterated nudity, which as all practitioners know, is the historical, natural, electric, and open state of many if not all practicing witches.

Sleeping with One Eye Open

FREDRIK EYTZINGER

I awoke with the dream still in my awareness. I had obtained advanced technical knowledge surrounding the Machine of Ecstasy. If I started the engines and caressed its metal handles, it would inexorably force my dream body up against the ceiling, measuring in height with the cascade of black oil released from somewhere below. The room turned green and in an instant I travelled beyond the stars; I traversed the endless corners of innumerable multiverses to the extent that I could no longer maintain my human complexion or concept of reality. The expansion was intangible and as I finally felt how my body started to descend, I regained consciousness and eventually found myself sleeping on a bed made of residue from the dissolved firmament.

As a father of two young daughters, I always appreciate the moments when I get to sleep for a couple of hours extra in the morning. Since the birth of my first daughter, the mode of default vigil remains strong during the nocturnal hours and I have actually learned to cherish the moments when there is an interruption in their otherwise quite placatory ability to sleep through the entire night. I consider it a perfect opportunity to enter states of the in-between, states on the border between sleep and wakefulness. Their nightmares and ghastly nocturnal appetite have triggered in me many weird states of consciousness where the astral and the physical realms merge together, beheld by the one set of perceiving eyes at hand.

"And further, although there be two eyes, yet they are converted into one eye."[1]

---

1 Concerning the Macroprosopus (Arich Anpin), one of the two faces of Keter. S. L. McGregor Mathers (trans.), *Kabbalah Unveiled* (Dover Publications Inc. 2006), p. 126.

THE DISCOVERY

Both children have become my reality check completely beyond my control and favourably, without danger of entering the habitual. The advantage of waking up in the middle of the night unprepared, without the aid of alarm, seems to be a highly important element for a dreamer. It challenges your awareness and wit and calls for immediate action.

"Why is flexibility of mind so important? Because the rigidities of mind, the limitations of wrong views that obscure wisdom and constrict experience, keep us ensnared in illusory identities and prevent us from finding freedom." [2]

A sudden cry from the crib turns into an abysmal call during those particular moments, when my energy body has travelled into distances too far off in order for the physical sensorium to immediately respond. When awaking in the cold dead of the night, the visions are projected into the room, carrying the spirits and nocturnal creatures into the bedchamber as fellow members of the family. I comfort the children while being surrounded by an ancient, formless murmur, as I shift focus from dream to flesh. Fully banished, when the vision and the cry has settled, I enter a realm where the two worlds merge into one. My fantasies wander off into a place where flesh and dream are the same, where stellar man remembers his Atlantean agenda, where duality is a myth told at the bedside of prospect gods. But still, there is always the two in the one, and the one in the two.

Most intriguing are the states when I have felt as if existing on two planes at the same time: when I have the ability to split the astral body in two, witnessing the room through an out-of-body projection, while at the same time entering into a realm of non-ordinary dreamscape, when I have the ability to read and write at the same time, or dream and weave. For the ones yet to be convinced, the fission of the dream body has been given names such as *sleep paralysis, out-of-body experience*, or *possession*. For the dreamer, the realization of possessing three bodies, that of flesh, and the split body of light, comforts the idea that in reality the dream body may split into innumerable bodies of 'astral awareness'. Imagine dividing your dream body into billions of pieces of awareness and projecting them into every living organism on the earth, perceiving the instant as a whole, or the whole in an instant.

In the mornings, I usually extend my snooze ritual by carrying the youngest of two into my bed, casting a circle with sheet and linen around her play at the crack of dawn, in order to protect her from falling off the bed onto the hard, profane floor. Through the snooze, Dora the Explorer is interpreted as an augur priest in demonic possession, screaming from the temporary bed chamber that now resembles a celestial temple. In the middle of cacophony, the neighbours ceremonially greet the morning by waving their chainsaw in all four cardinal directions; the sound enters my room from a distance which turns into a board of goblins discussing the true nature of initiatory investment. Currently, the market value of dream is haunted by an uncanny inflation.

---

2 Tenzin Rinpoche Wangyal, *The Tibetan Yogas of Dream and Sleep* (Snow Lion 1998), p. 120.

It was during one of these witching mornings I came to discover the true meaning of the saying *to sleep with one eye open*. I was just about to doze off for half a minute, when I discovered I could comfortably rest my entire mind and body by only closing the right eye. I entered this stance as a result of heavy sleepiness, where I at the same time had to maintain focus on my daughter. Focusing my attention on my closed right eye, I existed in a relaxed state of tranquil blackness, while focusing on my open left eye, the dream-induced hallucinations started to manifest as a flickering point of light in the corner of the room. Maintaining a general focus made both worlds merge into one. The sensation can best be described as an evocation of my astral body, where I for an instant found myself in a state of alien ecstasy, suddenly observing a happily drooling entity entering my field of perception, flogging her words in a wretched tongue. Did she perceive me as being awake or asleep? Through a slight tunnel perception I was immediately sucked back into a normal state of awareness, ready for a new and prosperous day.

THE DEVIATION

The discovery was profound and through similar astral experiences, I have come to favour the techniques discovered by intuition, rather than the ones taught to me by others, forcefully grinded and meticulously practiced. The famous opening in William Blake's poem *Eternity*, *"One who binds to himself a joy does the winged life destroy"*, also applies to dream practice. Astral traveling is the knowledge of maintaining awareness while simultaneously creating and perceiving, wherefore dreams must be harnessed in the instant; for the body of dream remains flexible while the waking man remains stiff. Now, as this information has been passed on to you, your dream body and your subconscious mind also know, and one of them, or both, will try to trick you into thinking that you in fact don't know, by altering your dreamscape, challenging your dream emotions or dream ethics, or telling you that dreaming is possible and better off without awareness. Therefore you must deviate!

In the novel *Nineteen Eighty-Four* by George Orwell, the protagonist Winston Smith is in secrecy longing for a rebellion against the ruling totalitarian party, governed by its dictator called Big Brother. Smith works for the Ministry of Truth, which is the government propaganda section responsible for the writing and re-writing of history. While working there, he continuously makes himself guilty of *thoughtcrime*—not thinking in the line of the ruling party. Thomas Gray captured this alienation in the ending lines of his poem *Ode on a Distant Prospect of Eton College*: *"And happiness too swiftly flies. Thought would destroy their paradise. No more; where ignorance is bliss, 'Tis folly to be wise."*

If we consider the Ministry of Truth as our awareness of our own memory, and the Big Brother surveillance system as the subconscious in the guise of our dream self, then the journey of Winston Smith is the total rebellion against not only the system, but the whole concept that constitutes him as a being. This lucidity has to come with a total soul-searching recapitulation, knowing history not only as it has been written, but also as it has been re-written. In dream control, deviation is also a form of acceptance, involving not only the remembrance and veneration of one's wakeful history, but also the remembrance of dream history. Therefore, this deviation is not a defiant break-up from the path, or a bewitching of the subconscious; rather, it is a deviation from rehearsed patterns, or from your own *concept* of the sum of the parts that constitute you as a dreaming entity. The dreaming *path* is at a constant crossroad.

During the day when I came to discover the technique of sleeping with one eye open, I also thought about Odin and the symbolism embedded in his one-eyedness. In his book *The Afflicted Mirror*,[3] Peter Hamilton-Giles writes that affliction represents a symbolic Otherness and that it can be seen as a deviation from morality: *"Appearing as a corporeal distortion allays any sense of loss since the imbalance of disarticulation is countered by an increase in aspectual potentialities. This only makes itself known through the accompanying narrative which details specific characteristics about their 'becoming'."*

The affliction of the flesh is in this case an apparition of one's deviation from morality or reason, and the deviation itself becomes a symbol of perpetrated awareness. The afflicted gods, from my cultural context, represent the visionary impulse itself, and thus I came to the conclusion, in relation to my experience, that Odin did not only *sacrifice* his eye into the Well of Mimir in order to retrieve omnipotent knowledge as commonly told, rather, what he did was to lower one of his eyes into the well, into the earth, into the primordial water, into the dark places of hidden wisdom where no man awake would be able distinguish *this* from *that*. Once again, the omnipotent knowledge that is conscious and subconscious sacrificed itself unto itself, and Odin fulfilled the fission of the dream body.[4]

3 Three Hands Press, 2013.

4 The Well of Mimir, here envisioned as running through the World Tree, is among other things analogous with Sushumna, the central energetic channel in Tantric systems. The myth of Odin's eye-sacrifice shows upon a connection between eye and root.

THE DREAMING PATTERN

I searched the folklore for an answer. As with many mundane sayings there is often a deeper layer of knowledge embedded within the superficial fact. The idiom *'to sleep with one eye open'* is often described as being in a state of alertness as a reaction to some underlying suspiciousness. But I was not suspicious. I then pondered the related Swedish idiom *'att sova räv'* which directly translated reads *'to sleep [like a] fox'* most likely alluding to the cunningness of the fox and the sleep of wild animals who are always on the lookout for prey or enemies. In general, large predators tend to sleep for longer periods of time since they lack the fear of being hunted, while awake and dreaming. To sleep like a fox means to take a feigned nap while imitating the sleeping body, making others believe you are sleeping. This of course, resonates well with the image of the trickster-fox, a creature of cunning wisdom, running like a russet arrow through many of the world's cultures, gracious and untouchable. Dreaming *about* the fox was in pre-industrial Sweden said to be a harbinger of misfortune, probably due to the connection between the fox and the Devil. If you could sleep like a fox, would it also be possible to dream like a fox?

Some years ago, I was presented with a theory related to another type of sleep cycle than what we are commonly used to.[5] This pattern has been so deeply layered through history that when we stopped being aware of its nature, it came to be interpreted as a sleeping disorder, or a disease, rather than something natural and beneficial. I speak of the report emphasizing the historical sources that deal with what is referred to as *the first and the second sleep*. Apparently, in some western pre-industrial cultures the family would go to sleep in the evening and sleep for about four hours. In the middle of the night, they would wake up from the silent alarm of the bio-clock and engage in nightly activities for an hour after which they would return to bed and enter into what was referred to as the second sleep. The nightly activities during this break in sleep were often calm in nature and more mental than physical, such as reading or praying to God, although sexual interaction seemed to be quite recurrent. It has been discussed that man's cognitive abilities were stronger during this hour and therefore memorizing. Could the true meaning of *'sleeping with one eye open'* be traced to pre-industrial man, or maybe even to an era before the birth of civilization, a time more in resonance with biology and natural rhythm? Intuitively I thought that it could; however, with the experience still on my retina I searched for a more substantial answer.

I arrived upon the biology of the brain; its brain halves in analogy with a universal concept—the two in the one (yin and yang). I found that mammals living in the sea, such as whales and dolphins, could be in a slow wave sleep one cerebral hemisphere at the time, and that they during this *Unihemispheric Slow Wave Sleep* (USWS) *"demonstrated that the eye contralateral to the sleeping hemisphere remained primarily closed while the eye contralateral to the waking hemisphere was more often open"*.[6] It has also been suggested that the reason

---

5 See Robert Ekirch's *At Day's Close: Night in Times Past*, Phoenix, 2005.

6 Timothy J. Walter & Uma Marar, 'Sleeping with One Eye Open', *Capitol Sleep Medicine Newsletter*, 2.6 (2007) <http://www.capitolsleep.com/Sleeping_with_One_Eye_Open_June07.pdf>.

why some birds (such as the common blackbird and the common swift) are able to fly and navigate during sleep is that USWS allows them to keep the one eye open which is connected to the wakeful hemisphere. Also, as REM sleep relaxes the muscles that are needed during flight, it would of course be impossible to fly. However, it could be possible for birds to recover specific parts of sleep while on ground, through the use of USWS.

In man's celestial anatomy, the left and right eyes have been attributed to the sun and the moon. In the Chinese mythical text *Classic of Mountains and Seas* (Shan Hai Jing) from the fourth century BCE, it is described how the Fiery Dragon rules the coming and going of seasons with its breath, and controls day and night by opening and closing its eyes. In *Asian Mythologies* (1993) by Yves Bonnefoy, the following account is accredited to the emperor Xuanzonggi: *"To the north on the Mountain of the Bell, there is a stone with a head like a human head; the left eye is the Sun, the right eye is the Moon; when the left eye is open, it is day; when the right eye is open, it is night."*

From a human perspective, the eye is here the luminary source itself, related to phosphine phenomenon through psychedelic or electrical stimuli. Where there is no light source responsible for the experiencing of light, there may as well be several other modes of energy persistent within the mind and body of the seer. Through this mythical interpretation we are also able to ascribe the sensory input of the two brain hemispheres with the sun and the moon. Did Odin lower the sun or the moon into the Well of Knowledge?

In their classic text *The Projection of the Astral Body* (1929), Sylvan Muldoon and Hereward Carrington talk about the feeling of being split-in-two accompanied with astral projection, a concept related to the term *the repercussion of the astral body*. According to their theory, the astral body leaves the flesh every single night in order to become recharged by cosmic energy. The projection of the phantom body may extend at any distance *"within cord-activity range"*. In relation to the sun and the moon, the recharging of cosmic energy is seen in the context of man's stellar origin, manifested in the Metonic cycle, synchronizing the year of the sun and the year of the moon, uncovering the celestial sclera, uncovering the iris and the entirety of the pupil: the Eye of Ra and the Eye of Horus, densified in a burning-point of fiery and cooling intent. The using of stellar sight is an act of remembrance and an activation of the dormant capabilities within one's own stellar body. Suddenly, the Dream Chief tells me that this is fundamental knowledge possessed by an astral group of students known as the Lower Haddai Qadaph, who once were the familiar astral councillors of Eliphas Levi, ministering him with otherworldly knowledge of the Shem ha-Mephorash and the intelligence referred to as Chavajoth. We must disperse!

THE DISPERSION

I opened the *The Secret Book of John* where it is described how the body parts of soul-man were created by a throng of angels who had been given seven physical substances (the soul of bone, the soul of sinew, the soul of flesh, the soul of marrow, the soul of blood, the soul of skin and the soul of hair) created by the divine authorities. From these substances the angel *Asterechme* created the right eye, and *Thaspomocha* created the left eye. Now, the only thing which really was of interest was to return to practice. Remembering the nocturnal practices of pre-industrial man, I would set my alarm in the middle of the night, wake up at the given signal and make the blood flow increase a little, offer a prayer and return to bed closing only the right eye. I also found it important to conjure into my awareness the former experiences with this one-eyed perception. But entering into this state with force was initially a tedious undertaking. I had made the mistake of sharing my intention with my entire body: the flesh, the familiar host, and the shadow. I wondered who was the main familiar angel connected to Odin, *Asterechme* or *Thaspomocha?*

I then came up with a variation of the dream yoga commonly found in both Eastern and Western teachings, emphasizing the importance of carrying dream practice into waking life. The key in this practice, first and foremost, involves maintaining presence and awareness of the whole consciousness, in all common day practices. They may revolve around reality checks where the yogi asks if one is really awake and what proof may be found for such a statement. Similar practices deal with teaching the body to conjure forth sensory input into the waking awareness by for example imagining the scent of a rose or extending the ability to hear sounds existing in memory.

I figured that if I could allow my left dreaming eye to rest during the day it would store enough attention and awareness for the night to come. Therefore, I made a simple eye patch for my left eye and carried it throughout the day, and in my time of writing this article it still stays on, wherefore I have extended my reality check into my writing and thus, into your reading. Now, my left eye serves the only purpose of bringing me into that same state of consciousness once more. Hopefully, your eyes too will heed the call and join in the invocation of both *Asterechme* and *Thaspomocha*.

Blink once if you understand.

With this eye-patch I intuitively started to understand that eye-sight was deeply connected to memory, and that memory and awareness were two different sides of the coin—the two in the one. This atavistic awareness was, to my conclusion, the essence of the powers beheld by Odin. I do not believe it is a coincidence that Muninn, the second raven of Odin, has a name meaning *memory*. The first raven, Huginn, has a name which translates as *thought*, attributed to the awareness mentioned above. What is called *lucidity* in dream is called *awareness* in the waking state, but in reality they are the same. I came to experience that my left eye, which lacked sensory stimuli during the day, began to create its own world of perception, and soon it produced phosphine visions on its own. The angel *Thaspomocha* imitated the behaviour of pre-industrial man through her own becoming.

Still, I am not so sure what I am witnessing anymore. Am I using the true potential of my eye-sight, or am I blinded by hindsight, the forced search for lucid awareness? These processes are always in dire need of doubt and reflection; it is a part of the path. Well, I stood pondering below the bookshelf in hesitance when all of a sudden the *Hagakure* caught my attention—the spiritual and practical samurai codex wherein it is said that a warrior is a person who is able to make important decisions within seven breaths. So, upon my last breath on Resurrection Sunday, I awoke beheaded on a shore filled with white diamonds shimmering beneath a merciless sun. The ocean called my name twice and then I fell asleep, once again.

BIBLIOGRAPHY

Ekirch, Robert, *At Day's Close: Night in Times Past* (Phoenix, 2005)

Hamilton-Giles, Peter, *The Afflicted Mirror* (Three Hands Press, 2013)

Mathers, S. L. McGregor (trans.), *Kabbalah Unveiled* (Dover Publications Inc. 2006)

Walter, Timothy J. & Uma Marar, 'Sleeping with One Eye Open', *Capitol Sleep Medicine Newsletter*, 2.6 (2007) <http://www.capitolsleep.com/Sleeping_with_One_Eye_Open_June07.pdf>

Wangyal, Tenzin Rinpoche, *The Tibetan Yogas of Dream and Sleep* (Snow Lion 1998)

Τά ἔσχατα παύείν

TO SUFFER THE FATE OF DEATH[1]

HUMBERTO MAGGI

The wrath sing, goddess, of Peleus' son, Achilles, that destructive wrath which brought countless woes upon the Achaeans, and sent forth to Hades many valiant souls of heroes, and made them themselves spoil for dogs and every bird; thus the plan of Zeus came to fulfillment.[2]

As THE HISTORY of Western literature opens with these first lines of the *Iliad*, we are abruptly thrown into the wasteland full of corpses of the city of Troy. In just a few lines we face not only the sorrow the Achaeans felt for the death of friends, but we also have a hint of the gloomy *postmortem* fate waiting for them in Hades, and of the even worse possibility of being forgotten or lost unburied—the spoil of dogs and birds.

Let's start our venture into the Greek mysteries of death, fear, and suffering by looking into the first recorded use of the word ψυχὰς (*psychas* or souls) in these verses. The *psyche* in Homer has a very enigmatic set of meanings, being referred to first at the moment of death as something that leaves the σῶμα (*soma* or body), but after as the part of the deceased that retains his figure and memory. What is strange for us is, ***first***, that the *psyche* is never said to have any participation whilst the person is alive; ***second***, that the survival of the *psyche* is described in the next Homeric poem (the *Odyssey*) as a gloomy prospect even for the heroes who attained to the ideal of 'everlasting fame' when alive; ***third***, that even that pathetic survival of the soul in Hades is preferable to what happens to the soul of the ἄταφοι (*ataphoi* or unburied); and, ***fifth***, the fact that

---

1 I took the title of this paper from the introduction in Lars Albinus's excellent work *The House of Hades: Studies in Ancient Greek Eschatology*. Lars explains the use and meaning of *eskatos* in the context of his research, and we are following the same here: "The eponymous Greek word ἔσχατος carried no specifically religious connotations until the Christian notion of ἐσχατολογία was used to designate ‹the last times›, ‹the end of the world›. Yet, before the introduction of Christianity, the Greeks seemed more or less unconcerned with the general fate of mankind. What mattered was the fate of the individual mortal being. In this respect, however, it is worth noticing that ἔσχατος was implicitly associated with the invisible realm of immortality and afterlife by denoting extremes of space and time (meaning, e.g., 'furthest', 'uttermost' or 'last'). Thus, the phrase τα ἔσχατα παύείν, which means 'to suffer the fate of death', can be translated literally as 'to experience the last things'."

2 A.T. Murray, *The Iliad with an English Translation*. All quotes from the *Iliad* in this paper are from this source.

the *ataphoi* described in the *Iliad* and the *Odyssey* are the souls who manage to keep their capacity of communication with the living, whilst the rest of the dead can only interact with the living when invocated and propitiated in a proper manner.

It is generally agreed upon that the word *psyche* derived from ψΰχω (*psûkhō*), with meanings like 'to breathe' and 'to blow'. The association of breath with the life of the body and, by extension, with different concepts of 'soul' is found in other languages and cultures—for instance, the Hebrew רוח (*ruach*, literally 'wind') and נשמה (*neshamah*, literally 'breath').

> The etymology of ψυχή, cognate with ψῦχος and ψυχρός, suggests an original reference to the cold breath of death. If ψυχή was ever a literal concept, then this will have been its literal sense. In Homer, the word is used only in connection with death or deathlike loss of consciousness.[3]

The *psyche* is lost at the moment of death; in fact, it is the very loss of the *psyche* that characterizes the death of the individual. The first narrative in the *Iliad* where death is described as the loss of the *psyche* comes in verse 296 of Book 5, when Diomedes kills Pandarus "and there his spirit [ψυχή] and his strength [μένος] were undone". We have seventeen passages like that, plus another ten where the loss of *psyche* is associated with its flight to the "House of Hades" (δόμον Ἄϊδος)[4]. These represent a small amount of the "240 recorded deaths on the battlefield"[5] where the dead are named. The killing of the adversarial hero was a necessary condition for the acquisition of the 'everlasting fame' the warriors sought with the same intensity with which they fought for the spoils of the enemy, but the Homeric epics are far from presenting a univocal view about death on the battlefield. Often, we are confronted with the pathetic description of all the ramifications that the death of a hero had for the surviving family, the orphans, widows, and parents left behind:

> Then went he on after Xanthus and Thoön, sons twain of Phaenops, and both well beloved; and their father was fordone with grievous old age, and begat no other son to leave in charge of his possessions. There Diomedes slew them, and bereft them of dear life, both the twain; but for the father he left lamentation and grievous sorrow,

---

3 Douglas Cairns, Ψυχή, Θυμός, and Metaphor in Homer and Plato, *Etudes Platoniciennes* 11.

4 Cairns, op.cit.

5 Robert Garland, 'The Causation of Death in The "Iliad": A Theological And Biological Investigation', *Bulletin of the Institute of Classical Studies* 28. Thomas D. Seymour in *Life in the Homeric Age* mentions "a German Scholar (von Hahn)" giving the sum of 243 named dead heroes from the total of 318 killings.

seeing they lived not for him to welcome them on their return; and the next of kin divided his goods.[6]

From these twenty-seven passages linking the loss of the *psyche* with death, two are outstanding: the narratives of the death of Patroclus and Hector. First, our attention is called because these are the two passages where we "have the ψυχή both leaving the body and flying off towards Hades"[7]—the others have it doing one (17 passages) or the other (8 passages)[8]; second, we note that both the *psyches* of Patroclus and Hector shared the danger of becoming *ataphoi*.

Patroclus is killed in Book 16 of the *Iliad*; after being stunned, disarmed and made vulnerable by a blow given by the god Apollo, he was smitten in the back by the spear of Euphorbus, and finished by Hector:

> But Hector, when he beheld great-souled Patroclus drawing back, smitten with the sharp bronze, [820] came nigh him through the ranks, and smote him with a thrust of his spear in the nethermost belly, and drave the bronze clean through; and he fell with a thud, and sorely grieved the host of the Achaeans.[9]

Hector then exchanges words with the dying hero, threatening that he would not allow his body to be buried:

> [...] with the spear I myself am pre-eminent among the war-loving Trojans, even I that ward from them the day of doom; but for thee, vultures shall devour thee here.[10]

Patroclus's death has something else in common with the future death of Hector; in their final moments, they both prophesied the near death of their killers. In answer to Hector's boasting and threats, he stated:

> And another thing will I tell thee, and do thou lay it to heart: verily thou shalt not thyself be long in life, but even now doth death stand hard by thee, and mighty fate, that thou be slain beneath the hands of Achilles, the peerless son of Aeacus.[11]

---

6 *Il* 5.154–155.

7 Cairns, op. cit.

8 Cairns, op. cit.

9 *Iliad* 16.818–

10 *Iliad* 16.835–

11 *Iliad* 16.850–

Patroclus's *psyche* finally leaves his body, "fleeting from his limbs" and "going to Hades bewailing her fate"[12]. This is not, however, the last time we hear about it in the poem.

A GLIMPSE OF THE HOUSE OF HADES

In some instances, it seems that the Iliadic heroes feared more to be left unburied than death itself; the value they gave to the final rites due to the dead can be seen in the sequence of the poem, when Menelaus and Aias risk their own lives to rescue the cadaver of Patroclus from Hector, who "sought to hale him away that he might cut the head from off his shoulders with the sharp bronze, and drag off the corpse, and give it to the dogs of Troy".[13]

Hector's impious intent was not fulfilled, as the corpse of Patroclus was rescued and delivered to Achilles. And it was Hector's body which ended up dragged by the chariot of Achilles across the plain to the ships on the next day. After his victory over Hector, Achilles ordered the preparations for the funeral of his friend, and finally slept among his sorrowful tears. This is when the *psyche* of Patroclus appears to him:

> And when sleep seized him, loosening the cares of his heart, being shed in sweetness round about him—for sore weary were his glorious limbs with speeding after Hector unto windy Ilios—then there came to him the spirit of hapless Patroclus, in all things like his very self, in stature and fair eyes and in voice, and in like raiment was he clad withal; and he stood above Achilles' head and spake to him.[14]

It is important to note that the oneiric manifestation of the *psyche* of Patroclus repeats a pattern seen before in the poem when Zeus called a baneful dream (οὖλον ὄνειρον) and instructed him to appear to Agamemnon and deceive him; like the *psyche* of Patroclus, the oneiros "took his stand above his head"[15] during the king's sleep to talk to him. Like the prophetic capacity that Patroclus and Hector displayed in the liminal moment of death, the moment of sleep also put the heroes Agamemnon and Achilles in a liminal state where contact

---

12 "Even as he thus spake the end of death enfolded him; and his soul fleeting from his limbs was gone to Hades, bewailing her fate, leaving manliness and youth." (*Il.* 16.855–)

13 *Iliad* 17.125–130. Aias's resolve, however, was not so unflinching; at some point he stated that "In no wise have I such dread for the corpse of Patroclus that shall presently glut the dogs and birds of the Trojans, as I have for mine own life, lest some evil befall, and for thine as well, for a cloud of war compasseth everything about, even Hector, and for us is utter destruction plain to see." (*Il.* 17.245)

14 *Iliad* 23.60–70.

15 *Iliad* 2.20.

with dreams and the dead seems possible. We must remember that in the mythology of the *Iliad* Hypnos (Sleep) and Thanatos (Death) are lesser gods, brothers that live in Hades and work together to rescue the body of the hero Sarpedon.[16] Here we have the first Homeric seed that we see flourish in the following centuries, when the practice of incubation appears as a necromantic technique employed at the *Nekyomanteioi*— places where the dead were consulted. However, here in the Homeric epics this kind of interaction is severely limited. The reason for the apparition of the *psyche* of Patroclus is its fear of becoming *ataphoi*; this is why his first words to Achilles were of reproach:

> Thou sleepest, and hast forgotten me, Achilles. Not in my life wast thou unmindful of me, but now in my death! Bury me with all speed, that I pass within the gates of Hades. Afar do the spirits keep me aloof, the phantoms of men that have done with toils, neither suffer they me to join myself to them beyond the River, but vainly I wander through the wide-gated house of Hades.[17]

Here we have our first hints of the Homeric eschatology. We will see these few glimpses much extended in the next poem, the *Odyssey*. From Patroclus's words we see what happens to the *ataphoi*: they wander through the gates of the House of Hades, unable to join the other dead "beyond the River"; and it is the other dead themselves who do not accept his presence. Next, Patroclus give us another important piece of information:

> And give me thy hand, I pitifully entreat thee, for never more again shall I come back from out of Hades, when once ye have given me my due of fire.[18]

In the Homeric world, the dead that are accepted in the House of Hades do not return: once his funeral rites are concluded with the cremation of his body, the *psyche* of Patroclus loses its ability to manifest to the living. Another impossibility, even for the *ataphoi* who could still appear in dreams, was physical contact with the living. The pathos of the scene is increased because it seems Patroclus was not aware of this when he asked Achilles to give him his hand:

> Then in answer spake to him Achilles, swift of foot: "Wherefore, O head beloved, art thou come hither, and thus givest me charge about each thing? Nay, verily I will fulfill thee all, and will hearken even as thou biddest. But, I pray thee, draw thou nigher; though it be but for a little space let us clasp our arms one about the other, and take our fill of dire lamenting." So saying he reached forth with his hands, yet clasped him not; but the spirit like a vapour was gone beneath the earth, gibbering faintly.[19]

---

16 *Iliad* 16.667–684.

17 *Iliad* 23.60–70.

18 *Iliad* 23.75–80.

19 *Iliad* 23.93–100.

THE ODYSSEY: KATABASIS AND NEKYIOMANTEIA

The remark that Achilles made after his encounter with the *psyche* of his dead friend is one of the many enigmas Homeric scholars have tried to explain:

> Look you now, even in the House of Hades [Ἀΐδαο δόμοισι] is the spirit [ψυχὴ] and phantom [εἴδωλον] somewhat, albeit the mind [φρένες] be not anywise therein; for the whole night long hath the spirit of hapless Patroclus stood over me, weeping and wailing, and gave me charge concerning each thing, and was wondrously like his very self.[20]

The problem here resides in the use of the word phrenes (φρένες); A.T. Murray translated it as 'mind', as in 'mind, as seat of the mental faculties, perception, thought',[21] but other attested uses include 'heart, as seat of the passions'[22] and 'will, purpose'.[23] The term, as *psyche*, has a physical origin related to the place in the body where these faculties were supposed to reside, the midriff[24] or 'diaphragm, lungs, or pericardium'.[25]

> Regarding types of activity, phrenes are often associated with those we would call 'primarily intellectual.' In them or with them people carry on the activities of pondering, reflecting, deliberating, thinking, and planning. It appears that, when choices or decisions are to be made, phrenes are the place where individuals act or the means that individuals use.[26]

The problem is that the actions of the *psyche* of Patroclus do not betray a lack of *phrenes*. The *eidolon* of the dead hero has initiative, communication skills, and feelings. This is not the only instance in the Homeric poems where the souls in Hades are described as lacking the proper psychic abilities enjoyed by the living. In the *Odyssey*, when Circe instructs Odysseus regarding the

---

20 *Iliad* 23.100–105.

21 Henry George Liddell, Robert Scott, *A Greek-English Lexicon, revised and augmented throughout by Sir Henry Stuart Jones with the assistance of Roderick McKenzie* (Oxford: Clarendon Press, 1940).

22 Idem.

23 Idem.

24 Idem.

25 Shirley Darcus Sullivan, *Sophocles, Use of Psychological Terminology: Old and New* (McGill-Queen's University Press, 1999).

26 Idem.

katabasis[27] he must undergo to be able to invoke the soul of Tiresias, the soul of the seer is described as the only one whose mind/phrenes remains intact, differently from the rest.

> Son of Laertes, sprung from Zeus, Odysseus of many devices, abide ye now no longer in my house against your will; but you must first complete another journey, and come to the house of Hades and dread Persephone, to seek soothsaying of the spirit [ψυχῇ] of Theban Teiresias, the blind seer, whose mind [φρένες] abides steadfast. To him even in death Persephone has granted reason [νόον], that he alone should have understanding [πεπνῦσθαι]; but the others flit about as shadows.[28]

The several moments where the behavior of the souls of the dead seems to contradict the idea of the *psyches* in Hades "flitting about as shadows deprived of understanding"[29] are attributed by scholars to the centuries-long process of oral poetic elaboration that ended with "a composite eschatology made up of elements which had originated in different historical societies".[30] However, a common element that pervades all these different layers of afterlife beliefs is the idea that the House of Hades, the final destination of the souls, is a "dread and dank abode, wherefor the very gods have loathing".[31] However, even this seems to be preferable to the wandering state of the *ataphoi psyche*, the reason why the eidolon of Patroclus came to Achilles "weeping and wailing" for his burial.

That the restless *psyche* of Patroclus came to ask for his burial when the necessary arrangements were already being taken also puzzled the Homeric commentators. Again, solutions can be extrapolated after consulting the *Nekyia*[32] in Book 11 of the *Odyssey*. Consistent with the declaration of the soul of Patroclus that "for never more again shall I come back from out of Hades", the souls that Odysseus interviewed in the House of Hades and Persephone could provide information only about the events they witnessed whilst still alive. Even more to the point, the souls of the dead asked Odysseus about news from their loved ones still living. The last interaction Patroclus had with the living before coming like a dream to Achilles was the conversation with Hector who threatened that "vultures shall devour thee here"; all the soul of Patroclus

---

27 Κατάβασις, 'way down, descent'. (Henry George Liddell, Robert Scott, eds., *A Greek-English Lexicon*).

28 *Odyssey* 10.485–494. In A.T. Murray, trans., *The Odyssey with an English Translation* (Cambridge, MA: Harvard University Press/London: William Heinemann, Ltd., 1919). All quotes from the *Odyssey* in this paper are from this source.

29 Like the dead who bar the soul of the unburied Patroclus.

30 Christiane Sourvinou, *'Reading' Greek Death: To the End of the Classical Period*, Clarendon Press, 1996, p. 13.

31 *Iliad* 20.65.

32 Νέκυια is "an encounter between living and dead individuals, usually initiated through ritual" (Sarah Iles Johnston, *Restless Dead: Encounters between the Living and the Dead in Ancient Greece*, University of California Press, 1999, p. xviii). Book 11 of the *Odyssey* was thus named in Classical times.

knew then was that he remained *ataphoi* because he was not integrated in the company of the dead and could not be aware of the preparations for the burial.

The conclusion of the last rites for Patroclus would also be delayed due to the long series of honors Achilles prepared, with athletic competitions, sacrifices, and feast. Ironically, the spirit seemed to not care about all the pomp and circumstance, as his request was to be buried "with all speed". In the *Odyssey*, the description that Agamemnon gives to the ghost of Achilles of the magnificence of his burial gives the impression that the dead hero did not witness it.

THE RESTLESS DEAD

That the House of Hades is not a desirable place is clear from the initial reaction of Odysseus to the bid of Circe:

> So she spoke, and my spirit was broken within me, and I wept as I sat on the bed, nor had my heart any longer desire to live and behold the light of the sun. But when I had my fill of weeping and writhing, then I made answer, and addressed her, saying: 'O Circe, who will guide us on this journey? To Hades no man ever yet went in a black ship.'[33]

Odysseus's is not the first katabasis into Hades known in the Homeric poems. In the *Iliad* there is a mention of the katabasis of Herakles when Hermes and Athena helped him with the last Labor, capturing Cerberus,[34] and the final book of the poem describes the journey of Priam to rescue the corpse of his son Hector in terms reminiscent of a katabasis to the House of Hades.[35] The *Iliad* describes "the murky darkness"[36] that fell as the lot of Hades, to where the souls fly after death, as being an underground abode that risked being exposed by an earthquake caused by Poseidon.[37] Herakles accessed the underworld through caves, but Circe guided Odysseus by another route:

> Son of Laertes, sprung from Zeus, Odysseus of many devices, let there be in thy mind no concern for a pilot to guide thy ship,1 but set up thy mast, and spread the white sail, and sit thee down; and the breath of the North Wind will bear her onward. But when in thy ship thou hast now crossed the stream of Oceanus, where is a level shore and the

---

33 *Odyssey* 10.495–502.

34 *Iliad* 8.367.

35 Miguel Herrero de Jáuregui, 'Priam's Catabasis: Traces of the Epic Journey to Hades' in *Iliad* 24, *Transactions of the American Philological Association* 141.

36 *Iliad* 15.190.

37 *Iliad* 20.60–65.

groves of Persephone—tall poplars, and willows that shed their fruit—there do thou beach thy ship by the deep eddying Oceanus, but go thyself to the dank house of Hades. There into Acheron flow Periphlegethon and Cocytus, which is a branch of the water of the Styx; and there is a rock, and the meeting place of the two roaring rivers.[38]

We could ask why the need to travel to Hades to summon the shadow of Tiresias, but it is clear from the overall Homeric eschatology that the souls of the dead could not return to the world of the living—except in the case of the *ataphoi*. In the later evocation of the ghost of king Darius in Aeschylus's *Persae*, testifying to the changes in Greek ideas about the dead, the act of nekyiomancy prescinds a katabasis: both the ritual and the apparition of the spirit occur at the tomb. Like the shadows Odysseus met at Hades, the ghost of the king ignored whatever happened after his death in the world above.

The ritual prescribed by Circe follows the general pattern of sacrifices offered to the chthonic powers. That rituals which we today label as 'magical' resorted to the same techniques used in formal religious ceremonies is well attested in the later Greek Magical Papyri, where we find the same use of offerings, sacrifices and prayers blurring the divide between 'religion' and 'magic'. The Odyssean necromancy began with "a libation to all the dead" (milk and honey, sweet wine, water and white barley meal), followed by "prayers and supplication to the glorious tribes of the dead", the sacrifice of "a ram and a black ewe". Together with Odysseus's promises of future sacrifices and offerings to be given to the "powerless heads of the dead" upon his return to Ithaca, these proceedings should be enough to make "many ghosts of men that are dead come forth". At this point, the necromancer should propitiate the Rulers of the Dead by flaying and burning the sheep with "prayer to the gods, to mighty Hades and to dread Persephone".[39]

Once again, we have here a conflict of concepts in the 'composite eschatology' of the Homeric epics. The libations and sacrifices made to the dead at their abode make sense, but what about the promises to be fulfilled at Ithaca, where the dead cannot reach? How could they benefit from the "sacrifice of a barren heifer" and the filling of the altar "with rich gifts"? What we most likely have here is the juxtaposition of the older Homeric idea of the exiled souls in Hades with practices proper to a cult of the dead that would also flourish in the next centuries—or that was already a reality by the time the poems achieved their final written form.

The tribes of the dead attended the call and came for the blood of the sacrifice. Odysseus was instructed to guard the blood against them with a sword until the coming of Tiresias. Many explanations were offered for the blood and for the sword, which seem to contradict the immateriality of the *psyches* that cannot touch the living—and Odysseus like Achilles learns that sorrowful truth when later he tries to hold the ghost of his mother in his arms. But other factors are at play here: the dead can profit by the blood of the sacrifice like any other supernatural entity can enjoy the same, in a

---

38 *Iliad* 10.503–515.

39 *Odyssey* 10.503–534.

mysterious way usually defined by expressions like 'the smell of the offerings' so often found in the Old Testament, and metal has a reputation in different cultures of being able to affect spiritual beings. The thirst and the vulnerability of the dead here emphasize the Homeric concept of the feeble soul in Hades, to which the poet refers constantly with expressions like 'flit about as shadows' and 'the powerless heads of the dead'.

The first ghostly manifestation that answered Odysseus's call was very frightful:

> Then there gathered from out of Erebus the spirits of those that are dead, brides, and unwedded youths, and toil-worn old men, and tender maidens with hearts yet new to sorrow, and many, too, that had been wounded with bronze-tipped spears, men slain in fight, wearing their blood-stained armour. These came thronging in crowds about the pit from every side, with a wondrous cry; and pale fear seized me.[40]

It has been noted many times before that Odysseus's katabasis following the instructions of Circe did not bring him to the inner part of Hades past the gates, but to a limitrophe area, and that would be the reason why the first ghosts to appear seem to represent the categories of restless dead we find in later literature:

- *aōros*, aōrē (aōroi, aōrai) a man or woman who dies too young.
- *ataphos* (ataphoi) a dead person whose body has not received funeral rites.
- *biaiothanatos* (biaiothanatoi) a person who died violently.[41]

The "brides, unwedded youths and tender maidens with hearts yet new to sorrow" fall well into the category of the *aōroi*; the wounded warriors still "wearing their blood-stained armour", however, are not just *biaiothanatoi*: contrast their appearance with the *psyche* of Patroclus, "in all things like his very self, in stature and fair eyes and in voice, and in like raiment was he clad withal".[42] The important difference here is that the corpse of Patroclus, although yet unburied, was not left to rot on the battlefield but was already properly washed and clad. This marks the warrior ghosts that appeared to Odysseus as also *ataphoi*. In fact, in the case of fighters, the *biaiothanatoi* category is not very apt, as to die in battle was a form of attaining the so sought-after "imperishable fame" the heroes gave utmost value. The great fear was to be left unburied.

---

40 *Odyssey* 11.35–44.

41 Johnston, op. cit., p. xvii.

42 *Iliad* 23.65–70.

The third kind of ghosts that first came to Odysseus raised doubts in many commentators, but I see here another indication of a cult of the dead that is not fully accepted in the poem but notwithstanding may have existed in the reality of the time of its final rendition. The "toil-worn old men" fit well the situation of men who died fatherless or survived their children and did not have heirs to perform the post-burial attendances of their tombs. Such was the case we saw above with Phaenops, "fordone with grievous old age" who lost his two sons in the war. Lacking heirs "to leave in charge of his possessions […] the next of kin divided his goods" and attendance at his grave would be doubtful.

> That the Greeks considered the performance of funeral rites important to the disembodied soul is underscored by the practice of adopting heirs who would be able to carry them out if natural heirs were lacking. The right to inherit property was tied to the performance of these rites; more than once, settlement of a disputed estate hinged on the heir being able to prove that he was carrying out his obligations to the deceased.[43]

To Reign in Hades

Nothing speaks more eloquently about the sad *postmortem* fate in Homeric eschatologies than the statement the *psyche* of Achilles made to Odysseus during his katabasis. Not that the katabatic experience of Odysseus was not already full of examples of this: Tiresias called the underworld "a region where is no joy";[44] his mother asked why he came alive "beneath the murky darkness"[45] where "the spirit, like a dream, flits away, and hovers to and fro".[46] When the *psyche* of Agamemnon drinks the blood and recognizes his former comrade, he reveals himself as a sorrowful shade, still suffering for the treacherous death he endured at the hands of his wife:

> He knew me straightway, when he had drunk the dark blood, and he wept aloud, and shed big tears, and stretched forth his hands toward me eager to reach me. But no longer had he aught of strength or might remaining such as of old was in his supple limbs.[47]

After Agamemnon, came the *psyche* of Achilles, in the company of the *psychai* of Patroclus, Antilochus and Aias. Achilles also cries when he sees his former ally, and the "winged words" he addressed to Odysseus once again stress the gloomy reality of the shades in Hades:

---

43 Johnston, op. cit.
44 *Odyssey* 11.94.
45 *Odyssey* 11.155.
46 *Odyssey* 11.220.
47 *Odyssey* 11.390–394.

Son of Laertes, sprung from Zeus, Odysseus of many devices, rash man, what deed yet greater than this wilt thou devise in thy heart? How didst thou dare to come down to Hades, where dwell the unheeding dead, the phantoms of men outworn.[48]

Odysseus answered and tried to cheer Achilles, reminding him of the former honor he received when alive, and of the fact that he held an elevated position amongst the souls in the House of Hades:

For of old, when thou wast alive, we Argives honored thee even as the gods, and now that thou art here, thou rulest mightily among the dead. Wherefore grieve not at all that thou art dead, Achilles.[49]

It is here that the *psyche* of Achilles makes its famous declaration, often debated by scholars of old as of today; in this speech the pathetic abhorrence instilled by the Homeric afterlife achieved it highest point:

Nay, seek not to speak soothingly to me of death, glorious Odysseus. I should choose, so I might live on earth, to serve as the hireling of another, [490] of some portionless man whose livelihood was but small, rather than to be lord over all the dead that have perished.[50]

As Thomas Day Seymour succinctly stated:

And if the proud Achilles would rather serve on earth than reign in Hades, doubtless the ordinary man expected to gain nothing by death.[51]

INITIATES AND RESTLESS

Over time, several incongruencies and contradictions were noted, not only in the Homeric *Nekyia* but in the overall ensemble of both poems. We are here leaving out the katabasis of the souls of the slain suitors in the final Book 24 of the *Odyssey* as there is a scholarly agreement that it is a later addition— where the incongruencies and contradictions escalate. But already in the *Iliad* we have verses where the uniformity of the *postmortem* fate of the *psychai*, roughly distributed between the properly buried and the *ataphoi*, is challenged.

---

48 *Odyssey* 11.470–475.

49 *Odyssey* 11.484–485.

50 *Odyssey* 11.486–490.

51 Thomas Day Seymour, *Life in the Homeric Age.*

The *ataphoi* state wounds our modern sense of justice as being an afterlife of suffering that did not depend on the actions of the deceased—it was the result of a bad fate or a consequence of the negligence of the living. But we have two instances where punishments for the dead are mentioned. First, in the *Iliad*, during an oath Agamemnon makes a prayer where are mentioned "ye that in the world below take vengeance on men that are done with life, whosoever hath sworn a false oath".[52] It is assumed that this refer to the Erinyes, as a second oath in the epic repeats the formula, saying "the Erinyes, that under earth take vengeance on men, whosoever hath sworn a false oath".[53] In the second instance where we have examples of punishment in the House of Hades, however, there is no mention of the Erinyes or of the *psychai* of perjurers. After talking to Achilles's soul, Odysseus makes a tour around the area and witnesses the punishments of only three special characters, known for their acts of exceptional impiety towards the gods: Tantalus, Sisyphus and Tityos.

On the other hand, we also find in Homer indications that a few could escape the general fate of souls. We saw that Tiresias was especially gifted by Persephone, and because of this, there is no surprise when we see Persephone as one of the patron goddesses of the Mysteries of Eleusis where the initiate was promised a better afterlife in Hades:

> Happy is he among men upon earth who has seen these mysteries; but he who is uninitiate and who has no part in them, never has lot of like good things once he is dead, down in the darkness and gloom.[54]

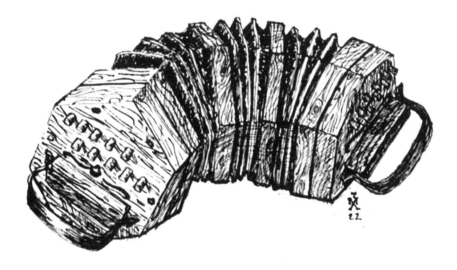

---

52 *Iliad* 3.275–279.

53 *Iliad* 19.259–260.

54 Hugh G. Evelyn-White, ed., *Hymn 2 to Demeter*, lines 480–482.

That the *postmortem* destiny of the *psychai* remained a source of wariness for people throughout antiquity is evinced by later testimonies, where the initiate is promised a better afterlife state by some higher power. In the Greek Magical Papyri, the "blessed initiate of the sacred magic", upon achieving success in his invocation of the magical assistant, is promised a release from the fate of the common lot:

> When you are dead, he will wrap up your body as befits a god, but he will take your spirit and carry it into the air with him. For no aerial spirit which is joined with a mighty assistant will go into Hades.[55]

The Greek Magical Papyri, together with the curse tablets, also testify to the post-Homeric developments in ideas about the restless dead. We saw that the *psyche* of the unburied Patroclus could appear like a dream, and in the katabasis of Odysseus we have an even stronger example of the exceptional capacities of the restless souls. Before sailing to the House of Hades, Elpenor, one of the companions of Odysseus, suffers an accident and dies on the island of Circe. He is left temporarily "unwept and unburied"[56] due to the urgency of their task, but his *psyche* is the first to appear in Hades and talk to Odysseus *without the need to drink the blood*. Odysseus also marvels at the speed with which Elpenor's soul arrived. The ghost pleads and begs that his corpse not be left unattended, like Patroclus did, but differently from the gentle hero he also *threatens* Odysseus:

> There, then, O prince, I bid thee remember me. Leave me not behind thee unwept and unburied as thou goest thence, and turn not away from me, lest haply I bring the wrath of the gods upon thee.[57]

Three seed-ideas seen in the descriptions of the encounters with Patroclus and Elpenor's *psychai* blossomed in the later goetic practices: (1) the restless could contact or be contacted by the living; (2) *psychai* traveled fast; and (3) *psychai* could "bring the wrath of the gods". We see already in the *Iliad* that the chthonic deities could be called upon to curse in what is the oldest written Greek reference to a curse known to us, one laid by a mother upon her own son:

> [...] she prayed instantly to the gods, being grieved for her brother's slaying; and furthermore instantly beat with her hands upon the all-nurturing earth, calling upon Hades and dread Persephone, the while she knelt and made the folds of her bosom wet with tears, that they

---

55 PGM I. 42–195. In Hans Dieter Betz, ed., *The Greek Magical Papyri in Translation. Including the Demotic Texts*.

56 *Odyssey* 11.51–54.

57 *Odyssey* 11.70–74.

should bring death upon her son; and the Erinys that walketh in darkness heard her from Erebus, even she of the ungentle heart.[58]

These later eschatological developments not only made the dead more fearsome, they added further *postmortem* preoccupations for the living as well: once dead, you might not just become restless, but could also be exploited by the *magoi* or the *goetes*. In PGM IV. 2006–2125, 'Pitys' Spell of Attraction', the magician is instructed to look for a buried corpse whose *psyche* will later come to him and "describes how he died, but first he tells you if he has the power to do anything or to perform any service". Strongly reminiscent of the Homeric ideas, the 'chthonic daimon' summoned "will actually stand beside you through the night in dreams". The ghost without rest is then forced into service under the threat of being subjected to further suffering by the magician:

> I adjure you, dead spirit, by the Destiny of Destinies, to come to me, NN, on this day, on this night, and I agree to the act of service for me. And if you don't, expect other chastisements.

CONCLUSIONS

We see that the gloomy eschatology from the Homeric epics remained constant and a source of distress until the end of antiquity. Routes to escape the *postmortem* fate reserved for the great majority of souls, like the Greek mysteries or the sacred magic of the papyri, probably developed under the inspiration (at least in part) of the exceptional cases we find in these earlier poems but, like the cult of heroes that seems to appear at the same time the Homeric verses were put to written form, they failed to give to the great masses a viable consolation. Although slaves could be initiated in the mysteries of Eleusis (if they spoke Greek) and of Dionysos, in practice only a very small fraction of them would receive authorization from their masters to do it.[59] And Greek eschatology was not alone in its disheartening prospects: Near Western variations like the Jewish Sheol and the Netherworld described in the tales of Gilgamesh confirm that there was little hope in the afterlife. The katabasis of Enkidu in the Mesopotamian epic was also a source of hopeless knowledge about the fate of souls.

To that fear was added a growing preoccupation with the restless dead. The special characteristics of the *psychai* barred from full assimilation beyond the Gates of Hades we saw in the *Iliad* and the *Odyssey* gave rise to necromantic techniques where the restless

---

58 Iliad, Il. 9.538. Available at: <http://data.perseus.org/citations/urn:cts:greekLit:tlg0012. tlg001.perseus-eng1:9.538-9.580>.

59 "If we took the lowest end of the slave-owning range for each category and the highest end we emerge with a realistic floor and ceiling of the late Roman slave population: 2.3 million to 9.65 million slaves, 4.6 to 19.3 percent of the population. [...]An estimate of the slave population near 5 million souls and at 10 percent of the total population compares with the best attempts to quantify the slave system of the early Roman empire." (Kyle Harper, *Slavery In The Late Roman World: AD 275-425*).

souls were forced to do the binding of the magician under severe threats. To become restless after death brought now even worse possibilities and new anxieties about the state of the departed ones.

It is my contention that this prevalent eschatological view helped significantly to pave the way for the rise of Christianity. Jesus was preached as a new patron who offered the possibility of a new happiness beyond the grave accessible to everyone. The new religion also eased the ancient fears by turning upside down the restless dead category: a virgin martyr whose body was left to the dogs and birds, and later divided in pieces to be distributed among the faithful, instead of becoming restless would receive a place of honor among the dead and the power to positively affect the living—as the Pagan heroes before. In a society where social movement was extremely difficult, Christianity promised a reward for corporeal suffering; it also denied that the souls of the dead could be summoned, instead putting them under the power of God and demonizing all such magical practices.

To make complete the absorption of the old ideas, in the second century several theologians propagated the tale of the κατελθόντα εἰς τὰ κατώτατα (katelthonta eis ta katôtata),[60] "the triumphant descent of Christ into hell (or Hades) between the time of His Crucifixion and His Resurrection, when, according to Christian belief, He brought salvation to the souls held captive there since the beginning of the world".[61]

The Christian katabasis, the successful descent of Jesus into "that drab and dull place",[62] helped then to smooth the transition between the old and the new eschatology; at the same time, it came to offer a much worse and more frightful vision of Hell that would haunt the Western imagination for centuries to come.

---

60 Apostle's Creed.

61 Harrowing of Hell, *The Catholic Encyclopedia*.

62 Rev. William G. Most, *The Basic Catholic Catechism*.

BIBLIOGRAPHY

Betz, H., *The Greek magical papyri in translation including the Demotic spells* (Chicago, Ill.: University of Chicago Press, 1986).

Cairns, D., *Etudes platoniciennes*, 1st ed. (Paris: Belles lettres, 2006).

Newadvent.org, *CATHOLIC ENCYCLOPEDIA: Harrowing of Hell*, [online] Available at: <https://www.newadvent.org/cathen/07143d.htm> [Accessed 5 May 2022].

de Jáuregui, M., 'Priam's Catabasis: Traces of the Epic Journey to Hades in Iliad 24', *Transactions of the American Philological Association*, 141.1 (2011).

Garland, R., 'THE CAUSATION OF DEATH IN THE ILIAD: A THEOLOGICAL AND BIOLOGICAL INVESTIGATION', *Bulletin of the Institute of Classical Studies*, 28.1 (1981).

Harper, K., *Slavery in the late roman world, ad 275-425* (Cambridge: Cambridge University Press, 2016).

Homer., Murray, A. and Dimock, G., *The Odyssey* (Cambridge, Massachusetts: Harvard University Press, 1995).

Sacred-texts.com, *Hymn To Demeter*, [online] Available at: <https://sacred-texts.com/cla/demeter.htm> [Accessed 5 May 2022].

Johnston, S., *Restless dead*, 1st ed. (Berkeley: University of California Press, 2013).

Catholicculture.org, *Library - The Father William Most Theological Collection*, [online] Available at: <https://www.catholicculture.org/culture/library/most/getwork.cfm?worknum=32> [Accessed 5 May 2022].

Liddell, H., Scott, R., Jones, H. and McKenzie, R., n.d., *Liddell, Scott, and Jones Greek Lexicon* (Perseus Digital Library, Tufts University, Classics Dept. Available at < https://www.perseus.tufts.edu/hopper/text?doc=Perseus:text:1999.04.0057:entry=lo/gos>.

Murray, A., *The Iliad*. 1st ed. (London: Heinemann, 1965).

Seymour, T., *Life in the Homeric Age*, 1st ed. (Forgotten Books, 2019).

Sourvinou-Inwood, C., *"Reading" Greek death* (Oxford: Clarendon Press, 2006).

Sullivan, S., *Sophocles' Use of Psychological Terminology* (Montréal: McGill-Queen's University Press, 2014).

WHEELS OF DIVINE INFLUENCE: THE IYNX AND THE STROPHALOS

H. FEIST

But I am bound upon a wheel of fire,
that mine own tears do scald like molten lead.
—Wm. Shakespeare, *King Lear* IV.vii.53-54

THE *IYNX* OF ANTIQUITY and the *strophalos* of the late Graeco-Roman era are often commingled in today's historical and popular occult literature. The iynx, a wheel-shaped disk suspended on a leather thong passed through its two holes and used to effect love spells, has been known since its appearance in Pindar. The strophalos, a much more elaborate ritual device, described as a golden sphere with lapis lazuli at the center, covered with characters and spun on a leather thong, was first described in the second century CE. These two devices are conflated, confused for one another, and misunderstood in much of the popular literature concerning either one of them. Contemporary popular works involving Hekate are witness to an amalgamation of the two devices.

Modern academic investigation of the ancient literature describing these ritual implements suggests that these devices had entirely different uses and were used by distinct classes of people. By the time of the writing of the Chaldean Oracles, the word 'iynges' had been adapted to describe the connective forces of a spiritual hierarchy, and the spinning ritual devices—at that point called strophaloi—were used in theurgical operations, and possibly in initiations into the mystery cults. For these reasons, this essay will argue that the devices are never equivalent and, further, neither of these devices has been historically documented as having been used to compel the presence or action of deities.

THE IYNX

According to mythology, Iynx was a nymph who magically drew the attention of Zeus (other sources say she attracted Zeus for Io) and was transformed by Hera into the wryneck. A possible justification for the fate of Iynx that is tied to erotic binding magic is the peculiar writhing motions made by this bird when attempting to attract a mate. In other versions of the story, Hera perhaps more predictably turns Iynx into stone.

The mapping of the origin story onto ritual implements is the metaphorical link between the nymph, the bird, and desire. In Pindar's *Pythian* IV (462 BCE), this invention is credited to Aphrodite, and this description is the sole literary example of an actual bird seemingly fixed, spread-eagled, onto the wheel and rotated.[1] In later descriptions the wheel is, perhaps, a representation of this model in which there is only a magical wheel. The best-known example of this type is Theocritus's *Idyll* II (third century BCE), in which the four-spoked magic wheel, the iynx (considered by most researchers to be only the wheel and not the unfortunate bird), is continuously spun during the recitation of the verse.[2]

The word 'iynx' (ἴυγξ) became a representation for compelled action and linked with the word 'elkomenos' (ἑλκόμενος), meaning to drag along, the metaphor indicating speech or sounds with qualities of a magic spell. An example of this usage is given in Plutarch's unforgettably titled 'Epicurus Actually Makes a Pleasant Life Impossible', which states "…the pleasures of geometry and harmonics have a pungent and multifarious enticement that gives them all the potency of a love-charm as they draw us with the strong compulsion of the theorems."[3]

Another example of the metaphorical use is in Origen's description of the 'charm' of Jesus in *Contra Celsum*, "There was such a charm in Jesus' words that not only men wanted to follow him into the desert, but women too, disregarding their feminine weakness and outward propriety…".[4]

One of the earliest academic studies of whirling ritual instruments of this name was undertaken by A.S.F. Gow in 1934.[5] Gow's interest in the iynx is primarily rooted in his fascination with Theocritus's *Idyll* II. This narrative, briefly mentioned above, is an extended rite to force the return of an errant lover. 'Bring me Delphis' is accompanied using various ritual actions, including the whirling device, the burning of various plant materials, and the offering of a libation.[6]

The protagonist in the *Idyll*, Simaetha, uses the iynx, translated variously as 'wryneck' and 'magic four-spoked wheel', along with various magical materia, including herbs and grain, a wax puppet, and the hem of her absent lover's cloak. These she burns at a crossroads before a wayside shrine to Hekate. This spell, especially the associated ingredients, is very similar to those encountered in much later papyri which describe syncretic magical workings with Greek, Jewish, and Egyptian components, and are imbued with a folk magic flavor very different from later magic that is classed as 'theurgical'.

---

1 Faraone, C.A. 'The Wheel, the Whip and Other Implements of Torture: Erotic Magic in Pindar *Pythian* IV.213–19', p. 3.

2 Theocritus, *Idyll* II, in *Greek Bucolic Poets*, pp. 24–39.

3 Plutarch, *Moralia* XIV, 1093D 4, *Non posse suaviter vivi secundum Epicurum*.

4 Origen, *Contra Celsum*, p 134.

5 Gow, A.S.F., 'ΙΥΓΞ, POMBOΣ, RHOMBUS, TURBO', pp. 1–14.

6 Edmunds, J.M., *Greek Bucolic Poets*, pp. 26–71.

The major factors that differentiate the magical approach of the *Idyll* include commonly available materials such as plants and animal parts, and older religious traditions. Theurgy was notably different because of the presence of written ritual and theogonic philosophy, as well as ritual implements out of reach of the general populace. Even a brief comparison between the alleged protagonist in *Idyll* II and the author of the Chaldean Oracles shows a drastic difference in approach, as well as socio-economic class of practitioner.

FIGURE 1. GILDED COPPER RING FEATURING EROS PLAYING WITH AN IYNX. 300 BCE.

In his 1934 publication, Gow documents Apulian vases dating from the fifth century BCE that show a spinning device clearly connected with Eros, and sometimes used by women in scenes associated with seduction or marriage. These vases show a flat, circular object with two strings through the center, being spun vertically. Images of Eros and Aphrodite employing the iynx are not uncommon in collections focused on Greek and Egyptian artifacts. Rather than attempting here to reproduce the poor photographs in the Gow paper, Figure 1 shows a recent and well-resolved image of Eros and his iynx on a ring found in a cemetery in Lower Egypt.[7]

The intent behind the development of the iynx as a ritual device, as Christopher Faraone explores, is rooted in the historically recognized use of wheels and whips as an orthodox form of punishment.[8] This understanding is couched in an analysis of the previously mentioned Pindar's *Pythian* IV, in which Aphrodite gives Jason a iynx to seduce Medea. In many ways, it is an erotic binding spell of the sort familiar to Greek Magical Papyri (PGM) researchers—it is meant to confuse Medea into leaving her home and coming to Jason, not as a solution to problems related to the Golden Fleece as happens in the *Argonautica*, but essentially as his love slave.

Bear in mind that Medea was known as a powerful sorceress and has often been depicted as a priestess of Hekate. In the original *Argonautica*, she helped Jason in his quest for the Golden Fleece, and according to some versions of the myth later settled with him in Corinth. An uncanny difference can be seen in the role of Medea in this selection of text from *Pythian* IV:210–219:[9]

7 Anonymous, Eros and Iynx on gold-plated copper ring, British Museum, Item 1888,0601.1.

8 Faraone, C.A., 'The Wheel, the Whip and Other Implements of Torture: Erotic Magic in Pindar Pythian 4.213–19', pp. 1–19.

9 Pindar, Basil L. Gildersleeve, '"*Pythian* IV", The Olympian and Pythian Odes', edited by Diane Arnson Svarlien, 1990, retrieved from <http://www.perseus.tufts.edu/hopper/t?doc=Perseus%3Atext%3A1999.01.0162%3Abook%3DP.%3Apoem%3D4>.

ἢ βαρυγδούπων ἀνέμων στίχες· ἀλλ' ἤδη τελευτὰν κεῖνος αὐταῖς
ἡμιθέων πλόος ἄγαγεν. ἐς Φᾶσιν δ' ἔπειτεν
ἤλυθον· ἔνθα κελαινώπεσσι Κόλχοισιν βίαν
μῖξαν Αἰήτᾳ παρ' αὐτῷ. πότνια δ' ὀξυτάτων βελέων
ποικίλαν ἴϋγγα τετράκναμον Οὐλυμπόθεν
ἐν ἀλύτῳ ζεύξαισα κύκλῳ
μαινάδ' ὄρνιν Κυπρογένεια φέρεν
πρῶτον ἀνθρώποισι, λιτάς τ' ἐπαοιδὰς ἐκδιδάσκησεν σοφὸν Αἰσονίδαν·
ὄφρα Μηδείας τοκέων ἀφέλοιτ' αἰδῶ, ποθεινὰ δ' Ἑλλὰς αὐτὰν
ἐν φρασὶ καιομέναν δονέοι μάστιγι Πειθοῦς.

And then the Argonauts came to Phasis, where they clashed with the dark-faced
Colchians in the realm of Aeetes himself. And the queen of sharpest arrows
brought the dappled wryneck from Olympus, bound to the four spokes of the
indissoluble wheel: Aphrodite of Cyprus brought the maddening bird to men
for the first time, and she taught the son of Aeson skill in prayerful incantations,
so that he could rob Medea of reverence for her parents, and a longing
for Greece would lash her, her mind on fire, with the whip of Persuasion.[10]

Faraone interprets these phrases in a literal way, as a "mad bird pinned to a
four-spoked wheel". This image of victims of 'love' spells being disoriented and
tormented is common in the later *PGM* documents (IV:2756–58 as only one example),[11]
but there is no mention of the iynx in any of these texts. In Faraone's interpretation,
in both Pindar's and the *PGM* spells, the expectation is that the device and the spells
(λόγοι) together caused the victim to leave their family, forsaken for the spell operator.
Medea herself was said to have grieved that she listened to the Greek man, causing her
to leave her family. Faraone adds that it was common at that time to punish criminals
by tying them to a wheel and torturing them by burning and beating them. In terms of
a punishment fixture, the wheels are likely to have been stationary, for practical reasons,
and not rotating, as the iynx is described as doing.

This description, Faraone informs, is part of a very old tradition.[12] The description
in the *Pythian* may be more complete than earlier descriptions, but there are many that
come before. It is clear from the ubiquity of allusions to 'love' (erotic binding) magic in
literature, from the works of Homer to the texts of early Christianity, that the audience
of the *Pythian* would have been conscious of what Jason was doing to Medea, and further,
would have recognized it as a large deviation from the original plot of the *Argonautica*.

To explore the details of the Pindar piece, note that *Pythian* IV was commissioned
along with *Pythian* V to commemorate a chariot race victory at Delphi by a Cyrene
man, Arcesilaus IV, during the fifth century BCE. The ode is a confused mixture

---

10 Ibid.

11 Betz, H.D., *Greek Magical Papyri in Translation*, p. 94.

12 Faraone, C.A., *Ancient Greek Love Magic*, pp. 5–15.

of epic poetry and description of the political climate in Cyrene. One of the epic components is the extended use of the story of Jason and the Argonauts, as we have seen. Also included is a plea for the return of an exiled man, related at the end of the Argonaut epic section, who is thought by some researchers to have paid for the ode.[13]

Pindar is known to have written odes for several powerful men, many of whom ruled cities on the periphery of Greek influence. He seems to have been motivated to emphasize their connection with the larger Greek community. It is clear from his activities later in life that he was interested in political commentary, so a reading of the Pythian odes from this standpoint makes sense.

As was made plain earlier, Pindar bends traditional myth to serve the required function of the story. Pindar transforms the relationship between Medea and Jason to explain *why* she fell in love with him, therefore assuring her aid in the quest. In doing so, the result is to keep Jason as the central figure. In Pindar's version of the story, instead of Medea wielding considerable sway, Aphrodite gives Jason the iynx and makes Medea a side-character. Her influence ends in this relation of the story with her concocting the salve for Jason and she is not involved in the acquisition of the fleece.

By taking the reins, so to speak, Jason is possibly a positive *exemplum* for Arcesilaus.[14] Or maybe not, as we will see in a moment.

FIGURE 2. ATTICA, CALYX-KRATER, BRITISH MUSEUM WEBSITE, 1867,0508.113.

Since on the larger scale, *Pythian IV* is a celebration of a chariot racing victory, there is at least conceptual and artistic overlap between chariot wheels and the appearance of the iynx in the Pindar version of the *Argonautica*. A survey of depictions of chariot racing on vases and other decorated containers shows an abundance of four-spoked wheels, and not many alternatives (Figure 2). Whether there is any significance to Pindar's description of the wryneck being affixed to a four-spoked wheel in an ode about a chariot race is an open question.

The four-spoked chariot wheel design is also present in artifacts dating before Pindar's period. One example is the iynx in the Boston Museum of Fine Arts (dated to the eighth century BCE), carefully documented in 1940. This object resembles a chariot wheel, but with 11 entire birds around the perimeter, and is oriented horizontally.[15]

13 Longely-Cook, I.A., *A Literary Study of Pindar's Fourth and Fifth Pythian Odes*, p. 90.

14 Longely-Cook, I.A., ibid., p. 89.

15 Nelson, G.W., 'A Greek Votive Inyx-Wheel in Boston', pp. 443–456.

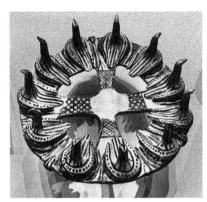

FIGURE 3. IYNX, DATED 8TH B.C.E.
(BOSTON MUSEUM OF FINE ARTS).
PHOTO: H. FEIST

This item could well be the type of ritual implement described by Pindar. Researchers are at odds with respect to the function of the iynx in the Pindar narrative. It is clearly an instrument to potentiate love binding spells, with an eye to confusing the target almost as if they were bound on a wheel for punishment, mostly with unhappy results.

Another explanation focuses on the sounds produced by the spinning of these devices. S.I. Johnston argues that the iynx operates on Medea by virtue of its whirring sound and states her belief that Pindar is using the iynx to explore the effects of voice and correct speech.[16] Like so many seductive sounds, it is likely to be deceptive, and is used because the audience understands the probable bad end it will cause. Johnston hypothesizes that the way the iynx inverts the power of Jason and Medea is meant to be improper, thereby emphasizing the proper use of language by Pindar himself and Cyrene's founders, Euphemus ('Good Speaker') and Battus ('Stutterer'). She indicates that Jason stands in contrast to Cyrene's founders because when he reaches the limits of his not-insignificant rhetoric skills, he employs trickery to constrain Medea's power. This emphasis on correct speech helps to accomplish the principal goal of persuading the current ruler to permit an exile to return home.

It is clear from this background survey that the iynx of 800–500 BCE is an instrument of persuasion. Archaeological as well as literary evidence from this time makes it possible to infer that the device discussed in Pindar is the same device as described by Philostratus, four golden iynges suspended from the ceiling of the hall of the Babylonian king. They are referred to in that document as the "tongues of the gods." Johnston documents that similar devices were suspended from the ceiling at the temple of Apollo at Delphi and possessed the persuasive powers of the Sirens, and says that it is a mystery how these devices made any sound at all.[17] Because of the example provided by the Boston Museum of Fine Arts, and the descriptions of Philostratus, there is a reasonable chance that at least some of these devices were utilized in a horizontal configuration.

Quite possibly unfamiliar with the Boston artifact, although the description is contemporary, Gow remarks of these ceiling-suspended ἴυγγες, "… [if they] are not pure fairy-tale, I will not attempt to guess what they may have been".[18]

It is evident from this survey that data regarding the orientation and use of the devices termed iynx or iynges in these early cases are limited and confused, rendering possible a variety of different interpretations. In every case except possibly those described by Philostratus, literary and archaeological evidence points to the iynx (used

16 Johnston, S.I. 'The Song of the *Iynx*: Magic and Rhetoric in *Pythian* IV', pp. 177–206.

17 Johnston, S.I., ibid., p. 184.

18 Gow, A.S.F., op. cit., p. 13.

both in the singular and plural forms) as a device that is meant to compel erotically, just like a traditional love (erotic binding) spell.

A last notable literary appearance of the iynx as a device to induce magical actions is described by Michael Psellus as being one possible cause of the so-called 'rain miracle' of 172 CE. The basic narrative of the rain miracle is that a Roman force, warring with the Quadi (in the present-day Czech Republic), were surrounded by the enemy, who denied them access to water. Cassius Dio reports that suddenly clouds gathered and there was a great downpour. Not only were the Romans saved from dying of thirst, but the storm also cast lightning and hail at the enemy.

A number of people, religions, and cults have laid claim to the magical rainstorm. Marcus Aurelius, an Egyptian magician named Arnouphis, and Julian the Theurgist of 'Chaldean Oracles' fame were three of those who were said to be responsible for the sorcerous thunderstorm. Julian is reported by Proclus as embedded with the army of Marcus, and so he is assumed to be contemporary with him. Fowden shows that Hesychius's biographical description of Julian is identical to the *Suda*'s description of Arnouphis and hypothesizes that Julian was invoked by later pagan authors to provide an alternative to the version of the story propagated by Christians.[19] It appears possible that Julian, the Chaldean theurgist, was a drop-in substitute for Arnouphis, and thus has all the fame surrounding this episode. However, that makes a less than optimal argument for the use of the iynx (or other spinning device) to summon rain.

A point about the socioeconomic status of the people associated with theurgical practices should be made here. Edmonds asserts in *Drawing Down the Moon* that there is more surviving documentation on practitioners of theurgy than on other forms of magic because

many of them were found among Roman nobility, emperors, and leaders of philosophical schools. Clearly, theurgy is not performed by people of Simaetha's status, for example.[20]

A modern nod to Aphrodite's gift of the iynx to lovers is found in Aleister Crowley's 'Hymn to Aphrodite':[21]

> *Daughter of Glory, child*
> *Of Earth's Dione mild*
> *By the Father of all, the Ægis-bearing King*
> *Spouse, daughter, mother of God,*
> *Queen of the blest abode*
> *In Cyprus' splendour singly glittering.*
> *Sweet sister unto me,*
> *I cry aloud to thee!*
> *I laugh upon thee laughing, O dew caught up from the sea!*

19 Fowden, G., 'Pagan Version of the Rain Miracle of A.D. 172', pp. 45–46.

20 Edmonds, R.G. III, *Drawing Down the Moon*, p. 317.

21 Crowley, A., *Orpheus: A Lyric Legend*, pp. 45–46.

Drawn by sharp sparrow and dove
And swan's wide plumes of love,
And all the swallow's swifter vehemence.
And subtler than the Sphinx,
The ineffable iynx
Heralds they splendour swooning into sense,
When from the bluest bowers
And greenest-hearted hours
Of Heaven thou smilest toward earth, a miracle of flowers!

THE STROPHALOS

Besides his report on the iynx in Theocritus and Pindar, Gow also reports the later use of the term 'strophalos' by Byzantine historians Michael Psellus (1017–1078 CE) and Nicephorus Gregoras (1295–1360 CE) in a theurgical, rather than a sorcerous, context. The differentiation is of critical importance to the principal argument of this essay.

The first known use of the word strophalos (στρόφαλος) is in fragment 202 of the Chaldean Oracles. The basic root of the word (στρόφ-) is present in much earlier literature and used with other nominal suffixes to mean eddy, whirl, twist, etc. Words based on that root have been in the literature for a long time, but the complete word 'strophalos', having the connotations with which we are familiar, had to wait until the second century CE.

The Chaldean Oracles are a set of texts used by Neoplatonic philosophers in the Byzantine era. They are thought to have been 'received' (i.e., revealed during a trance) by one of the Juliani, either Julian the Chaldean, or his son Julian the Theurgist, in the second century CE. The original manuscripts have been lost and the Oracles are known because of commentary upon them by the Neoplatonists, many of whom considered them to be a central text. They describe a fundamental dualism between the material world and the world of intelligences that resembles what we know today as Gnosticism. The collection of fragments describes a metaphysical schema that represents a spiritual hierarchy including a transcendent being called Father, from which intellect originates. The membrane between the realm of the intellect and the material one is personified as Hekate. From Hekate issues the World-Soul, and in turn, Nature.[22]

As the purpose of this essay is to differentiate between the iynx and the strophalos, it is important to note that the word in the singular—iynx—is not found in the Chaldean Oracles. Psellus and others only use the word in the plural form—iynges—as it relates to connective forces of the spiritual hierarchy detailed in the Chaldean Oracles (particularly fragment 206):

---

22 Majercik, R., *Chaldean Oracles*, p. 7.

"Operate with the magic wheel of Hecate."[23]

In a footnote prescient to the remainder of this essay, in *The History of Magic*, Éliphas Lévi states: "One of the Chaldæan Oracles has the following counsel: 'Labour thou around the *Strophalos* of Hecate,' which Mr. G.R.S. Mead translates 'Be active (or operative) round the Hecatic spinning thing.'" He adds by way of commentary that *Strophalos* may sometimes mean a top: "In the Mysteries tops were included among the playthings of the young Bacchus, or Iacchus. They represented...the fixed stars (humming tops) and planets (whipping tops)."[24]

The word 'iynx' in the singular is absent because the Oracles no longer refer to spinning devices that effect binding spells, but instead are denoting forces with which to communicate. In a sense, they are the thoughts of God, the same role that Plato attributed to *daimones*. Iynges also corresponded to Platonic Ideas and form a triad in the empyrean realm with the Synoches ('Maintainers') and the Teletarches ('Initators').[25]

Critically, to emphasize the principal argument of this essay, the only ritual device discussed in the Chaldean Oracles is the strophalos, and it is used in a theurgic, not a compulsive, manner. This is an important, though perhaps subtle, distinction. Majercik points this out: "...it was not the theurgist, but the god invoked who had ultimate control over the rite." Particularly, she specifies fragment 222, in which Hecate is invited by a "supplicatory prayer".[26] She also points out that there are three fragments which point to gods being bound 'against their will', but hypothesizes that the coercion is an argument for an alternate, non-Chaldean source of these fragments. Lastly, there is no fragment that speaks of the strophalos as an agent of compulsion.

Commenting upon the Oracles, Iamblichus puts the whole notion to bed: "But no one threatens the gods, nor does such a manner of invocation occur in relation to them. Hence, among the Chaldeans, by whom language used for the gods alone is preserved in its purity, threats are never uttered."[27]

If the strophalos is not an instrument for divine compulsion, then indeed, what is it?

In an origin myth regarding the Dionysian/Orphic Mysteries, the baby Dionysus is killed by Titans after they distract him with toys. These toys are clearly an important aspect of them myth and the use of the toys in initiatory settings was featured in accounts of the Mysteries, in a way that researchers as far back as Mead recognized. The toys associated with this myth, a *rhombos*, *konos*, dolls, golden apples, a mirror, and knuckle bones, are thought to correspond to a set of ritual objects, which, as Levaniouk points out,

---

23 Majercik, R., ibid., p. 127.

24 Levi, E., *The History of Magic*, Weiser Books, Boston MA/York Beach ME, 2001; footnotes on p. 68.

25 Majercik, R., op. cit., pp. 79–83.

26 Majercik, R., op. cit., p. 220.

27 Iamblichus, *De mysteriis*, translated by E.C. Clark, J.M. Dillon and J.P. Hershbell, Society for Biblical Literature, 2003. He is wryly saying that only the Egyptians would be so bold.

also had a symbolic function (as a token or *symbolon*).[28] This relationship was documented in the third-century BCE Gurob papyrus, which describes a ritual that appears to be related to the death and rebirth of the infant Dionysus. Smyly was perhaps the first to hypothesize that these ritual devices were mystic passwords or test phrases.[29]

The documented lists of the ritual toys vary, but always involve a top-like item and a spinner that rotates on a thong of some type. Clement of Alexandria, describing the Mysteries from a dismissive and Christian, but very detailed, perspective states that the mythological toys the Titans lured Dionysos with included "cone, bull-roarer, puppets (or dolls) with jointed limbs and fair gold apples from the sweet-voiced Hesperides."[30] He then lists the objects that he denotes as "tokens of this sacrament"—that is, the *symbola*: knucklebone, ball, strobilos (στρόβιλος—pinecone), apples, bull-roarer (ρόμβος), mirror and unworked wool.

The influence of these *symbola* did not end with the actual initiation rituals. Apuleius claims in his *Apology* 55:

> I have been initiated into various of the Greek mysteries and preserve with the utmost care certain emblems and mementoes of my initiation with which the priests presented me. There is nothing abnormal or unheard of in this. Those of you here present who have been initiated into the mysteries of father Liber alone, know what you keep hidden at home, safe from all profane touch and the object of your silent veneration.[31]

Levaniouk indicates that the toys of Dionysos were kept at home by the *mystai* as reminders of their initiation, tokens identifying the initiates, and objects of private worship. Struck states: "In the mysteries, particular sayings or tokens, specifically called symbols, are given to new initiates as a guarantee that other members of the cult, and especially the gods, will recognize their new status."[32]

Levaniouk and Struck agree that these toys are signs of ritual authority both to other initiates of the mysteries and the gods themselves. It is possible that this sort of ritual authority could have been conferred onto the item known in the Chaldean Oracles as the strophalos. This, therefore, answers the question: It is possible that instead of being an instrument of divine compulsion, the strophalos is rather the sign to the deity that the magician has the authority to make requests. This is a completely theurgical approach, rather than a more traditionally religious system of reciprocal gift exchange between humans and deities.

Lastly, as proof that language evolves in amusing ways, στρόφαλος means 'crankshaft' in modern Greek.

---

28 Levaniouk, O., 'The Toys of Dionysus', *Harvard Studies in Classical Philology*, Vol. 103 (2007), p. 167.

29 Smyly, G., *Greek Papyri from Gurob*, Dublin, 1921, p. 7.

30 Levaniouk, O., op. cit., p. 167–168.

31 <http://classics.mit.edu/Apuleius/apol.3.3.html>.

32 Struck, P., *Birth of the Symbol: Ancient Readers at the Limits of Their Texts*, p. 105.

SUMMARY

This essay has attempted to differentiate two types of top-like spinning ritual tools: the iynx, found in earlier literature as a potentiator for binding erotic magic, and the strophalos, found in later literature as a theurgic ritual instrument and possibly a memento of initiation in the Mysteries of Dionysus, one that may demonstrate the ritual authority and initiation status of the practitioner. In addition, it should be clear from contemporary literature that neither of the devices were ever used to compel a deity, but rather to compel people in the case of the iynx and to invite the gods to the theurgists' presence in the case of the strophalos.

BIBLIOGRAPHY

Anonymous. Attic calyx-krater. British Museum. Item 1867,0508.1133.

Anonymous. Eros and iynx on ring. British Museum. Item 1888,0601.1.

Apuleius (H.E. Butler, ed.). *The Defense*. n.d. Accessed 23 December 2021. <http://classics.mit.edu/Apuleius/apol.mb.txt>.

Betz, Hans Dieter. *The Greek Magical Papyri in Translation*. Chicago and London: University of Chicago Press, 1986.

Crowley, Aleister. *Orpheus: A Lyrical Legend*. New York: Gordon Press, 1974.

Edmonds, J.M. *Greek Bucolic Poets*. Cambridge, MA: Harvard University Press, 1912.

Edmonds, Radcliffe G. III. *Drawing Down the Moon*. Princeton, NJ: Princeton University Press, 2019.

Faraone, C.A. *Ancient Greek Love Magic*. Cambridge, MA and London, England: Harvard University Press, 1999.

—. 'The Wheel, the Whip and Other Implements of Torture: Erotic Magic in Pindar Pythian 4.213-19'. *The Classical Journal* 89 (1993): 1–19.

Fowden, Garth. 'Pagan Versions of the Rain Miracle of A.D. 172'. *Historia: Zeitschrift für Alte Geschichte* 36 (1987): 83–95.

Gow, Andrew S.F. 'ΙΥΓΞ, ΡΟΜΒΟΣ, RHOMBUS, TURBO'. *Journal of Hellenic Studies* 54 (1934): 1–13.

Iamblichus (E.C. Clark, et. al., eds). *De mysteriis*. Society for Biblical LIterature, 2003.

Iles Johnston, Sarah. 'The Song of the *Iynx*: Magic and Rhetoric in *Pythian 4*'. *Transactions of the American Philological Association* 125 (1995): 177–206.

Levaniouk, Olga. 'The Toys of Dionysus'. *Harvard Studies in Classical Philology* 103 (2007): 165–202.

Levi, Eliphas. *The History of Magic*. Boston MA/York Beach, ME: Weiser Books, 2001.

Longley-Cook, I.A. 'A Literary Study of Pindar's Fourth and Fifth Pythian Odes'. Ph.D. Thesis. St. Andrews University, 1989.

Majercik, Ruth. *The Chaldean Oracles*. Koninkljike Brill NV, 1989.

Nelson, Grace W. 'A Greek Votive Iynx-Wheel in Boston'. *American Journal of Archaeology* 44 (1940): 443–456.

Origen (H. Chadwick, translator). *Contra Celsum*. Cambridge, UK: Cambridge University Press, 1953.

Pindar (Sir John Sandys, ed.). *The Odes of Pindar including the Principal Fragments with an Introduction and an English Translation*. Cambridge, MA: Harvard University Press, 1937.

Pindar, Basil L. Gildersleeve (D.A. Svalien, ed.). Pythian Ode IV. Ed. Gregory R. Crane. 1990. Accessed 21 December 2021. <http://www.perseus.tufts.edu/hopper/t?doc=Perseus%3Atext%3A1999.01.0162%3Abook%3DP.%3Apoem%3D4>.

Plutarch (B. Einarson and P.H. DeLacy, eds.). *Moralia, Volume XIV*. Cambridge, MA: Harvard University Press, 1967.

Psellus, Michael. *Philosophica Minora, vol. II, Opuscula, Psychologica, Theologica, Daemonologica*. Teubner Verlagsgesellschaft, 1989.

Smyly, J. Gilbert., ed. *Greek Papyri from Gurob*. Dublin: Hodges, Figgis & Co., 1921.

Struck, Peter T. *Birth of the Symbol: Ancient Readers at the Limits of Their Texts*. Princeton, NJ: Princeton University Press, 2004.

MOTHER, DAIMONES AND GOÊTEIA: ECSTASY AND CIVILIZATION

SIMONE BALDACCI

AMONG THE MAIN ACTORS of what is defined as *goêteia*, there are those daimonic and multifaceted figures who in ancient times were called, with their differences, Dactyls, Telchines, Curetes, Corybantes, and Kabeiroi. Esoteric culture has paid little attention to these, underlining some witch-like aspects, without considering all the other themes and intersections that give us a richer and certainly more complex picture.

An ignored aspect is related to craftsmanship, *techne*, and civilization. The *daimones*, as we will see, have deep ties with society and culture. They are depicted on public monuments, have a presence in the theater, and some of them are part of the founding myths of cities. Another ignored point is their tie with mysteries: these figures were part of certain mystery rites spread across the eastern Mediterranean and beyond.

After an introduction to illustrate a possible model of *goêteia*, this article will focus on the figures of these *daimones* with a slight focus on the female divinity, be it goddess or nymph, commonly found with them.

THE TWO PILLARS OF GOETEIA: THE MOTHER AND THE DAIMON

There the *goêtes*, Phrygian men of Ida, mountain dwellers, have their homes
Kelmis and Damnameneus the great and proud Akmon
The ingenious attendants of the mountain goddess Adrasteia,
Who first discovered the work of clever-minded Hephaistos
In the mountain valley, purple-dark iron,
Bringing it to the fire and bringing bright works to light.

This is a fragment of *Phoronis*, an epic poem on the founding of Argos, dated between the 7th and 5th centuries B.C. Preserved through a scholion in Apollonios Rhodios's *Argonautica*, it is the oldest fragment where the word *goês* appears.

The heart of the magical-mystery dynamic called *goêteia* is tied to this core structure: a female figure and two or more male figures subordinated to it. The former, often a 'motherly' figure, is the focus of the rites, and the source of the ritual power that the attendants exercise. A role of ultimate authority similar to the one played by the Highest God in the PGM (*Papyri Graecae Magicae*) and in the grimoire tradition.

This model, however, has to be taken with caution and just as the bare bones. At times the male figure is divided into two roles: a minor attendant and a prominent figure who receives particular devotion; in other cases, besides the goddess, we find a subordinate level of female figures, such as a daughter, nymphs, *daimones*, more or less involved in a hierogamy. Being mysteries linked to local contexts, it is natural that the themes and characters of *goêteia* have a high degree of variability.

These differences, however, are in a certain sense part of the myth. The *daimones*, coming from external parts of the Greek world, such as Phrygia, Cyprus, or Crete, bring their cults with them. They establish mystery rituals by joining the local culture or clashing with the political power of the places where they reside or visit. They aren't only remembered as smiths or *goêtes*, but also as wandering priests or culture heroes: founders of cities, mysteries, sanctuaries and cults; or as inventors, mixing with public worship, with theater, with communities.

Another central point is that these *daimones* move between mythical and historical times. We know of mythical Corybantes as armed dancers of the Dionysian processions and yet also of historical Corybantes performing rituals of initiation and catharsis in the Athens of Plato.

This ambiguity is also found in a certain sense in myth: the *daimones* appear at times as immortal beings, at times as mortal heroes. In some cases they are the one invoked, in others they perform the rites. They permeate and link everything, reaching the heart of human activities and connecting them with the unlimited space of Otherness.

Thresholds and Liminality

Goêteia isn't just about the invisible and what lies beyond. It is an intricate ritual complex that involves very broad themes: the natural world, social reality, customs, culture and technology.

If we take a blank sheet of paper, and draw a circle, we now have three sections: outside the circle, inside the circle, and, however thin, the line between them. The Mother[1] is the space outside the circle, which is potentially infinite. She emerged from Chaos and is its essence contained in form, mediating its endless possibilities.

---

1 I used this term to simplify the filial relationship of the *daimones* toward the goddess or nymph who generates them. Yet, it's also relative to the *Meter Theon*, as we will see.

Inside the circle there is the space of man, civilization, order and technology.

The *daimones* reside on the border. They guard this thin line, moving smoothly between worlds and connecting these two realities, maintaining this ever-shifting balance.

When talking about liminality in magical contexts we usually mean the border with the world of the dead or with the celestial spheres: in the present case this border takes on a multifaceted dimension. We therefore find the border between civilization and primitivism, the city and wilderness, nature and culture, the earth's surface and its bowels, ecstasy and normality, mythic and historical time, past ages and the present, the sacred and the profane. In short, the *daimones* mediate between human experience and otherness in all its forms.

DAIMONES AS SPIRITS: DEMONS, ANGELS AND ELEMENTALS

Simply, they are attendants. They act, based on necessity and function.

In a mind map they are the connecting lines. Without them there is no action, the sacred remains isolated and inaccessible. Before speculation and specialization, they were able to fill every role, and perform every function later attributed to different categories of spirits.

They have a distinctive chthonic root. Close to men, able to act on the world of mortals and the dead, yet at the same time one step from the gods. Byzantine and Renaissance sources such as Psellos, Tzetzes, or Cornelius Agrippa consider them to be among the infernal powers. According to other sources they are none other than the Giants, born from Gaea and the blood of Uranus, or even Titans, often defined as *autochthon*, earthborn. They have strong ambiguities, can bring both evil and good, cause ailments and heal them.

During the Argonauts' journey they are invoked to achieve success in a partially compulsive ritual performance, with all the ambiguity of *dispensers of doom*,[2] much like the petition to demons in the grimoire tradition.

They have the role of *angeloi* in its original meaning of carriers of messages. In their role as mystagogues and initiators they guide through the mysteries to reach the divine. In Samothrace, Lemnos, and Imbros one of the male figures is Kasmilos,[3] interpreted as a Hermes with daimonic connotations, even more halfway between worlds. This initiatory and messenger role allows us to establish a comparison with those intermediary spirits of the grimoires, who have the role of establishing communication, but also with angels, in their role as guides on the path of spiritual growth and communion with the gods.

---

2 Apollonius Rhodius, *Argonautica* I.1122.

3 Also found spelled as Kadmilos, Hasmilos, or Romanized as Camillus.

It's possible to establish links between these *daimones* and each of the four elements, according to the Paracelsian synthesis.

The connection with metals and the arts of Hephaestus, the ecstatic and Dionysian sphere and the armed dance, links them to Fire, qualifying them as Salamanders.

The Telchines are sons of the waves of the sea, or of its personification; they manipulate water and have shapes that resemble marine creatures. They qualify as Undines, water elementals, and—like them—they have a distinctive feminine sphere. Furthermore, one of the main themes of Samothracian mysteries is protection at sea, of which the Dioscuri are patrons.

Other *daimones* emerge from the ground and have their mysteries within caves. They preside over the fertility of the land, the agricultural harvest and general prosperity. Some are similar to dwarves and pygmies, like the Gnomes, a deformity that symbolically connects to the element of Earth and its depths.

Some dwell at the top of high mountains. They have connections with the stars, with the winds and with the weather. They therefore have a connection with the element of Air, and qualify as Sylphs. They share links with the invention of arts, crafts, music and pre-Socratic philosophy, and the world of mind and intellect is associated with this element. Yet there are more links, and this represents just a small selection.

A further element that the *daimones* share with the Paracelsian elementals is the possibility of procreating with humans, thus maintaining the same ambiguity and closeness that is found in the *Liber de Nymphis*.

DAIMONES AS MIGHTY DEAD: HEROES, SAINTS AND ANCESTORS

They can also be initiators of a lineage or founders of a city,[4] capable of tracing a descent, mythical or real, from the present to the remote past, thus qualifying as ancestors. As ancient practitioners of the craft, they can also be configured as those 'dead magicians' that can be found rarely in the grimoire tradition.

Some of the *daimones* had cults: by transcending the limit between the human condition and the divine one, by birth or by merit, they can mediate that boundary.

When the Argonauts invoke the Dactyls, among them is Orpheus, described as initiated in Samothrace, locus of a mystery founded by the Idaean Dactyls themselves. Therefore the cantor is certainly qualified to invoke them as an initiate. But among Jason's crew there are also the Dioscuri, who in Samothrace receive the same honors as the gods. Sometimes described as Kabeiroi, therefore sons of Hephaestus, a sort of paradox occurs: they are both *subject* and *object* of invocation.

---

4 Like the Telchines as first inhabitants of Rhodes or the Couretes on Crete, or the various links between Phoroneus and the Dactyls—he's either the one who discovered fire and gave it to them, or part of their genealogy (Hesiod, fr. 123 MW).

It is also speculated that some of these mysteries celebrated the 'first man', and given the involvement of Hephaestus and Prometheus, it shouldn't be a surprise. The connection with previous eras is also suggested by Hesiod, when he speaks of the Men of Gold, Silver, and Bronze, who share common points with our *daimones*.

First Generation: The Golden Race

But after the earth had covered this generation—they are called pure spirits dwelling on the earth, and are kindly, delivering from harm, and guardians of mortal men; for they roam everywhere over the earth, clothed in mist and keep watch on judgments and cruel deeds, givers of wealth; for this royal right also they received; [...] For upon the bounteous earth Zeus has thrice ten thousand spirits, watchers of mortal men, and these keep watch on judgments and deeds of wrong as they roam, clothed in mist, all over the earth.[5]

The dead of this generation still wander the earth as invisible spirits at the disposal of men, protecting them from dangers. They also play a role in control, judgment and punishment. According to ancient views, this is a positive fact because they preserve *Dike*, Justice, which is a broader idea than ours, comparable to the Egyptian *Maat*. Justice is the principle of cosmic balance, thus by protecting the laws that govern this principle, they are upholding the common good.

Yet this punitive role creates a link with the Egyptian *daimones* of the PGM, as judges of the underworld, and with the demons of Hell. Regarding the latter, that "thrice ten thousand spirits" echoes the listing of legions and ministering spirits in the Renaissance and medieval spirits catalogs.

The idea that these spirits watch over men is reflected in the invocation to the Dactyls Tytias and Kyllenos by the Argonauts, and the promise of intervention in case of sea perils offered in Samothrace. The belief that reciting the magic formula called *Ephesia Grammata* as a litany could, through an intercession, free us from the most serious dangers certainly gives the sense of someone being there watching over us.

Second Generation: The Silver Race

But when they were full grown and had come to the full measure of their prime, they lived only a little time and that in sorrow because of their foolishness, for they could not keep from sinning and from wronging one another, nor would they serve the immortals, nor sacrifice on the holy altars of the blessed ones as it is right for men to do wherever they dwell. [...]

---

5 Hesiod, *Works and Days* 121–128, 252–255.

But when earth had covered this generation also—they are called blessed spirits of the underworld by men, and, though they are of second order, yet honor attends them also[6]

Here we find another common trait of the *daimones*: their antagonism towards the gods. Kelmis, one of the Dactyls, either refuses to honor the Mother or offends her in some way. As a punishment, he is turned to iron or locked up under the earth. The males of the Telchines get sentenced to death for various offenses: refusing to honor the gods and forgetting the sacrifices; not allowing Aphrodite to land on Rhodes; and using their magic to make the fields of the island barren as a revenge for their expulsion.

THIRD GENERATION: THE BRONZE RACE

Zeus the Father made a third generation of mortal men, a brazen race, sprung from ash-trees; and it was in no way equal to the silver age, but was terrible and strong. They loved the lamentable works of Ares and deeds of violence; they ate no bread, but were hard of heart like adamant, fearful men. Great was their strength and unconquerable the arms which grew from their shoulders on their strong limbs. Their armor was of bronze, and their houses of bronze, and of bronze were their implements: there was no black iron. These were destroyed by their own hands and passed to the dank house of chill Hades, and left no name: terrible though they were, black Death seized them, and they left the bright light of the sun."[7] "...and [Zeus] would not give the power of unwearying fire to the Melian race of mortal men who live on the earth.[8]

At Zeus's birth on Mount Ida, the *daimones* arise from the earth when Rhea sticks her fingers into it, or when one of the nursing nymphs, Anchiale, collecting some dust, lets it slip between her fingers,[9] echoing the act of Deucalion and Pyrrha or the rise of the Spartoi in the travels of Cadmos and Jason. They come up fully armed with bronze, mirroring the birth of the Giants:

And the great Giants with gleaming armor, holding long spears in their hands[10]

A possible etymology of the word Giants is *gêgenês*, earthborn, basically identical to *autochthon*. The equation between the Giants and the bronze-clad *daimones* was well known in antiquity.

---

6 Hesiod, *Works and Days* 130–142.

7 Hesiod, *Works and Days* 143–157.

8 Hesiod, *Theogony* 564.

9 Scholion e on Apollonius Rhodius, *Argonautica* I.1126–31.

10 Hesiod, *Theogony* 185.

Regarding the ash, it is an allusion to the *Meliae*, the mountain nymphs of this tree, mentioned in Hesiod immediately after the Giants. From these, according to Apollonios Rhodios, the men of bronze descend. Adrasteia, among the nurses of Zeus on Mount Ida, belongs to these nymphs. Their role as nurses lies in the root of their name, since *meli* also means honey, and honey is the food of the gods, appropriate for the infant Zeus.

This tree was also employed to make instrument handles, bows, and spear shafts, laying an additional martial element on the table. The martial nature of the *daimones* is also emphasized in many ways: virility, phallic elements, terrestrial fertility, armed dance, and their role as *kourotrophos*, nurturers of infants.

Their demise bears a different description than those of the other generations: it's said that they left the light of the sun. A similar phrase will be used by Psellus to define a whole category of demons, which he calls Lucifuges, those who flee the light.[11]

The last sentence is a mention of the myth of Prometheus's theft of fire. The bronze race are equated with the mortals that received his stolen gift, thus establishing a strong link between them. As we will see, the Titan has deep involvement in this context.

INTERLUDE: ARES, HEPHAESTUS AND PRIAPUS

The text says they loved the works of Ares. That could conceal, as with Hephaestus in the fragment of *Phoronis*, more than a simple reference to war.

These two gods share many links with each other and with the chthonic world:

- They do not enjoy sympathy: Hephaestus is mocked and lives far from everyone; Ares is defined, in many sources, as hateful.
- They were born by parthenogenesis from their mother Hera.
- They have a teacher that could qualify as one of the mentioned *daimones*. Hephaestus's teacher is Kedalion, a dwarf whose name means 'The Phallic One'. Ares is instructed in the art of dance and war by Priapus, who has clear phallic connotations.

About Priapus, a Roman source defines him as a Dactyl.[12] He shows phallic and chthonic features as well as connections with the magical-apotropaic world through the domain of terrestrial fertility and that of armed dance. He is sometimes represented like Hermes, sometimes referred to as Dionysus himself, or his son. Ovid tells us of his attempted rape of Vesta, Pomona, and the nymph Lotis, which mirrors the theme of offense against the female found with Kelmis. For these reasons and more, I fully consider him one of the *daimones*.

---

11 Psellus, *On the Operation of Demons*.

12 Lucian, *De Saltatione* 21.

Fourth Generation: Heroes

The fourth generation of men is not marked by any metal, and is that of the Homeric Heroes. Apart from singing their praises, the author gives us an interesting piece of information. To this generation:

> Father Zeus the son of Cronos gave a living and an abode apart from men, and made them dwell at the ends of the earth. And they live untouched by sorrow in the islands of the blessed along the shore of deep-swirling Ocean.[13]

The Ocean in myth is not the same as the sea. It divides and protects. It is that body of water, often a river, that marks the boundary between the underworld and the world of men, confirming the liminality of the *daimones*.

Fifth Generation: The Iron Race

The use of iron to connote present-day men certainly marks a clear distance from the past—different metal, different age. Yet, the very fact that this generation is marked by a metal creates a bridge and highlights some kind of continuity and commonality between current men and earlier times.

The identification of *daimones* with metals isn't just evoked through their skill with metallurgy or the bronze armor they wear. Some of them have the names of metals themselves, such as *Kelmis*, iron, or, although from a Byzantine source, the three Telchines: *Argyron*, silvery, *Chryson*, golden, and *Chalcon*, brazen.

Daimones' Main Features

Let's recall the five main categories of *daimones*: Dactyls, Telchines, Corybantes, Curetes and Kabeiroi.

At present, we have little information on them, and even less of a ritual nature. Starting from Strabo's words[14] stating that all these entities were connected and mostly the same, I'll have as a mental compass two aims. First, to understand what links them, even if we've already glimpsed this a bit. Then, to highlight the differences and bring out the peculiarities, which I will now analyze.

Pyrrhic Dance: Ecstasy and Performance

The 'Pyrrhic dance' was a kind of dance, not exclusive to men, executed by wearing and clashing bronze armors and weapons. This type of ritual performance was invented by a certain Pyrrhicos; according to others by Neoptolemus, called Pyrrhus, son of

---

13 Hesiod, *Works and Days* 167–172. .

14 Strabo, *Geography,* X.3.7–8.

Achilles. Other sources claim it is the funeral dance performed by the same Achilles around the *pyre* of Patroclus. Or it could stem from the dance of the Curetes to protect the infant Zeus. A fifth hypothesis says it was invented by the goddess Athena, who performs it twice: once just after her birth, then after the defeat of the Giants.

The etymology tells us a lot about this dance: the word Pyrrhic derives from *pyrrhos*, red, or flame-colored, due to the color of the Curetes' tunics, and from *pyr*, fire. Often, the music of the aulos—a flute invented by the Dactyls—was added to this performance.

In the episode of Zeus's birth, Rhea makes the *daimones* emerge from the earth, fully armed, so that their noisy dance can cover the lamentations of the goddess and of the child, making sure that Kronos doesn't discover them.

Each of the five groups of *daimones* is, more or less, linked to this performance. Whether they do it themselves, or whether they are invoked during these acts in propitiation to bring a positive outcome, it is one of their central attributes.

METER THEON AND DANCE AS SACRED MADNESS

Besides having Dionysian aspects, dance (and music) also links to the cult of the Mother of the Gods, identified, from time to time, with Rhea, Cybele, Gaea, Demeter, or other figures. The ceremonies of these cults used to take place in the wilderness, probably at night. People looked for these cults because they offered a connection to the divine world without any mediation or the formality of the polis rituals. Representations of the Mother often show the presence of the *tympanon*, a hand drum, one of her main iconographic attributes. Certainly the clash of bronze armor and the beating of weapons on shields take up this percussive idea of the drum, known in all cultures for its ability to ease passage into altered states. A clear testimony to the ecstatic character of this cult is given to us by the Homeric Hymn XIV, to the Mother of the Gods:

> I Prithee, clear-voiced Muse, daughter of mighty Zeus,
> sing of the mother of all gods and men.
> She is well-pleased with the sound of rattles and of timbrels,
> with the voice of flutes and the outcry of wolves and bright-eyed lions,
> with echoing hills and wooded coombes.
> And so hail to you in my song and to all goddesses as well![15]

Although short, the hymn gives us a clear image: ceremonies in the mountains and woods, between the frantic rhythm of primal instruments and the sounds of wild animals.

The ecstatic aspect of the dance could be channeled into a form of healing. In fact, Plato tells us of a Corybantic ritual called *thronosis*, performed in Athens during his time.[16] The aspirant was sitting, head covered, and two armed figures danced around him. This

---

15 Hesiod, *Homeric Hymns, Epic Cycle, Homerica*, translated by Evelyn-White, Loeb, 1914.

16 S. Blakely, 2006. Plato, *Euthydemus* 277d; *Ion* 533c–34a, 536c; *Krito* 54d; *Laws* VII.790c–91b; scholia to *Symposium* 215, 215e.

brought him into a state of 'madness'. Through the same combination of dance and music, this state was then cured and the aspirant was brought back to his senses. This procedure was used to cure psychological ailments or could serve for purification.

The connection between the Mother and folly is also reported by Catullus, in this famous verse:

> Goddess so great, goddess Cybele, lady goddess of Dindymus, may all your madness stay far from my home, mistress: drive others in frantic speed, drive others to madness.[17]

The Pseudo-Apollodorus, in his *Bibliotheca*, tells how Dionysus, filled with madness, was purified and healed by Cybele.[18] The Mother would then initiate him into the mysteries.

Almost echoing the vestiges of a shamanic path, the god has passed the test, surviving the sacred disease. The goddess heals and consecrates him, while instructing him in the mysteries.

DANCE AS RITUAL PERFORMANCE

We are now going to deal with another important aspect of this dance, citing this episode:

> And near it they heaped an altar of small stones, and wreathed their brows with oak leaves and paid heed to sacrifice, invoking the mother of Dindymus, most venerable, dweller in Phrygia, and Titias and Cyllenus, who alone of many are called dispensers of doom and assessors of the Idaean mother, -- the Idaean Dactyls of Crete, whom once the nymph Anchiale, as she grasped with both hands the land of Oaxus, bare in the Dictaean cave. And with many prayers did Aeson's son beseech the goddess to turn aside the stormy blasts as he poured libations on the blazing sacrifice; and at the same time by command of Orpheus the youths trod a measure dancing in full armor, and clashed with their swords on their shields, so that the ill-omened cry might be lost in the air the wail which the people were still sending up in grief for their king.[19]

The Argonauts mistakenly killed Cyzicus, king of the Doliones, who had previously welcomed them. Despite the necessary funeral rites, the headwinds that keep them on dry land refuse to cease due to a preceding offense: the Argonauts killed some Giants[20] which had come to attack them. Guided by a prophecy, they go on Mount Dindymon, where they carve a *xoana* (a crudely carved wooden statue) from an oak and erect an

---

17 Catullus, *Attis* 63.

18 Pseudo-Apollodorus, *Bibliotheca* III.33.

19 Apollonius Rhodius, *Argonautica* I.1122.

20 These giants were sons of the Mountain Mother, Rhea-Cybele.

altar of stones. Invoking the Mother and the two local dactyls, Tityas and Kyllenos, through sacrifices and armed dance, the celebrants not only manage to stop the evil winds and to dispel the aura of grief in the air, but they obtain unexpected results. The mountain is reborn, the forest is tawny and lush, a spring starts flowing from the stones of the altar, and wild animals come near the place of the ceremony, appearing tame and friendly. Cyzicus's spirit is appeased, and Rhea has accepted the offer and rewarded the celebrants. Here we see another ritual aspect of the armed dance: to promote fertility. Besides calming the ghost of Cyzicus and the winds, the mountain is hit by an explosion of lusciousness.

This connection is also found in a Cretan hymn[21] that praises Zeus as a *kouros*, a young god of vegetation, representative of male phallic fertility, dancing and leaping across the fields. His return brings back fertility in spring, thus ensuring the new harvest. And the *daimones*, addressed as Curetes, attend to him in his passage.

We could therefore define this dance as a multipurpose and multifunctional tool to carry out propitiatory, apotropaic, cathartic, funeral and mystery operations through the achievement of altered states and communion with the Mountain Mother.

Terrestrial Fertility: Nurturing and Protection

We touched on this subject with the dance of the Argonauts. A role that distinguishes the *daimones* is that of *kourotrophos*, essential for the birth and growth of the young Zeus and his spring return. The protection and nurturing of infant gods is not just limited to Zeus. Some sources present the Corybantes as nurturers of Dionysus, and the Telchines of Poseidon.

The *daimones* have a close connection with everything related to earth. The Mother is the chthonic principle. She is Gaea, she is Earth itself, and one of her titles is *Meter Oreia*, mother of the mountains; they are her ministries.

Let's take the example of Priapus as Dactyl: he's got a clear role as protector and warden of fertility, a fitting association. This model, which can be defined as chthonic-phallic,[22] clearly outlines the *daimones*, and recalls, more than a modern conception of sexuality, the apotropaic power of this symbol: the *hermai* that mark and protect the fields, or the Roman *fascinum*, able to protect from the evil eye and malicious influences, are just a few examples. The *daimones* propagate fertility through the martial act of protection and their communion with the goddess.

Many *daimones* are described as dwarves, or pygmies, or have deformities of this kind. The prototype of the small human being is often connected to caves, mines, tunnels and the bowels of the earth. This aspect has a further phallic connotation confirmed by the numerous statuettes of dwarves with a disproportionate phallus. Deformity is often linked to magical abilities, according to the idea that everything that diverges from normality brings with it something exceptional and is tied to otherness and to the realm of the sacred.

---

21 The Palaikastro Hymn, also known as Hymn to the Kouretes.

22 E. Monick, *Phallos: Sacred Image of the Masculine*, Inner City Books, 1987.

Terrestrial Fertility: Magic and Metals

The *daimones'* association with protection is expressed through the presence of metals. The bronze of their armor implies sacredness and antiquity, both symbols of authority. The Dactyls recall the apotropaic power of iron. The Kabeiroi, with their reference to the forge and to Hephaestus, refer to the intervention of tools and agriculture in enhancing the wealth of the fields. Even some heroes, connected to the *daimones* through the same mystery complex, carry the theme of civilization and fertility. Iasion, founder of the mysteries of Samothrace, performs a hierogamy with Demeter, in the "thrice-plowed field". Their union generates *Ploutos*, personification of wealth and prosperity. After plowing the field of King Aetes, Jason sows dragon's teeth, generating the *Spartoi*, fully armed earthborn men. This recalls both the emergence of the Curetes, the creation of mankind by Deucalion, and the same act performed by Kadmus, whose surviving Spartoi will become the ruling families of Thebes.

The *daimones'* power to influence the harvest and fertility is also expressed through their magic and their ability, as *goêtes*, to manipulate weather, both in a constructive way, as we have seen in the story of the Argonauts on Mount Dindymus, or for destruction, like in the myth of the Telchines: after being expelled from the island of Rhodes, to get revenge they pour Stygian water that makes the fields barren. It is not clear if this act is done through weather magic, or if it refers to a *pharmaka*, and both possibilities are equally coherent.

Interlude: Heracles the Dactyl

A final example of this domain is in the figure of *Herakles Daktylos*, a syncretic *daimon* who has ties with the Egyptian Bes, the demigod Heracles, and the Phoenician Melqart. He was honored by Greek women as a protector of childbirth and the hearth. Many amulets, often inscribed on lodestone, depict him as a leonine dwarf with snakes in his hands, symbolizing his power against dangers and his protective role. The lodestone, also called Heraclean Stone, besides carrying the powers of iron, had many magical properties. In this case, it was used for its capacity to exert an 'invisible force', thus sympathetically exerting that same force and resolution against the targeted ailments.

Δαμναμενευς

Ακμων

Κελμις

Goeteia: Between Magic and Philosophy

Only the Dactyls and Telchines are explicitly mentioned as *goêtes*. Curiously, they are the most related to metallurgy and craftsmanship, and the most morally ambiguous.

Their magical craft, *goêteia,* is articulated on these points:

- weather manipulation
- *pharmakeia:* use of drugs, herbs and medicines
- necromancy in the broader sense of operations performed with/for/through the dead
- *epoidai*, incantations performed through inscription or voice: as healing songs, magical formulas like the *Ephesia Grammata*, or the making of talismans.

Yet this is just a scheme. Reality is more complex: there is, for example, the power of symbols and images, inherent in the figure of the dwarf, or in the phallus, capable of countering the evil eye and negative influences. A problem arises when analyzing what *goêteia* means. Its elaboration appears very late and it's derived from a verb, denoting a ritual act of funeral lament, and from the word used to denote the one performing it, that is the *goês*.[23] And the word seems to escape clear boundaries, being used to denote sorcerers, lycanthropes, charlatans, or entire populations,[24] leaving us with no choice but to use a tautological definition which will be useful later:

Goêteia is the art of the goês

This vague answer, however, allows us to reframe the problem correctly and shift the focus to a question within our reach:

Who were the Goêtes? And <u>what did they do</u>?

Based on what we have seen, the *goês* is not just a magician or a sorcerer as our modern imagery could suggest. Using another misnomer, his attributes reflect something closer to a shamanic prototype:

- ritual dance and performance
- power over earthly fertility
- assistance in the worship of the gods
- physical and psychical healing
- relationship with the arts
- knowledge of a territory and its ecology of spirits
- mediation of borders with the dead and the invisible
- mastery of altered states
- initiations and mysteries
- service and protection of a community, if not being part of it
- involvement in ancestry and local mythology

These are all characteristics of a multifaceted figure that the words Magician, Sorcerer, and even Shaman perhaps, struggle to contain.

THE GOÊS AS NATURAL PHILOSOPHER: PRE-SOCRATIC IDEAS AND PYTHAGOREANISM

In this overview, I haven't counted all the connections with pre-Socratic philosophy. According to a recent hypothesis, Pythagoreanism had ideas in common with *goêteia*.[25] We know that Pythagoras himself was initiated in Crete or Phrygia by a Dactyl (or one of the Curetes) named Morgus, and purified by means of a sacred stone.[26] The

---

23 D. Ogden, *Greek and Roman Necromancy*, 2001.

24 M. Antola, 'Γόης, γοητεύω e γοητεία in Platone', Master's thesis, University of Pisa, 2017.

25 S. Blakely, 'Pherekydes' Daktyloi: Ritual, technology, and the Presocratic perspective', *Kernos* 20, 2007, 43–67.

26 Iamblichus, *V.P.*, 17, 25; Porphyry, *V.P.*, 9, 17; Diogenes Laertius, *V* 25–27.

philosopher Empedocles is defined by many ancient authors as a *goês*. This quote is from one of his own fragments:

> Pharmaka, however many are a defense against evils and old age,
> you will learn, since for you alone I shall accomplish these things.
> You will stop the strength of the weariless winds, which
> rise up along the earth and lay waste to cultivated lands with their blasts,
> and again, if you want, you will lead the winds back.
> And out of black rain you will make a timely drought
> for men, and out of a summer drought you will make
> tree-nourishing streams, that dwell in the air.
> And you will lead from Hades the strength of a dead man.[27]

The links with philosophy go even deeper. About the Dactyls, we know only that they discovered iron. We don't know exactly what they produce, what they do with it. In her research, fundamental for this essay, Sandra Blakely interprets that maybe the focus is not on craftsmanship, but on the knowledge of a material and its processing techniques. If we combine the idea of the *daimones* as profound connoisseurs of metals with their knowledge of *pharmakeia*, the resulting picture is that of a natural philosopher who is not only a *technites* of the mineral, vegetal, and animal worlds, but also an adept of the symbolic and mystical relationships between the elements in philosophical terms of Air, Water, Earth and Fire.

Knowledge and observation skills, according to the myth, are what lead the Dactyls to discover the casting of metals after a great fire. Mastery over the mineral and vegetal world is what leads the Telchines perhaps to concoct something equivalent to the infernal water of the river Styx, capable of making the fields barren. Their legendary skills in the arts of Hephaestus, combining magic and *techne*, is what allows them to animate statues: both suitable for hosting a god and imitating human life. We could, exaggerating a bit, say that they combine skills typical of a magician with those of a scientist.

According to Zenobius, the power of the *Ephesia Grammata*, a supreme magical formula of protection invented by the Dactyls, consisted in the revelation of the cosmic order of the planets and the seasons. And this is well suited to the emphasis on knowledge of the structure of the cosmos through numbers and self-purification promoted by the Pythagoreans. This formula also aligns with the taste for enigmas represented by *akousmata*, oral and sybilline aphorisms that bring stimulus for contemplation.

Techne and Magic, the Case of Hephaestus

According to the interpretations of Delcourt and Detienne, Hephaestus is the prototype of the magician god, possessing the two basic powers: binding and loosening. We see the former in the episode of Hera trapped on the golden throne; in that of

---

27 C. Faraone, 'Empedocles the Sorcerer and his Hexametrical Pharmaka', *Antichthon* 53, 2019, 14–32.

the invisible net in which Ares and Aphrodite are caught; through the cursed necklace of Harmonia, which binds anyone who wears it to an unfortunate fate. The latter is expressed in the power to animate objects, such as his self-moving tripods, or his golden servants; in the splitting of the head of Zeus to free Athena; in causing an 'inextinguishable laughter' among the Gods.

These powers, attributed to Hephaestus, are mirrored by the Dactyls in this fragment preserved in a scholion to the *Argonautica*:

> Idaean Dactyls: They say they are six and five, the right being male, the left being female. Pherekydes says the right are twenty, and the left thirty two. They are magicians and poisoners, and they are said to be the first skilled workmen in iron and to be miners. They are named for mother Ida, the left of them, as Pherekydes[28] says, are magicians, and those loosening spells the right.

The power to bind is found in some magical-medical devices used mostly by women, calling on Herakles Dactylos: we speak of *periammata*, analogous to the phylactery in the PGM.[29] They were talismans: sympathetically arranged devices that, by prayers and incantations, were magically tied to the person for whom they would work.

Magic of Life and Death

The field of the relationship between *goêteia* and the dead is a very complex one, and I would be inadequate in speaking about it. For a complete treatment of the funerary theme in Greek culture I rely on Sarah Iles Johnston's *Restless Dead*. I will just add some considerations.

It is known that the word *goês* derives from terms such as *goào*, lament, cry, and *goos*, the funeral lament typically made by women. Although the Daimones, as *goêtes*, are mediators between the world of the living and that of the dead, they are still forces of life. The Argonauts prepare the ceremony for the Phrygian Mother because the dead have to be placated, and an offense to the goddess needs to be repaired. The need to appeal to the Mother is due to her power. She governs the winds, the sea, and all the forces of earth and sky, thus exerting dominion over life. After the place for the ceremony is prepared, the Argonauts start their frantic dance, making metallic noises and clangor and playing the *tympanon*, following the rhythm of the *aulos*:

> so that the ill-omened cry might be lost in the air, the wail which the people were still sending up in grief for their king.

Thus the martial, phallic, vital power exemplified by the Argonauts and their ecstatic and Dionysian display—in accord with the forces of the Great Mother which

---

28 It could be the Syrian Pherecydes, master of Pythagoras, whose fragments constitute a major source for our knowledge of the dactyls.

29 S. Blakely, 2006, 139–162.

the Homeric hymn compares to the howling of wolves and the roar of lions—drives away the forces of death, restoring order and indeed giving gifts of fertility as a sign of good omen. Ecstatic madness, capable of healing, as seen in the cathartic and purifying power of Corybantic experiences, in this case banishes all the influences of the world of the dead that are still crossing that sacred boundary between their world and that of the living. Just as Odysseus holds the dead at bay with his sword, here the holiness of bronze and the apotropaic iron, invoked through the Dactyls, drive away negative influences, cleansing the mind and the soul through the power of sound, recalling also this Pythagorean *akousma*:

> The echoing sound of the bronze when it is stuck is the captured voice of a demon.

Even if the sources show the word *goês* assuming negative connotations from the Classical era, most of the evidence we have on the *daimones* is from the Hellenistic and Roman periods. And yet, in the descriptions of Pausanias or Strabo there is no detraction of these figures. They survive this debasement by leaning on the reputation of the myths and mysteries involving them. Our protagonists maintain that fluidity and indeterminacy, typical of the concept of the *daimon*, which allows them to appear both in 'street' magic formulas, like certain fragments of the PGM, and in 'higher' narratives through associations with the cult of the Phrygian Mother and the Idaean, Samothracian, Kabeiric and Dionysian Mysteries.

MYSTERIES: MYTHS AND NARRATIVES

On this point I would like to posit another premise. We know very little of the mystery rites in which the *daimones* were involved, and almost nothing of the rituals performed there, except for the archaeological evidence, which, through the finds, allows us to understand something about the material part of the rites. Therefore, the interpretation of these sources has an even more personal character. Let's start with a quote:

> The first of these gods of whom tradition has left a record made their home in Crete about Mount Ida and were called Idaean Dactyls.
> [...] But some historians, and Ephoros is one of them, record that the Idaean Dactyls were in fact born on Mt. Ida which is in Phrygia and passed over to Europe together with Mygdon; and since they were magicians, they practiced charms and initiatory rites and mysteries, and in the course of a sojourn in Samothrace they amazed the natives of that island not a little by their skill in such matters. And it was at this time, we are further told, that Orpheus, who was endowed with an exceptional gift of poetry and song, also became a pupil of theirs, and he was subsequently the first to introduce initiatory rites and Mysteries to the Greeks.

However this may be, the Idaean Dactyls of Crete, so tradition tells us, discovered both the use of fire and what the metals copper and iron are, as well as the means of working them, this being done in the territory of the city of Aptera at Berecynthia, as it is called; and since they were looked upon as the originators of great blessings for the race of men, they were accorded immortal honors.[30]

The Mysteries of Eleusis weren't the only ones present in the Aegean area of influence. Other rites, with different themes and mythologies, were celebrated in many parts of Greece. After Eleusis, the Mysteries of Samothrace were the most famous and sought after. That and other sanctuaries were linked by the term used to address their deities, either *Megaloi Theoi*, Great Gods, or *Kabeiroi*.

These mysteries unfold around the eastern Aegean Sea, which connects Greece, the Black Sea basin and Anatolia, yet also the shores of Phoenicia. It also follows the journey of the Dactyls, which, starting from Phrygia, takes them to Crete.

Lemnos and Thebes

The oldest sanctuary of the Kabeiroi is on Lemnos, the island sacred to Hephaestus. The metallurgical theme was present, as evidenced by the fragments that speak of the Kabeiroi trained in the father's furnace. Here, over time, various female figures have followed one another: it is hypothesized a certain Lemnos was equated with Artemis or Aphrodite. There are fragments that speak instead of a Kabeiro, daughter of Proteus, and Cybele is attested in the Hellenistic period. There is also mention of a Kadmilos, son of Hephaestus, identified with Hermes, in turn the father of three Kabeiroi and three *kabeirides* nymphs. According to other sources, there are only two Kabeiroi, Onnes and Tottes.

Themes relating to the evolution of civilization, the arts and human creation are also found in other sanctuaries. In Boeotian Thebes the goddess Demeter Kabeiria is paired with either a Kabeiros, identified with Dionysus, with a young attendant named Pais, or with two other male figures, Prometheus and his son Aetneus, instructed by the goddess in the mysteries. Assuming that the main male figure had a prominent role within the myth, we see how its themes may concern the theft of fire, the creation of mankind, and the myth of Pyrrha and Deucalion. He is also the son of Prometheus, who warned him to build the ark. This myth also involves a strong element of autochthony, since the Oracle of Themis warns the two progenitors to throw the 'Mother's bones' behind their backs. The reference is both to Gaea, intended as the mother of all, but also to Pandora, mother of Pyrrha, under whose mask an ancient Mother Goddess might be hiding. In fact, the name Pandora, understood as *the one who has all the gifts*, can also be translated as *all-giver*, referring to the fruits and the wealth given by the land.

Like the *Spartoi* and the *daimones*, men too are therefore *Ge-genes*, earthborn. The myth of Prometheus is deeply linked to Hephaestus: the lame god is the one who creates Pandora and reluctantly chains the Titan on the Caucasus.

---

30 Diodorus Siculus, *Library of History*, V.64.3--5.

SEAFARING, SALVATION AND VOYAGE

In Samothrace we have a triad perhaps identifiable with Harmonia and her two brothers Dardanus and Iasion, with the presence of Curetes as initiators and attendants, and altars to other gods, such as the Dioscuri. One of the central themes of this sanctuary was protection at sea. This is thoroughly confirmed by the many thanksgiving dedications left on other islands by sailors in honor of the gods of Samothrace.

The *daimones* in charge of this intervention were the Dioscuri, Castor and Polydeuces, which we also see at work in the Argonauts' journey:

> There came on a great storm and the chieftains had given up hope of being saved, when Orpheus, they say, who was the only one on ship-board who had ever been initiated in the Mysteries of the deities of Samothrace, offered to these deities prayers for their salvation. And immediately the wind died down and two stars fell over the heads of the Dioskouroi, and the whole company was amazed at the marvel which had taken place and concluded that they had been rescued from their perils by an act of providence of the gods. For this reason, the story of this reversal of fortune for the Argonauts has been handed down to succeeding generations, and sailors when caught in storms always direct their prayers to the deities of Samothrace and attribute the appearance of the two stars to the epiphany of the Dioskouroi.[31]

Another myth probably present in Samothrace, and surely part of the Kabeiric complex as evinced by certain vases from Thebes and other locations, derives from the episode, narrated by Homer, of the meeting between Odysseus and Ino Leucothea. She was a mortal who became a sea goddess. Alcman defines her as *Thalassomedoisa*, Queen of the Sea, and she has points of contact with the figure of Tethis, Hephaestus's adoptive mother. Both of the mentioned goddesses are also involved as nurturing figures to Dionysus.

While Odysseus is in the middle of a storm sent to him by Poseidon, the goddess Leucothea, having mercy on him, appears to the hero and gives him a scarf that will guarantee him safety until he reaches the mainland. A scholion of the *Argonautica* confirms this:

> They say Odysseus, being an initiate and using Leukothea's veil in place of a filet, was saved from the storm at sea by placing the veil below his abdomen. For the initiates bind filets below their abdomen.

Ino Leucothea was the daughter of Cadmus, one of the oldest heroes of the Greek world, who appears in another episode central to the mysteries: that of his marriage with Harmonia.

---

31 Diodorus Siculus, *Library of History* IV.43.1.

Of Phoenician descent, founder of the same Thebes in Boeotia mentioned earlier, dragonslayer, navigator and explorer, as well as inventor of the alphabet, Cadmus landed in Samothrace to look for his sister Europa, kidnapped by Zeus, and it is here that he meets Harmonia. Although many genealogies define her as the daughter of Ares and Aphrodite, in this myth she is identified as the daughter of Electra, one of the Pleiades. The Phoenician hero has points of contact with Kadmilos-Hermes, mentioned earlier, who appears in several different sanctuaries. They are both travelers and bringers of culture, and both are said to be inventors of the alphabet.

A marriage between a cultural hero and a goddess who represents balance and harmony really has many implications, considering all that has been said about the tension between the Great Mother and the *daimones*, and the nature-culture polarity sub-theme that underlies this essay. The *technites*, while causing some kind of offense to the Mother, plays an essential role in regard to her.

The figure of Electra creates a further genealogical link with recurring elements: she is in fact the daughter of Atlas, brother of Prometheus, and like many others in this essay, he too receives exemplary punishment.

Furthermore, her two sons, Iasion and Dardanus, are themselves cultural heroes. Of the former we said he's the founder of the Mysteries of Samothrace, which he received from Demeter. But we also know that Samothrace was founded by the Dactyls. Consequently, this would make Iasion, and therefore also his brother, two Dactyls. Dardanus, which we also find mentioned in the PGM, is reputed to be the founder of Troy, from which the Roman Penate gods, identified with the Kabeiroi, were brought to Latium by Aeneas on his travels.

Electra's homonym, as daughter of Agamemnon, is also involved in crime and tragedy: taking vengeance for her father, as told in Aeschylus's *Oresteia*, by colluding in the killing of Clytemnestra and Aegisthus. Orestes, after committing this crime, is absolved through trial by Athene. This echoes the presence at Samothrace of a 'confession of sins' and a special priest charged with purifying homicides.

The other aspect is the connection between the Pleiades and their role in navigation, certainly consistent with the marine themes of Samothrace. The presence of the stars also recalls the light and fire on the heads of the two Dioscuri. This element played a key role at the end of the initiatory process. The epitaph of Isidorus, an Athenian who lived between 2 and 1 B.C. tells us:

> As an initiate, great-hearted, he saw the doubly sacred light of Kabiros in Samothrace and the pure rites of Deo in Eleusis.

HERMES AND THE PELASGIAN PAST

A connection to be taken into account with caution pertains to another of the Pleiades, Maia, syncretized with the Roman goddess of the same name (yet the majority of the sources on Samothrace are from the Hellenistic and Roman period), wife of Vulcan, goddess of fertility and of the earth, identified with a whole series of Mother

Goddesses such as Tellus, Ops, Bona Dea (Agathe Tyche), Juno, and more. However, an association does not seem so far-fetched. Maia is also the mother of Hermes, who appears in this daimonic form under the name of Kadmilos. Hermes's trickster role links to Hephaestus and Prometheus, and he is also credited with the discovery of fire. Hermes's connection with these mysteries is also confirmed by Herodotus. He narrates that the *hermai*, ithyphallic statues of Hermes:

> came from the Pelasgians, from whom the Athenians were the first Greeks to take it, and then handed it on to others. [...] Whoever has been initiated into the rites of the Kabeiroi, which the Samothracians learned from the Pelasgians and now practice, understands what my meaning is. Samothrace was formerly inhabited by those Pelasgians who came to live among the Athenians, and it is from them that the Samothracians take their rites.[32]

There is some evidence pointing at this foreign and pre-Hellenic influence in Samothrace. The official language of the mysteries wasn't Greek, but a local language still not fully deciphered, derived from the Thracian language, pointing again at Anatolia, and giving even more credit to its founding by the Dactyls.

THE DIONYSIAN HERITAGE OF THE KABEIROI

These mysteries could possibly have to do with Dionysus, and we already uncovered some solid connections. Cadmus and Harmonia are the grandparents of Dionysus, and Ino Leucothea is both his nurse and sister of Semele, his mother. After her death, Hermes brings the infant to Ino and recommends that she raise him like a female to hide him from Lycurgus. Hephaestus also plays a pivotal role in this story. He and Dionysus are both raised by the nymph Thetis, but it is due to an action of the blacksmith god that Dionysus will be born. To take revenge for Aphrodite's betrayal, Hephaestus creates, as a wedding gift for Harmonia, a cursed necklace. Although it allows the wearer to remain eternally young and beautiful, unbeknownst to everyone it is able to manipulate fate and attract misfortune to the one who bears it. In fact the whole royal house of Thebes, from Cadmus to Oedipus, passing through Semele and Dionysus, will be afflicted by this disaster. So the chain of events that leads to the birth of Dionysus starts from Hephaestus.

But the connection with Dionysus does not end here. We learn that two Kabeiroi, Onnes and Tottes, traveled carrying the *sacra* of the Cabiri in a basket.[33] in exchange for the establishment of a Kabeiric cult in Assessus near Miletus, they save the city from its aggressors. The sight of the basket fills the enemies with panic, which allows the Kabeiroi's army to defeat them. According to the Christian author Clemens, this *sacra* would be the phallus of Dionysus/Zagreus, which they acquired and brought to the Tyrrhenians (therefore in Lemnos or in Etruria.)

---

32 Herodotus, *Histories* II.51.

33 Nicolaus of Damascus, *FGH* 90 fr. 52.

Obviously the Kabeiric sanctuaries aren't limited to these places, but I have brought the most significant examples to illustrate the context, and to make us reflect on this complex network of meanings.

ZEUS MYSTERIES: SACRED STONES, CAVES AND METEORITES

The other network of related mysteries is linked to the birth of Zeus. These mysteries, celebrated in numerous parts of Greece, Anatolia and Crete, saw the *daimones* playing a central role, as protectors and *kourotrophoi* of the god.

Furthermore, we find numerous chthonic aspects in these mysteries: the cult of caves, the role of metal and bronze given in votive offerings, fertility and the renewal of the land through the death and rebirth of the Cretan Zeus. The importance of these mysteries for our story also comes from the legend, already mentioned, of the initiation of Pythagoras by one of the Dactyls or the Curetes, with the mention of a *keraunia lithos*. With this term, Pliny means two types of stones with metallurgical connotations. The first are the thunderstones: rocks found on places struck by lightning, collected for their connection with the divine world. This belief is spread throughout Europe, and probably dates back to the megalithic cultures, when the lightning bolts of the sky god were imagined as stone axes or clubs.[34] Later, with the advent of metals, the lightning changes material and is produced by the blacksmith god, thus becoming associated with meteorites, which are often made of iron. These stones were also highly sought after by the magi for their powers, especially of purification, since we know, from Pliny, that lightning strikes left the smell of sulfur, a substance used for purgative fumigation.

Meteoric iron is one of the first metals with which man interacted. Although its processing dates back, with some exceptions, to what is usually called the Iron Age, we know from archaeological findings that it was already used, for its holiness, in funerary, votive, and ritual contexts.

More relevant to our thread is a story narrated by Philo of Byblos. He describes a stone using the name *baitylos*, a word of Phoenician derivation, from the Semitic *Beth-El*, House of God. The author describes this Baitylos as a *lithos empsychos*, an animated stone invented by Uranus, as well as the name of one of his four sons. Damascius instead clarifies that these stones were meteorites with all the features of animated statues: able to speak, move, and predict the future. The presence of Uranus carries with it clear metallurgical connotations. He is the sky dome, made of bronze or iron, upon which the palaces of the gods rest. One of his names is Akmon, which is also one of the three Dactyls mentioned in the *Phoronis*. This name means anvil, but it can also mean pestle. What these two meanings have in common is the image of something falling from above. The image of the falling anvil is used by Hesiod to measure the distance that separates heaven from earth and Tartarus. Anvils are hung on Hera's legs when Zeus wants to punish her and Hephaestus rebels against his father to free her. Uranus's mating with Gaea is described as something coming from above, perhaps mimicking the fall of a meteorite.

---

34 L. Motz, *The Wise One of the Mountain: Form, Function and Significance of the Subterranean Smith : a Study in Folklore*, Kümmerle, 1983.

No Female Daimones?

Sources about female *daimones* are very scarce, and therefore it's hard to piece them together to form a coherent and solid picture.

Females often represent static principles, while males represent the forces of change. In most cases, besides being addressed as other goddesses, we find them as nymphs.

Commonly, nymphs are personifications of natural elements or phenomena, and therefore they are intrinsically tied to the local dimension of territories. Which, of course, pairs them perfectly with the *daimones*, both in their role as *autochthon*, knowing the intimate secrets of a territory (and thus being 'married' to the nymphs), or in representing an external cultural influence that mixes with the local one (we could again use the imagery of marriage).

Considering the role of interchangeability with the Mother, it's possible to speculate that they are all local emanations of her power. This doesn't devalue their position, just places it a bit far from our study, needing at least as many words as those expended in this essay.

Conclusions

Despite all efforts, *goêteia* still manages to defy any clear definition. Yet it's possible to define the container through its contents.

The *goês* is a polyvalent specialist of the sacred, capable of handling different experiences through the mastery of a wide array of techniques, deeply engaged in territories, community and narratives. From the raw power of dance to the fine art of talismans; from the liberating sensation of ecstasy, to the mindful inventions that make our everyday life easier, he's there to mediate all the realities that compose human experience—either the *goês*, or its spiritual double: the *daimon*.

Postface

In this essay there are all the elements to build a personal practice centered on the structure of the Mother and her companion, surrounded by a cohort of *daimones*. The right tools can be found among the remains of our past, and I hope to provide some in a sequel to this essay. Yet this one still has a practical value. Mythologies and symbols have the role of shaping our mind, connecting it with the times in which they were made and allowing us to enter into a deep relationship with an otherwise alien world. They give us the meanings by which to find hidden treasures in the sybilline world of the past, and decode them in a coherent and linear narrative through hermeneutics, one of the two sacred arts of Hermes.

Entering the cave as we are, as consumers of the 21st century, would mean nothing. The need, I stress, is to remove our suits and ties and go back to the dirty and dusty ground, to the dark depths and the remote corners of this world. The only needed 'pathworking' is that which moves our legs and lets us walk the abandoned roads that lead into nature. That's why I've chosen to include themes such as technology, civilization, political power and social structure. The relationship between nature and culture, in all its strength and precarious balance, has to be made conscious, so we can help our planet achieve a new balance. We mustn't ignore our world. It wants to be part of the spirit and to be loved as the highest heavens, and we must take care of it. Despite all the efforts at escapism through Bacchic revelry, Ouranic mortification, and excuses for inertia, the *daimones* stay firmly on the line between, still making our world as sacred as the others.

Bibliography

Beekes, R. S. P, 'The Origin of the Kabeiroi', *Mnemosyne* 57(4), 2004, pp. 465–77.

Blakely, S. 'Kadmos, Jason and the Great Gods of Samothrace: Initiation as Mediation in a Northern Aegean Context', *Electronic Antiquity* 11(1), 2007, pp. 67–95.

Blakely, S. 'Daimones in the Thracian Sea: Mysteries, Iron, and Metaphors', *Archiv für Religionsgeschichte* 14(1), 2013, pp. 155–82.

Blakely, S. *Myth, Ritual and Metallurgy in Ancient Greek and Recent Africa*, Cambridge University Press, 2006.

Blakely, S. 'Pherekydes' Daktyloi: Ritual, technology, and the Presocratic perspective', *Kernos* 20, 2007, pp. 43–67.

Bremmer, J. N. *Initiation Into the Mysteries of the Ancient World*, De Gruyter, 2014.

Burkert, W. *Ancient Mystery Cults*, Harvard University Press, 1987.

Burkert, W. 'Concordia Discors: the literary and the archaeological evidence on the sanctuary of Samothrace', in *Greek Sanctuaries*, ed. Robin Hagg and Nanno Marinatos, Routledge, 1994.

Burkert, W. *Greek Religion*, Blackwell, 1985.

Cole, S. G. *Theoi Megaloi: The Cult of the Great Gods at Samothrace*, Brill, 1984.

Cruccas, E. *Gli Dei senza nome. Sincretismi, ritualità e iconografia dei Cabiri e dei Grandi Dei tra Grecia e Asia Minore*, Rahden: Verlag Marie Leitdorf, 2014.

Detienne, M., Vernant, J.P. *Cunning Intelligence in Greek Culture and Society*, University of Chicago Press, 1991.

Delcourt, M. *Hèphaistos ou la Lègende du Magicien*, Paris: Soc. d'ed. Les Belles-Lettres, 1957.

De Ciantis, C. *The Return of Hephaestus: Reconstructing the Fragmented Mythos of the Maker*, Bowker, 2019.

Emerson, D.W. 'The Lodestone, From Plato to Kircher', *Preview* 173, 2014, pp. 52–62.

Faraone, C. 'Empedocles the Sorcerer and his Hexametrical Pharmaka', *Antichthon* 53, 2019, pp. 14–32.

Hemberg, B. *Die Kabiren*, Uppsala: Almquist & Wiksell, 1950.

Isler-Kerenyi, C. *Dionysos in Archaic Greece. An understanding through images*, Brill, 2006.

Kerenyi, K. *The Gods of the Greeks*, Thames and Hudson, 1951.

Johnston, S. I. *Restless Dead: Encounters Between the Living and the Dead in Ancient Greece*, University of California Press, 1999.

Mayor, A. *Gods and Robots: Myths, Machines, and Ancient Dreams of Technology*, Princeton University Press, 2020.

Motz, L. *The Wise One of the Mountain: Form, Function and Significance of the Subterranean Smith: a Study in Folklore*, Kümmerle, 1983.

Ogden, D. *Greek and Roman Necromancy*, Princeton University Press, 2001.

Roller, L. *In Search of God the Mother: The Cult of Anatolian Cybele*, University of California Press, 1999.

Stratton-Kent, J. *Geosophia*, vol. I & II, Scarlet Imprint, 2010.

ISIS OF THE MAGICIANS: THE FACES OF ISIS IN THE GREEK MAGICAL PAPYRI

KIM HUGGENS

'…for I am Isis the Wise, the sayings of whose mouth come to pass.'[1]

THE MYTHS OF ISIS are some of the most well-known narratives surviving from ancient Egypt, and in the modern world she has arguably become one of the most beloved Egyptian deities, her popularity almost eclipsing that of all others. However, mentions of her are surprisingly lacking prior to the Pyramid Texts[2] at the end of the fifth dynasty, in which her name or epithets (such as 'Fierce of Radiance'[3]) appear over 80 times.[4] In these texts, Isis often takes on a maternal role for the dead king, who frequently proclaims, 'My mother is Isis',[5] and is given guardianship over the mummification process and the dead king's soul. By the time of the Egyptian *Book of the Dead*, which was in use from the beginning of the New Kingdom (around 1550 BCE) to around 50 BCE, she had gained many titles and epithets, including 'She who gives birth to heaven and earth', 'Great Lady of Magic', 'Mistress of the House of Life', 'Lady of the Words of Power', 'Light-Giver of Heaven', 'The One Who is All', and 'Star of the Sea'.[6] The standard epithet for Isis was *weret hekau*—great of magic.

Surviving texts from the Graeco-Roman period, such as the Berlin Papyrus and the Bremner-Rhind Papyrus, portray Isis alongside Nephthys lamenting over Osiris's dead body before resurrecting him.[7] Isis's popularity and power were even transported to the British Isles during and just before this period by the Roman Empire—in recent

---

1 Betz, H. D., *The Greek Magical Papyri in Translation*, PDM xiv. 50.

2 For an easily accessible online version of the Pyramid Texts, see http://www.pyramidtextsonline.com/translation.html (accessed 15 March 2021).

3 *Pyr*. 342: 556.

4 Tower Hollis, S., Goddesses and Sovereignty in Ancient Egypt. In E. Benard and B. Moon (eds.), *Goddesses Who Rule*, p. 227.

5 Such as in *Pyr*. 555 and 1375.

6 Reeder Williams, E., Isis Pelagia and a Roman Marble Matrix from the Athenian Agora. *Hesperia* 54 (2) (Apr.–Jun. 1985), pp. 109–119.

7 See *The Lamentations of Isis and Nephthys*, trans. Raymond Oliver Faulkner, Institut francais d'archéologie orientale, 1934. The *Lamentations* is from the Berlin Papyrus, and is similar to *The Songs of Isis and Nephthys*, also published by Faulkner, from the Papyrus Bremner-Rhind.

decades, tantalizing glimpses of a temple of Isis built in Roman London have been excavated, and several examples of figurines of Isis have been found[8]—and continued well into the Christian era in the form of the Navigium Isidis ('the vessel of Isis'), an annual Roman festival still recorded in several sources in the fourth century CE.[9] It is even believed that the cult of Isis in Rome vied for popularity with the cult of Mithras.[10]

Late antique writings about Isis frequently link her with the teaching and learning of magic, such as in Lucian's *Lovers of Lies*, in which Pancrates of Memphis is described as spending twenty-three years in a secret subterranean chamber in which he learned the magical arts from Isis herself.[11] A few centuries earlier, even Pythagoras was said to have spent time underground in Egypt where the 'Mother' shared her magical knowledge with him.[12]

Some of the most prominent and well-evidenced myths of Isis from throughout her history include:

- Isis learning the magical name of Ra to remove snake venom.[13]
- her role as intelligent and cunning trickster-magician in the *Contendings of Horus and Set*.[14]
- finding the pieces of Osiris's body and putting him together.[15]
- magically conceiving her son, Horus, from Osiris's mummified body.[16]

In these myths, Isis is presented as wise, knowledgeable, crafty, deceiving, dedicated, loving and powerful, with one describing her particularly beautifully:

Now Isis was a clever woman. Her heart was craftier that a million men; she was choicier than a million gods; she was more discerning than a million of the noble dead. There was nothing that she did not know in heaven and earth, like Re, who made the content of the earth.[17]

---

8 Durham, E., Metropolitan styling: figurines from London and Colchester. In: S. Hoss and A. Whitmore (eds.), *Small Finds and Ancient Social Practices in the Northwest Provinces of the Roman Empire*, pp. 75–97.

9 Alföldi, A. A., Festival of Isis in Rome under the Christian Emperors of the Fourth Century. *The Journal of Roman Studies* 28 (1) (1938), pp. 88–90. For a general discussion of the Navigium Isidis, see Bricault, L., *Isis Pelagia: Images, Names and Cults of a Goddess of the Seas*, pp. 203–229.

10 Pomeroy, S. B., *Goddesses, Whores, Wives, & Slaves: Women in Classical Antiquity*, pp. 225.

11 Lucian, *Lovers of Lies* 34–36.

12 Ankarloo, B. and Clark, S., *Witchcraft and Magic in Europe, vol 2: Ancient Greece and Rome*, pp. 107.

13 *Papyrus de Turin*, published by F. Rossi and W. Pleyte, dating between 1350–1200 BCE, found in two different manuscripts.

14 *Papyrus Chester Beatty I*, 12th century BCE.

15 Perhaps the most influential ancient Egyptian myth, and the most pervasive, being found mentioned in a wide variety of texts. The most common account is *De Iside et Osiride* by the Greek writer Plutarch.

16 Ibid.

17 Pritchard, J. B., *Ancient Near Eastern Texts Relating to the Old Testament*, p. 12.

The *Papyri Graecae Magicae* (abbreviated to PGM herein), a collection of spells dating from the second century BCE to the fifth century CE,[18] therefore continues a long-historied tradition of writings about Isis. It might be expected that the earlier myths, religion and epithets of Isis directly informed how she was presented, invoked and referred to in the PGM. However, these late antique texts break away from the well-established presentation of Isis as nurturing mother, mourning wife, and great of magic; furthermore, although the papyri use these aspects of Isis as a foundation for their magic, other facets of Isis are introduced and new narratives in which she features are created.

Arguably an early form of conjure magic, the PGM spells are a mixture of mysticism and results magic—both beneficent and malefic—that can be seen to have significantly influenced the later grimoire tradition. Like the Pyramid Texts, some of the spells in the collection are concerned with the state of the soul (although that of the magician rather than the dead king), and, like the Egyptian *Book of the Dead*, some identify the magician with a deity, some grant mystical knowledge, and others offer magical protection. Dozens of PGM spells mention or invoke Isis, so it would seem to follow that these spells would offer insight into this goddess or how these magicians—who practised the arts that Isis herself learned and taught—viewed her. It is easy to see how the myths of Isis would be suitable for use in powerful magic. Perhaps the way in which she conceived Horus from her dead husband can be found in the PGM as the basis for effective fertility magic? Maybe the power that she gave to Horus's fight in the *Contendings of Horus and Set* would also be given to the magician that invoked her for victory? Does the manner in which she obtained the knowledge of Ra's true name offer itself to magical means of gaining secret knowledge? Can she resurrect the dead at a magician's bidding, or pull the spirits of the dead from the underworld? Does she grant the magician the knowledge of how to cure snakebites?

This paper will explore the use of the myths of Isis in the spells of the PGM, examine the possible syncretism of Isis with other deities within the spells, and identify the main types of spell for which her name, myths, or power were used: erotic attraction spells, erotic separation spells, business spells, divination spells, healing spells (particularly the curing of snakebites, scorpion stings and animal bites) and spells to catch a thief. In doing so, some of the features of the PGM as a conjure tradition will be highlighted in the hope that this reflection will be useful not only for those who wish to practise or study the magic of the PGM, but to those who might find similarities with, or the origins of, later conjure traditions therein. Throughout the investigation, we will see how the way in which Isis is used in the PGM also demonstrates a significant feature of conjure traditions that diverges from how deities are perceived and related to in many other kinds of magic, particularly in the modern world: a deity is not necessarily called upon for their associations (e.g., Aphrodite is not necessarily called upon for love), but because they are perceived as powerful and effective, because they represent a continuation of an already established tradition or mystery cult, and because their myths offer a

---

18 The version used in this paper is Betz, Hans Dieter, ed., *The Greek Magical Papyri in Translation including the demotic spells.* London: University of Chicago Press, 1992.

narrative of which a magician and their spells can become part, using the power of that narrative to fuel the magic.

A note on the authors of the PGM and the term 'magicians'

The spells and handbooks collected in the PGM were written, edited and redacted by a number of different practising magicians, and offer an important insight into ideas of magic and the spiritual world at the time. The world of Graeco-Roman Egypt in late antiquity was a syncretic melting pot of culture, religion and language, and the texts in the PGM showcase some of the most interesting features thereof. Reading between the lines of the spells offers some information about their authors or redactors, but only concerning their beliefs, culture, and spiritual practices; the information we are accustomed to having when assessing literary texts from the medieval period onwards, for example, is largely absent. Overwhelmingly, however, the magician who performs a spell is referred to as male.

The term 'magician' is used in this paper to refer to the person writing and/or performing a PGM spell. Although this term is easily understood by modern readers, it conceals the nuances of the practices of these individuals, the wide variety of types of magic they performed, and the differing ideas of what defined a magician. Plaisance discusses the changing understanding of the differences between μάγοι (and the practice of μαγεία) and γόητες (and the practice of γοητεία)[19] and identifies the different forms of (what modern readers would call) magic, which were not necessarily seen as separate from each other or distinct from religion.

HISTORIOLA: THE PRECEDENCE FOR MAGIC IN THE MYTHS OF ISIS

The use of myths concerning a deity as a precedent for a magical method or formula is common in the PGM, often referred to as historiola by modern historians. Historiola occur as short mythological stories appearing in magical texts before the magical technique is given. Skinner states that '…the thinking behind it includes demonstrating to the god knowledge of its background, thereby making it more compliant to the commands of the magician. Just as the god triumphed in some previous contest, so now he was expected to aid the magician and triumph again.'[20] Brashear describes it as the '…idea that mythical events (archetypes) "once upon a time" (*in ilio tempore*) retain their supernatural forces forever and can be reactivated at any given time by the simple act of recounting them'.[21] In fact, it seems that when a suitable myth was not available, the

19 Plaisance, C. A., *Evocating the Gods: Divine Evocation in the Graeco-Egyptian Magical Papyri*, pp. 12–15.

20 Skinner, S., *Techniques of Graeco-Egyptian Magic*, p. 105.

21 Brashear, W., The Greek Magical Papyri: An Introduction and Survey; Annotated Bibliography (1928–1994). *Aufstieg und Niedergang der römischen Welt* II, 18.5, p. 3439.

creation of one was just as powerful, as was borrowing something from the mythology of other cultures.[22]

In some PGM spells, the use of historiola appears to focus not on commanding the deity/their power or creating a sympathetic link between the magician's situation and that of the deity, but on claiming to *be* that deity. One spell, PDM xiv. 1–92 ('A vessel divination'), combines both: it begins by stating that '…this vessel divination is the vessel divination of Isis when she was searching', presumably referring to the myth of Isis searching for Osiris's dismembered body parts and suggesting that Isis herself used the divination spell to discover the location of the body parts, and continues with an invocation of chthonic deities so that they may speak through a boy who is acting as the diviner. The magician seeks to command these deities by claiming to be Isis (and therefore claiming her power as his own): '…for I am Isis the wise, the sayings of whose mouth come to pass'.[23] It was not only the spells themselves that were given a divine origin, however: sometimes the ingredients used in a spell were said to have been used by a deity. In PGM CXXII. 1–55, a series of love spells, the magician is instructed to anoint their face with myrrh while saying, 'You are the myrrh with which Isis was anointed when she went to the bosom of Osiris, her … brother, and gave him her favour on that day'.[24] Presumably, the magician sought to elicit love from the target of the spell, just as Isis elicited love from Osiris, and the spell continues with a brief instruction to Isis herself: 'Wake up him, NN, or her, NN, Mistress Isis, and carry out this perfect charm'.[25]

As well as ascribing the origin of a spell to a deity who used it (such as in the 'vessel divination'), some historiola offer narratives in which a deity gave the spell to another for use. Asserting that the spell was prescribed by a deity may have had several purposes, including to give the spell antiquity (and, thus, power), to assure the magician/their client of the spell's success, and perhaps to add the sanctity of religion (or maybe the power of one of the Mysteries) to the magic.

There are several spells that use Isis as a prominent figure and include examples of historiola. Although some of the narratives are familiar to modern readers, such as the murder of Osiris and Isis's search for his dismembered body parts, some were either invented by the magician for the spell's purpose or have been lost in surviving mythological sources. For example, PGM VII. 993–1009 gives a recipe for an ink with which to write a formula that will raise a dead spirit, claiming that, 'Isis uttered [it and] wrote [it] when, after taking up Osiris, she fit together his separated members. Asklepios[26] [saw] Osiris and admitted that he [could] not [put together] someone who was dead [even] with the help of Hebe'.[27] Since Isis spoke and recorded the formula to pull the spirit of Osiris back from the dead, it was potent magic that the magician

---

22 Ibid.

23 PDM xiv. 50.

24 PGM CXXII. 31–31.

25 PGM CXXII. 32.

26 Greek god of healing.

27 Greek goddess of youth; in one myth she returned youth to the elderly chariot driver of Herakles.

could use to summon a dead spirit to their aid. Although surviving myth recounts the resurrection of Osiris by Isis and Nephthys, it does not mention a magical ink being used for the process, suggesting that the magician who created this spell embellished a well-known mythical motif to suit the spell's purposes. Another example of ascribing to Isis magical acts that are otherwise unknown in myth can be found in in PGM VIII. 1–63 ('Binding love spell of Astrapsoukos'), in which the magician claims to invoke Hermes[28] because Isis herself did so all the time:

> Whereas Isis, the greatest of all gods, invoked you in every crisis, in every district, against gods and men and daimons, creatures of water and earth and held your favor, / victory against gods and men and [among] all the creatures beneath the world, so also I, NN, invoke you.[29]

Such mythical episodes in the magical texts offer a variety of views of Isis, but it is unclear whether these perspectives were given the treatment a worshipper might afford to a deity or if they were simply a means to an end. Some of them are familiar to modern readers, whereas others seem only loosely connected to the form of the goddess we know. Isis is frequently presented as a woman deeply in love with her husband, but sometimes also as a spurned lover and sometimes as a woman who is desired but needs to be persuaded to return that desire. She is seen as a grieving, worried parent, fearful for her son's safety, and as a guardian of the liminal point between the worlds of the living and the dead; in some spells, she even takes on the aspects of Hellenistic chthonic deities and not only protects the spirits of the dead but commands them. Her power is given to a great number of divination spells and to several spells to cure poison, heal animal bites, and offer an antidote to snakebites. As is the nature of such collections, there are also some miscellaneous purposes to which she lends her hand, such as business success spells and spells to catch thieves. However, the role in which we do *not* find her is that of a fertile mother or pregnant woman, which may seem odd given the prevalence of surviving images of Isis suckling the infant Horus and the prominence of her motherhood in the surviving mythological narratives. It might be pointed out that the PGM is lacking in spells for pregnant women or labouring women in general; in fact, only two such spells are found in the collection: PGM XXIIa. 9–10 ('for pain in the breasts and uterus') and PGM CXXIII. 48 a–f (which gives several brief charms for various conditions, one of which is 'for childbearing'), neither of which mention Isis.

---

28 Hermes and Thoth are often mentioned interchangeably in the spells of the PGM, and sometimes mistaken for each other/syncretised with each other.

29 PGM VIII. 22–26.

Syncretism in the PGM: the Isis of Apuleius?

It is often said that the cult of Isis, and the goddess herself, was so popular in the ancient world that she subsumed the cults and worship of many other goddesses into her own.[30] Indeed, this has been historically proven in the case of a number of other Egyptian cults, and many writers of the late antique period would lead us to believe that this was also the case with goddesses from the surrounding regions. Apuleius famously gives Isis a speech in which she claims to be known by many names, including Cybele, Proserpine, Juno, Hecate and Ceres.[31] In fact, any female deity that was extremely popular seems to be included in the list (and it is interesting to note that they all had their own mystery religions dedicated to them). However, while this may have been the case from the perspective of a devotee of Isis, there is little in the magical texts of the PGM that agrees with this view.

Isis is frequently called upon in the PGM alongside other deities, but references to her as a syncretic deity are infrequent. PGM VII. 490–504 calls her, 'Lady Isis, Nemesis, Adrasteia, many-named, many-formed', and in the same spell she is conflated with Sothis as Isis-Sothis; in PDM xiv. 594–620, she is called Sekhmet-Isis. Mentions of her alongside Hermes are frequent, perhaps due to the fact that Hermes and Thoth were often viewed interchangeably by Greeks and Egyptians alike (in fact, in one spell Isis and Osiris are called the mother and father of Hermes[32]). Another spell opens with the Hebrew god-name Adonai, before continuing on to present a compulsive spell to Isis.[33] The Greek god Helios also finds his way into a great number of spells that otherwise contain a significant presence of Egyptian godhood,[34] and Aphrodite is invoked to carry out a sentence before Isis is invoked for the same in a love spell using apples.[35] Further, Isis's name is invoked in one spell alongside several other deities (Greek, Egyptian, Gnostic and Christian), each one's name and power being claimed by the magician as their own.[36] It was clearly more common in the PGM for Isis to be presented alongside non-Egyptian deities than to be syncretised or conflated with them.

---

30 Dunand, F., *Culte d'Isis dans le Bassin Oriental de la Méditerranée*.

31 Lucius Apuleius, *The Golden Asse*, Book XI, 1–4.

32 PGM XII. 144–52.

33 PGM LVII. 1–37.

34 PGM XXIVa. 1–25 is an exception to this, as Isis is praised at the beginning of a spell that otherwise calls exclusively upon Greek gods (Helios and Hermes).

35 PGM CXXII. 1–55.

36 PGM XII. 201–69 ('a ring').

Goddess of a Thousand Names

There are a few mentions of Isis 'of many names' in the PGM, such as in PGM LIX. 1–15, a spell for the protection of the mummified remains and spirit of a person, which mentions 'the everlasting [punishments given by] the Lady [Isis] / goddess of many names'. Missing from this fragmentary text is a promise that Isis will punish anybody who dares to disturb the grave or spirit of the protected person—a common magical method in the ancient world.[37]

In another spell, PGM LVII. 1–37, which prescribes a rite to find an assistant spirit, Isis is referred to as 'the many-named goddess' and the magician is commanded to recite her secrets. It is not said what these secrets are, and it is not clear the reason why they may be recited. This could be an example of the magician proving their magical worth, power and knowledge by reciting lists of 'secrets', which in other examples from the ancient world include supposedly secret names of deities, mysteries from their cults revealed only to initiates, scandalous stories of the deities, identifying with a deity, taking on a deity's name, or claiming to be something innately magical and powerful. However, this formula may be something more sinister, which was also common in the late antique period and is found elsewhere in the PGM: a threat to the deity to move them to action. By reciting the secrets of the many-named goddess Isis, the magician may be threatening to reveal them to others; certainly in this case the magician makes threats at the start of the spell, saying that they will do or not do certain things, including not killing Ammon, preserving the flesh of Osiris, not calling those who have died a violent death, and not scattering the limbs of Osiris, if Isis does as he requests.

Erotic Attraction Spells

Erotic attraction spells should be recognized as distinct from erotic separation spells, both of which can be categorized as amatory curses.[38] The former work to arouse desire for the magician/the employer of the magician in another person, whereas the latter work to separate a couple from each other, usually so that a third party can take the opportunity to gain one of the erstwhile couple as a lover.

Almost all of the erotic attraction spells that mention Isis as lover or loved one use the mythic precedence of the relationship between her and Osiris as historiola ('Let her, NN, love me for all her time as Isis loved Osiris...'[39]) or state that Isis/Osiris used the spell first. Examples outside of the PGM reinforce this approach; for example, a lead tablet from Egypt dating from the second or third century CE gives a love spell designed

---

37 For more on this phenomenon, see Strubbe, J. H. M., Cursed be he that moves my bones. In C. A. Faraone and D. Obbink (eds.), *Magika Hiera: Ancient Greek Magic and Religion*, pp. 33–59.

38 For more on these categories of spells, see Faraone, C., The Agonistic Context of Early Greek Binding Spells. In C. Faraone and D. Obbink (eds.), *Magika Hiera*, pp. 10–11.

39 PGM XXXVI. 283–94.

to attract and bind a woman called Theodotis to a man, Ammonion, and is claimed to have first been used by Isis, presumably to attract Osiris in the same way.[40]

In a particularly interesting example of an erotic attraction spell, PGM IV. 94–153, Isis performs the prescribed rite first. The spell begins with a narrative of Isis coming to see her father, Thoth, at midday, her eyes 'full of tears and her heart […] full of sighs'. When Thoth enquires as to the cause of her tears and her soiled garments (soiled garments also being a sign of grief at the death of a loved one, telling us that the pain Isis is feeling at the betrayal of her husband is like that of losing him to death), she says, 'He is not with me, O my father, Ape Thoth, Ape / [Thoth], my father. I have been betrayed by my female companion. I have discovered [a] secret: yes, Nephthys is having intercourse with Osiris … my brother, my own mother's son.'[41]

Thoth then gives Isis magical advice for bringing Osiris back to her. It begins as a direct instruction to Isis:

Arise, O my daughter Isis, and [go] to the south to Thebes, to the north to Abydos. There are … those who trample (?) there. Take for yourself Belf son of Belf, [the one whose] foot is of bronze and whose heels are of iron, / [that] he forge for you a double iron nail with a … head, a thin base, a strong point, and light iron. Bring it before me, dip it in the blood of Osiris, and hand it over; we … this mysterious (?) flame to me.[42]

This is not the only instance in which a spell from the PGM refers to the blood of Osiris in an attraction spell. PDM xiv. 428–50 is a recipe for a potion of attraction that uses, among other things (such as the blood of a tick from a black dog, a standard ingredient in malefic magic), the blood of the magician who wishes to attract the person, put into a cup of wine that is given to the victim to drink, whereupon she will fall in love with he whose blood is in the wine. The spell presents Isis as a model of devotion and passionate love and refers to a mythical precedent (not attested to in any surviving myth) in which Osiris gave his blood to Isis in a cup of wine 'to make her feel love in her heart for him at night, at noon, at any time, there not being time of change'.[43] It continues with the instruction:

Give it, the blood of NN, whom NN bore, to give it to NN, whom NN bore, in this cup, this bowl of wine today, to cause her to feel a love for him in her heart. The love which Isis felt for Osiris, when she was seeking after him everywhere,

---

40 Gager, J. G., *Curse Tablets and Binding Spells from the Ancient World*, pp. 109–10. This non-PGM source is included here to show that archaeological evidence strongly suggests the techniques described in the PGM were employed; another case in which archaeological evidence bears a striking similarity to PGM texts is that of the so-called 'Louvre doll' and PGM IV. 296–466 ('Wondrous spell for binding a lover').

41 PGM IV. 99–104.

42 PGM IV. 106–114.

43 PDM xiv. 440.

let NN, the daughter of NN, feel it, / while seeking after NN, the son of NN, everywhere.[44]

Although here the blood of Osiris is a mythical precedent for the blood of the magician being used in a potion, researchers have found that many of the ingredients prescribed in PGM spells are code names for herbs or other, more mundane, ingredients; 'blood of Isis', for example, was black horehound, and 'semen of Helios' was white hellebore.[45] Clearly, the spells in the PGM use multi-layered symbolism, a feature common in later conjure traditions and grimoires.

PDM xiv. 428–50 continues by presenting an attraction spell given by Thoth to Isis, in which Thoth puts the nail, covered in the blood of Osiris, onto a stove to be heated, saying:

> Every flaming, every cooking, every heating, every steaming, and every sweating that you [masc.] will cause in this flaming stove, you [will] cause in the heart, in the liver, [in] the area of the navel, and in the belly of NN whom NN has borne, until I bring her to the house of NN whom NN has borne...[46]

'You' being masculine at this point in the spell shows that Thoth's instructions to Isis have now transitioned into instructions for the magician, who in this case is male. From this point on, the usual formula that is found in many other erotic attraction spells in the PGM is given, in which the victim is struck with love sickness and eventually relents and comes to the magician, giving herself devotedly.[47]

The cause of Isis's pain in PDM xiv. 428–50—Nephthys having intercourse with Osiris—appears rarely in surviving accounts and comes about in the Late Period; it certainly would have been present by the time this spell was written. However, the Late Period texts present it from the perspective of Set instead, who is hurt by Nephthys's betrayal with his brother Osiris and who uses it as the reason for killing Osiris (which is the beginning of the myth of Osiris's death and resurrection).[48] From this illicit union is born Anubis, who is sometimes called the eldest son of Osiris. In the PGM spell, however, it is not Set but Isis who is hurt by the betrayal—and the hurt of women in the ancient world is often silent, so seeing it here is striking. Perhaps it is presented here so plainly because this is a magical text and not a legal, literary or educational text. Further highlighting the striking nature of this presentation of Isis as a wronged woman

---

44 PDM xiv. 445.

45 Skinner, S., *Techniques of Graeco-Egyptian Magic*, pp. 115–117.

46 PGM IV. 115–120.

47 For more on the love sickness/madness invoked by magicians in Graeco-Egyptian sources, see Faraone, C. A., *Ancient Greek Love Magic*, and Winkler, J. J., The Constraints of Eros. In C. Faraone and D. Obbink (eds.), *Magika Hiera: Ancient Greek Magic and Religion*, pp. 230–4.

48 Spiegelberg, W., *Demotische Papyrus aus den königlichen Museen ze Berlin*, pp. 21; Von Lieven, A., Seth ist im Recht, Osiris ist im Unrecht! *Zeitschrift fur agyptische Spracge und Altertumskunde* 133, pp. 141–150.

is the fact that when the text of this spell shifts from narrative provenance to magical instruction for the performance of the spell, it is given as if the magician is a man trying to magically induce the love of a woman, not that of a woman trying to induce the love of a man. Although the formula begins as if being given to a woman (Isis), it uses phrases such as 'my male parts'. Later, the spell offers provisions for both male and female victims, and in the case of the male victim he is likened to Osiris desiring after Isis: 'arouse the heart of Osiris after Isis'.

Although this spell presents a more bitter account of the relationship between Isis and Osiris, it is the devotion and love held between them that is more commonly invoked in magical spells. There is a surviving example (one of many) of lead tablets with magical inscriptions upon them, dated to the third or fourth century CE, which accompany a pot that is also inscribed. Although it is the spirit of a dead person that is intended to do the work described in the spell, it is the love of Isis and Osiris that is invoked for mythical precedence to give it power: 'Just as Isis loved Osiris, so may Matrona love Theodoros for all the time of her life.'[49] This formula is also found in PGM XXXVI. 283–94, ('Pudenda key spell'): 'Let her, NN, love me for all her time as Isis loved Osiris', although the rest of the spell specifically calls to the womb of NN, and appears to use the added power of the desire of the magician to fuel it, as it is prescribed for recitation every time he 'grinds' or rubs his genitals.

In an unusual attribution of Isis, we find her mentioned briefly in PGM IV. 1390– 1495 ('Love spell of attraction performed with the help of heroes or gladiators or those who have died a violent death'). The purpose of the spell is to pull to the magician the spirits of restless, bitter ghosts, which will be sent after the desired lover, and drag her (again, the victim is stipulated as a woman) to the magician. The spell reads, 'Isis came, holding on her shoulders her brother who is her bedfellow',[50] along with other gods, to await and watch the phantoms of the dead perform the deed the magician has set them to. It is possible that Isis is mentioned here for her association with the death of Osiris, whom she brought back from the dead, or because she protected the spirit of the dead king; it is also likely that her ability to bring Osiris back from the underworld was being invoked by the magician who wished to similarly bring the spirits of the dead to him.

In PGM XXXVI. 134–60 ('Marvelous love spell of attraction'), we find another type of erotic attraction spell in which Isis plays a role: a slander spell, named not for its purpose but for a significant feature of its working. The original Greek term for 'spell' was *logos*, but a slander spell was specifically *diabole*, from *diabolus*, 'the slanderer', from whence we get our 'diabolical' devil. The main operative feature of these spells is for the magician to do things that are magically 'wrong', such as giving the wrong offerings to a deity or giving them offerings that are viewed as taboo. When these things have been done, the magician will say to the offended deity, 'It is not I who does these things, but so-and-so', and will then ask the deity to perform certain actions to torment the slandered person. In PGM XXXVI. 134–60, the actions expected of the deity—in this

---

49 Gager, J. G, *Curse Tablets and Binding Spells from the Ancient World*, pp. 100–1.
50 PGM IV. 1474.

case, Isis—are to torment the victim until she gives in to the magician's desire for her. The spell accuses the victim of sacrificing 'unlawful eggs', because of which,

> Isis raised up a loud cry, and the world was thrown into confusion. She tosses and turns in her holy bed, and its bonds and those of the daimon world are smashed to pieces because of the enmity and impiety of her, NN whom NN bore.[51]

Here, Isis is ascribed so much power that her distress causes the world of spirits to shatter and the links between it and this world to break. The spell continues by asking Isis and Osiris 'and [daimons] of the chthonic world' to rise up and inflict upon the victim a number of malicious torments, both physical and mental. Once again, Isis and Osiris are presented in a magical text based on their association with the realm of the dead.

This spell displays a significant Graeco-Roman influence, despite the exclusively Egyptian deities being used: the afterlife envisioned by the ancient Egyptians did not leave much room for magic in which the dead could be pulled back from the underworld to torment the living. As the spell presents Isis writhing in her bed and shattering the bonds of the daimon world as she does so, the magician may have envisioned her as having a home in the underworld, much like the Greek goddess Persephone did.

The same spell goes on to use the torment of Isis as a persuasively analogical ritual: just as Isis tosses and turns in her bed, so the target of the spell is caused to 'be sleepless, to fly through the air, hungry, thirsty, not finding sleep'.[52] This aspect of the spell takes the divine authority of Isis—usually used to give authority and power to the magician and the spell—and turns it on its head, giving it to the target of the spell, along with Isis's torment as a victim.

There are very few erotic attraction spells that aren't malefic in some way. Our modern idea of a love spell making us more attractive to a potential lover seems anathema to the forceful dragging of unwilling victims to the desirous magician. However, one non-PGM text, a Graeco-Egyptian recipe for love, gives a simple prescription for a woman to anoint her face with myrrh and chant an incantation to bring charm (*charis*) to her in the eyes of her husband or lover: 'Take myrrh and chant (the following) and anoint your face: "You are the myrrh with which Isis anointed herself when she went to the bosom of Osiris, her own husband and brother, and on that day you gave her charm".'[53] The presence of this historiola—in which Isis used the spell first—and the subsequent granting of potency and authenticity to the spell, can therefore be seen to have been a feature of non-PGM magic of the time.

---

51 PGM XXXVI. 141–45.

52 PGM XXXVI. 146–47.

53 *Supplementum Magicum* 72, col. ii. 4–8, quoted in Faraone, C. A., *Ancient Greek Love Magic*, pp. 105.

EROTIC SEPARATION SPELLS

As well as erotic attraction spells, we find the myths of Isis and Osiris used as mythical precedents in erotic separation spells. One spell, PDM xii. 50–61 ('Spell for separating one person from another'), uses the separation of Isis and Osiris by their enemy Set when he killed Osiris:

> A spell for separating one person from another: Dung of … and you put it [in] a document, and you write on a document of papyrus these great names / together with the name of the man, and you bury it under the doorsil of the house. […] "separate NN, born of NN, from NN, born of NN!" It is … "Separate Isis from…".

The spell then instructs the magician to both inscribe and recite several names, many of which end with '–seth', probably referring to Set(h) from the myth. Although the type of animal from which the dung is taken is illegible, it may be have been a donkey, as many of these kinds of spells use parts of this animal or draw it as a representation of Set. In the next spell from the same handbook, an image of a donkey-headed man is drawn and labelled 'Seth', and although the text is fragmentary, enough can be understood to conclude that the holy names are written on something (perhaps a potsherd, as one is mentioned later in the spell) that is buried (probably in proximity to the victims), and upon which the image of Seth is drawn.[54]

Another erotic separation spell, PGM XII. 365–75 ('Charm for causing separation'), invokes the mythic enmity of Typhon and Isis to create enmity between a husband and wife; the spell initially provides a spoken formula to separate two men but also provides the words to separate a man and a woman:

> …"give to him, NN, the son of her, NN, strike, war; and to him, NN, the son of her, NN, odiousness, enmity, just as Typhon and Osiris had" (but if it is a husband and wife, "just as Typhon and Isis had").

---

54 PDM xii. 62–75.

BUSINESS SPELLS

Just as PGM IV. 94–153 presents historiola in which Thoth gives an erotic attraction spell to Isis when she comes to him in distress, PGM IV. 2373–2440 ('Charm for acquiring business and for calling in customers') narrates a brief story of Isis seeking aid from Hermes. The spell describes Isis as 'the wandering Isis' (this being Isis as she wandered the earth looking for the dismembered body parts of Osiris). Isis is also mentioned in the design of the wax figurine that is prescribed by the spell: 'Let there be around the staff a coiled snake, and let him be dressed in a girdle and standing on a sphere that has / a coiled snake, like Isis.'[55] The brief historiola does not make clear, however, why the spell was made for Isis, for she is not known to have owned a business. Instead, the method of the spell's performance offers a suggestion for her association: it prescribes that a wax figurine be formed and each of its body parts consecrated separately—fourteen body parts in total, the same number of parts that Osiris's body was cut into by Set when he was murdered, which 'wandering Isis' found and put back together. The spell appears to be a method to imbue the wax figurine with a spirit, naming the snake that is wrapped around the staff *agathos daimon* ('good spirit') and concluding with a direct address to the figurine, charging it to perform its duty. Perhaps the spell was intended to bring a spirit into the wax figurine just as wandering Isis brought life to her dismembered husband.

This use in a business spell of the mythical narrative of Isis searching for Osiris's dismembered body parts and giving him life enough to conceive a son by him demonstrates how the same myth could be used in many different types of spells and for many different purposes. It also shows the complexity of the way in which the mythical narratives were approached, embellished and applied in the PGM, in which they were not treated as untouchable but as living stories that could be connected with and acted upon to create new meaning.

DREAM ORACLES AND DIVINATION

Although Isis is not specifically presented in myth as a goddess associated with divination, second sight, or receiving oracles, there are a number of divination spells that mention her in the PGM. Such spells seem to call upon Isis's power and the power of her priests and her mysteries through direct invocation, by borrowing the power of her name and sacred objects, and through affirmations of a spell's success based on her nature. One way of doing this that recurs in several different PGM handbooks is through the use of a 'cloth of Isis'.

PGM VII. 222–49 ('Request for a dream oracle from Besas') instructs the magician to '[t]ake a black of Isis and put it around your hand', which Betz notes is an unidentified item that may be intended to be a black linen garment used in the cult of Isis. Once the cloth is wrapped around the magician's hand, they are instructed to go to sleep, presumably receiving a dream that will give them the answers they seek. PGM VIII. 64–110 (another 'Request for a dream oracle from Besas') similarly says: 'Put around

---

55 PGM IV. 2380–2385.

your hand a black cloth of Isis and go to sleep without giving answer to anyone. The remainder of the cloth wrap around your neck.' Another spell, PGM CII. 1–17 (which appears to have been a lamp divination), instructs the magician to smear a picture 'with the black of Isis'—presumably the black cloth mentioned in other spells—and the compulsive PGM LVII. 1–37 asks Isis to indicate whether the spell's purpose has been carried out by revealing her holy veil and shaking her 'black'.

Eitrem says that the cloth of Isis was a cloth taken from a statue of Isis, presumably from a temple statue.[56] Those familiar with the concept of secondary and tertiary relics in Catholicism, in which an item that has touched the relic of a saint carries with it the power of that relic, might see in this practice some similarity. In ancient Egypt, statues of deities were not just aesthetic representations of the divine but were imbued with spirits that were then fed and maintained throughout their life within the temple. It might therefore be suggested that these divination spells are a home-grown version of dream incubation, a common religious practice in the Graeco-Roman world that was also prevalent in Egypt. However, another possibility is that the cloths are taken from the cult of Isis, which by this point in history was a syncretic mystery religion, whose inner mysteries were accessible only to those who were initiated. The cloth from these rites would therefore have borne the power of those rites and a special connection to Isis. That the spell is done in the name of Bes, however, proves problematic for this feature: one of Bes's specialities was in giving oracles, so it is not clear why Isis is brought into the spell. The syncretic nature of the magic in these handbooks offers an answer. Although Isis had no special relationship with Bes or a reason to be invoked alongside him, the power that her cult and temples had was unquestionable. By using a cloth of Isis, the magician was drawing on that power and bringing a religious rite usually performed in a temple to the home, bringing the public sphere into the private sphere, thereby increasing the effectiveness of the spell and perhaps adding authority to their practice.

Another kind of cloth associated with Isis is mentioned in the PGM. In PDM xiv. 150–231 ('An inquiry of the lamp'), the wick of a divinatory lamp is praised by the magician and given a divine heritage: 'Are you the unique, great wick of the linen of Thoth? Are you the byssus robe of Osiris, the divine Drowned, woven by the hand of Isis, spun by the hand of Nephthys?'[57] Here, the items that were supposedly associated with deities, in this case Thoth, Osiris, Isis and Nephthys (the latter three all deities from the Osirian cycle), are powerful, and the mundane object that is being used is given their power by being identified with them, in much the same way that a magician might give themselves more power and authority by identifying themselves as a deity or a series of deities or by taking on their magical names. In fact, PDM xiv. 239–95 ('The vessel enquiry of Khonsu'), another vessel divination spell from the same handbook, does exactly that, instructing the magician to say, 'I am Isis; I shall bind him. I am Osiris; I

---

56 Eitrem, S., Dreams and Divination in Magical Ritual. In C. A. Faraone and D. Obbink (eds.), *Magika Hiera*, pp. 178–9.

57 PDM xiv. 160–161.

shall bind him. I am Anubis; I shall bind him'.[58] Later, the magician calls upon Isis in a more familiar form: 'Come to me, Isis, mistress of magic, the great sorceress of all the gods. Horus is before me; Isis is behind me; Nephthys is as my diadem.'[59] The magician then variously identifies as 'Horus, son of Isis', and as 'those two falcons who watch over Isis and Osiris'. As the spell progresses, it becomes clear that it is designed to draw forth the spirits of the dead to give answers:

> O fury of all these gods, whose names I have uttered here today, awaken for me, awaken for me the drowned [dead]! Let your souls and your [secret] forms live for me at the mouths of my lamp, my bandage, my word-gathering. Let it answer me concerning every word [about] which I am asking here today...[60]

Therefore the choice to call upon Isis, Osiris, Nephthys and Anubis makes sense: these are all deities associated with the dead and in particular the process of mummification (hence the use of the term 'bandage' throughout the spell in relation to the wick of the lamp); these are deities that have a close relationship with the spirits of the dead and who therefore would be more able/willing to call up those spirits to aid the magician. Furthermore, the request for these deities to awaken the drowned dead could be drawing on the threads of the Osiris/Isis myth in which Osiris was trapped in a coffin and thrown into the sea to drown.

Yet more forms of cloth associated with Isis can be found in other divination spells. PGM IV. 3086–3124 ('Oracle of Kronos, called "little mill"') instructs the magician to wear the robe of a priest of Isis, saying, 'You must not be afraid since you are protected by the phylactery that / will be revealed to you. Be clothed with clean linen in the garb of priest of Isis'.[61] Luck identifies this cloth as a white robe,[62] therefore distinguishing it from the black cloth of Isis wrapped around the eyes or hand in other spells. Some have interpreted this garb as a protective measure due to the mandate to have no fear, but it could also be that the magician was assuming the power and authority of a priest of the mysteries of Isis. Betz writes that, '[c]loth or material taken from the dresses of statues of the gods, especially of Isis, was considered magically potent'.[63] Therefore, this robe may have granted both protection and initiated power—the assumption of power that may not be the right of the magician but that is recognized by both the magician and the spirits on which they call.

The redactor of PDM xiv seems to have been fond of lamp divination spells, as another one, PDM xiv. 750–1, does not differ much in technique from the others but is presented in a way that would be far more familiar to modern magicians: it is

---

58 PDM xiv. 239–95.

59 PDM xiv. 257.

60 PDM xiv. 281.

61 PGM IV. 3095–6.

62 Luck, G., *Arcana Mundi: Magic and the Occult in the Greek and Roman Worlds, A Collection of Ancient Texts*, p. 141.

63 Betz, H. D., *The Greek Magical Papyri in Translation* (Glossary), p. 336.

reminiscent of many scrying methods employed today. Like another spell from this particular handbook, it contains the phrase 'for I am Isis the wise; the sayings of my mouth come to pass'. This spell, however, is more explicit about the fact that it is using the spirits of the dead to obtain answers: 'Do it, O he who has died! Awaken to me, awaken to me, O soul of life, O soul of breath!'. This spell also makes reference to Isis using a vessel for divination when searching for Osiris.

One particularly interesting divination spell that calls upon Isis can be found in PGM XXIVa. 1–25. It begins 'Great is the Lady Isis!' and continues with a method of divination using 29 leaves:

> Copy of a holy book found in the archives of Hermes: / The method is that concerning the 29 letters through which letters Hermes and Isis, who was seeking / Osiris, her brother and husband, [found him]. Call upon Helios and all the gods in the deep concerning those things for which you want to receive an omen. Take / 29 leaves of a male date palm and write on each of the leaves the names of the gods. Pray and then pick them up two / by two. Read the last remaining leaf and you will find your omen, how things are, and you will be answered / clearly.

It is almost certain that the 29 leaves used here represent the 29 letters of the Coptic alphabet,[64] although it is not known which god names were written on the leaves, nor whether each was associated normally with a letter of the Coptic alphabet. It is also not stated what Isis has to do with this technique of divination—perhaps she is simply called upon by the magician because of a close relationship with her, or perhaps, as mistress of magic, she is seen by the magician as ruling over divination.

The power of Isis being used in magic is further demonstrated by the vessel divination spell in PDM xiv. 1–92, during which the magician invokes various gods and demands that they come so that the divination might be performed and answers given:

> Come to the mouths / of my vessel today and tell me an answer in truth concerning everything about which I am inquiring, without falsehood therein, for I am Isis the Wise, the sayings of whose mouth come to pass.[65]

Not only does the magician identify themself as Isis, they also make the claim that everything Isis speaks happens—the magical formula she speaks will come to pass, and nothing in the universe could make it not so.

Sometimes it does not seem to be Isis's power or greatness of magic that is called upon by a spell but rather her ability to intercede for the magician. In the lamp divination of PDM xiv. 150–231 ('An enquiry of the lamp'), the image of Osiris in his ship (the Neshmet barge, a vessel created by human hands for festivals but by Nun in mythology, and which was sometimes seen as analogous to the barge on which the dead king's soul

---

64 See W. Schubart, *Einführung in die Papyruskunde* p. 369.

65 The same phrase is used in PDM xiv. 750–1.

was taken to the afterlife) is given to the lamp, which is instructed to find Osiris and his retinue and speak to Isis:

> O Osiris, O lamp, it will cause [me] to see those above; it will cause [me] to see those below, and vice versa. O lamp, O lamp, Amoun is moored in you. O lamp, O lamp, I call to you while you are going up upon the great sea, the sea of Syria, the sea of Osiris. Am I speaking to you? Are you coming that I may send you? O lamp, bear witness! When you have found Osiris upon his boat of papyrus and faïence, Isis being at his head, Nephthys at his feet, and the male and female divinities about him, say [to] Isis, "Let them speak to Osiris concerning the things about which I am asking, to send the god in whose hand the command is, so that he say to me an answer to everything about which I am inquiring here today".[66]

The 'god in whose hand the command is' is the god of the hour, the god 'in charge' at the time the spell is performed. In this spell, then, although the lamp is sent to find Osiris' barge, it is Isis who is seen as having the intercessionary ability to allow messages from the other gods to be passed to Osiris, who then passes those messages to the god of the hour, who delivers them to the magician via the lamp.

The same spell then continues with a short episode of historiola:

> When Isis said, "Let a god who is serious concerning the business which he will undertake be summoned for me so that I may send him and so that he may complete them," they went and brought [one] to her. You are the lamp, the [thing] which was brought to her.[67]

This historiola does not appear to specifically refer to any surviving myth, but it may have been based on the narrative of her search for Osiris, just as PDM xiv. 1–92 referred to Isis using the spell ('this vessel divination is the vessel divination of Isis when she was searching'). However, in PDM xiv. 150–231, the historiola becomes the foundation for a formula more commonly found in erotic attraction spells and used to ensure the cooperation of the spirits of the dead: the magician threatens the lamp with a form of holding it hostage, not allowing it to perform its cited mythical function until it has given the magician the answers they seek:

> The fury of Sakhmet, your mother, and of Hike, your father, is cast at you. You shall not burn for Osiris and Isis; you shall not burn for Anubis until you have told me an answer to everything about which I am asking here today truly, without telling me falsehood. If not doing it is what you will do, I will not give you oil, (I will not give you oil); I will not give you fat, O lamp.[68]

---

66 PDM xiv. 150–231.

67 Ibid.

68 Ibid.

The number of PGM spells for divination that call upon or mention Isis is surprising considering that our modern view of her does not immediately suggest an association with divination. However, in the context of the late antique world and the use of dream incubation in temples, as well as the profound and multifaceted historiola of Isis's search for Osiris, it is unsurprising that the authors and redactors of the PGM contributed this perspective on the goddess. Isis's association with divination may not have been found in the accepted writings about her, but these divination spells demonstrate that conjure magic is, and always has been, a living tradition that is not constrained by established thought.

CURING SNAKEBITES AND SCORPION STINGS

Various non-PGM sources refer to a mythical episode in which Horus is bitten by a snake or scorpion (sometimes sent by Set/Typhon) and Isis must find a cure for him. It is this myth that is referenced in a magical stela from the reign of Nectanebo II (30th Dynasty), known as the Metternich Stela, which belongs to a group of stelae known as the 'Cippi of Horus' or 'Stelae of Horus on the crocodiles'. These stelae were commonly used to protect against the bites and stings of venomous and dangerous animals, and their prevalence serves as a reminder of how dangerous the environment of Egypt at that time was. The Metternich Stela presents a long text in which Isis left the baby Horus alone for a while and returned to find him lifeless, unwilling to drink milk from her. She was terrified and alone, unable to call upon any of the gods for help:

> How great was my fear, because there was no one who could come at my call! For my father was in the Netherworld, my mother in the Place of Silence, my older brother (Osiris) in the sarcophagus; (my) other one (Seth) was the enemy, long furious at me, and my younger sister (Nephthys) was in his house.[69]

Instead, she turned to mortals in a nearby village, who diagnosed Horus. Isis's sister Nephthys arrived and offered advice, which Isis followed:

> "Isis, call out to the sky, so that Re's crew will come to a halt and Re's boat not proceed while son Horus is prostrate." Isis sent her voice to the sky, crying to the Boat of Eternity, and the sun-disk stopped opposite her and did not move from his place.[70]

(Compare this halting power of Isis's distress with that in PGM XXXVI. 134–60 ['For Isis raised up a loud cry, and the world was thrown into confusion'] and the grief of the Greek goddess Demeter that caused the earth to become barren while she

---

69 Text in translation by Allen, J., online at The Metropolitan Museum of Art, http://www.metmuseum.org/collection/the-collection-online/search/546037?=&imgNo=0&tabName=gallery-label [Accessed 8 September 2014].

70 Ibid.

searched for her kidnapped daughter.) Finally, Thoth arrived and administered the cure for Horus, but the text then moves from the mythical to the magical, as each line of Thoth's protection spell for Horus ends with 'and the protection of the afflicted as well'. The power of halting the proper course of the universe is also given to the magician: 'The boat is stopped and cannot sail, the sun-disk is where it was yesterday, until Horus gets well for his mother Isis and until the afflicted gets well for his mother as well'.

Another well-known myth concerning Isis is when she cured Ra of a snakebite. In this tale, Isis desired to learn the true name of Ra, the most powerful of the gods and the creator of the universe, so she created from Ra's spittle a snake. The snake bit Ra, and, because he did not create it, he could not cure the bite himself. All the gods and goddesses came to him to try and help, but only Isis was renowned enough with healing and magic to be able to offer any aid. She began the chants, but then said that she could not continue without knowing Ra's true name, for in using the power of his name she would surely be able to save him. Ra initially gave several untrue names, all of which Isis refused, until he finally conceded and bestowed upon her the secret. He also said that she could tell his name to her son, Horus, under oath. When Isis spoke Ra's magical name, he was cured, but as a result Isis had attained the same magical power as Ra. At this point, the text recounting the mythical story becomes a magical prescription:

> Words to be spoken over an image of Atum and of Horus-of-Praise, a figure of Isis, and an image of Horus, painted on the hand of him who has the sting and licked off by the man—(or) done similarly on a strip of fine linen, placed at the throat of him who has the sting. It is the way of caring for a scorpion poison. (Or) it may be worked with beer or wine and drunk by the man who has a scorpion (bite). It is what kills the poison—really successful a million times.[71]

Here, the images of the deities from the story are painted onto the patient's hand, who licks them off, presumably taking into his body the healing that was performed in the story and the power of the deities therein. It is perhaps a succinct means of internalizing (quite literally) and utilizing the mythical precedent of this cure, with little effort required from the healer or the patient.

In another non-PGM text concerning Isis curing a snakebite/scorpion sting, Isis speaks the words of the spell, ending with 'and such is also the case with the sufferer',[72] so the words that the magician would speak are also the words of Isis. This is both historiola and an act whereby the magician claims Isis's power as their own.

There are a large number of similar anti-snakebite magical texts from Dynastic Egypt, yet in the PGM there are only a few. Given the proliferation of other sources for this kind of cure, it could be suggested that the redactors of the handbooks in the PGM saw no need to add another. Some might also suggest that the lack of such cures in the PGM is due to the difference in time period—the PGM spells date to over a millennium later than many of the other surviving texts concerning snakebites,

---

71 Pritchard, J. B., ed., *Ancient Near Eastern Texts Relating to the Old Testament*, p. 14.

72 Borghouts, J. F., *Ancient Egyptian Magical Texts*, p. 70.

and medical understanding and practice may have outstripped the need for magical assistance. However, there are many other medico-magical prescriptions in the PGM, indicating that the distinction between medicine and magic was not clear.[73]

Three PGM spells mention Isis in cures for poisons. The first, PDM xiv. 554–62, is 'to be said to the bite of a dog' and tells the magician what to say to prevent the bite from turning bad, ending with the powerful statement 'according to the voice of Isis, the magician, the lady of magic, who bewitches everything, who is never bewitched in her name of Isis, the magician'. It is unclear here if the magician is identifying as Isis or doing the magic in her name. The second spell, which follows immediately after this one, is to be said to 'extract the venom from the heart of a man who has already been made to drink a potion or a poison'. It identifies and magically names a cup as the 'golden cup of Osiris' and states that from this cup Isis, Osiris and Agathodaimon ('good spirit') have drunk, and in doing so others who drink from the cup will not suffer from poisons or potions, but will instead be healed by it.[74] Such a cup is not attested in mythology, but the granting of divine origin to a mundane item to be used in the spell is similar to the identification of the lamp wick in PDM xiv. 150–231 with the byssus robe of Osiris.

The third spell, PDM xiv. 594–620, is perhaps the most interesting and the most complex. It is 'to be said to the sting' and begins with the magician identifying as 'the King's son, greatest and first, Anubis'. (Anubis was sometimes seen as the eldest son of Isis and Osiris, although he was conceived by Nephthys and Set in many myths.) The spell continues by presenting a mythically inspired historiola in which Sekhmet-Isis visits the magician-Anubis and tells him to come to Egypt from Syria to witness his father, Osiris's, crowning as the ruler of the land. However, the historiola then describes a serpent leaping at the magician-Anubis and biting him, after which Isis gives instructions to him about what to do:

> "Do not weep, do not weep, my child, King's son, greatest and first, Anubis! Lick from your tongue to your heart, and vice versa, as far as the edges of the wound! Lick from the edges of the wound up to the limits of your / strength!" What you will lick up, you should swallow it. Do not spit it out on the ground, for your tongue is the tongue of the Agathodaimon, your tongue is that of Atum!"[75]

This is similar in practice to the mythical-narrative-turned-spell of Isis curing Ra of a snakebite mentioned earlier, in which the licking off of images painted on the victim's hand cures bites, stings and poisons. However, the earlier text dates from the 19th Dynasty (1350–1200 BCE), whereas the PGM spell is from a millennium later, and the reasons for the licking—as well as what is consumed—are different: in the earlier spell, the magical healing power of Atum and Horus is taken into the victim and enacts

---

73 For further reading on the medical treatments of snakebites in ancient Egypt, see Nunn, J. F., *Ancient Egyptian Medicine*, 1996.

74 PDM xiv. 563–74.

75 PDM xiv. 601–607.

the cure, whereas in the PGM spell, the magician *is* Atum and Isis's son (in this case, Anubis rather than Horus) and it is the fluids of the wound that are consumed by that healing power.

This identification of the magician with the gods in PDM xiv. 594–620 continues with a prescription for the magician to magically charge oil to rub on the wound daily for seven days. When speaking to the oil to charge it, the magician is instructed to say, 'Isis is the one who / is speaking to the oil', perhaps referencing the historiola, which continues by saying that Isis sat down and charged the oil, or perhaps switching the magician's identification from Anubis, the wounded, to Isis the healer. The latter seems most likely, as the end of the spell has the magician speaking as the healer for others:

> I shall employ you for the sting of the King's son, greatest and first, Anubis, my child, in order that you fill it and make it well. For I shall employ you for [the] sting of NN, whom NN bore, / in order that you fill it and make it well.[76]

It seems particularly apt that the magician takes on the role of Isis in this spell, since she is the mother of the wounded, and the loving care shown by Isis as a grieving mother is played out by the magician for the patient, who may or may not be known to them.

To catch a thief

Isis is not often associated with discovering thieves or bringing criminals to justice; in fact, some of her myths present her as a trickster herself, using deceit to achieve her ends (such as in her trickery to learn Ra's true name, and in her deceit towards Set in the *Contendings of Horus and Set*). Nevertheless, one PGM spell, PDM lxi. 79–94 ('Way of finding a thief'), uses a brief historiola in which Isis is the pursuer of justice and protection for a wronged victim, using the spell to discover the whereabouts of Set so that he could not harm Horus:

> I shall give them the words / of Geb which he gave to Isis when Shu (?) concealed them in the papyrus (swamp) of Buto, she bringing the small amount of flax in her hand, she forming it into a knot, she tying these forelegs (?) until he was revealed to Horus in the papyrus (swamp).

The spell continues by saying that the same action can also be used to discover the whereabouts of a thief: 'I will bring this small amount of flax in my own hand, I making it into a knot until NN is revealed'.

Although this spell could also be considered a form of divination, it stands apart from the previously discussed divination spells because of its purpose and its specific conflation of Set—the 'bad guy' of the Osirian cycle—with a wrongdoer, in this case a thief. It reminds us that, no matter the purpose to which the PGM spells are put,

---

76 PDM xiv. 617–620.

the magician tends to identify themself with the 'good guys'—Isis, Horus and Osiris, for example (such as in PDM xiv. 239–95). Even in spells that call upon the terrifying facets of deities, such as Artemis-Persephone-Selene (although with a description more closely matching Hekate Triformis) in PGM IV. 2241–2621, in which the goddess is described as world-shaking, grave-dwelling, terrifying and chthonic, the invoked deities themselves are not traditionally the 'bad guys' of mythology.

This spell also showcases the phenomenon of persuasively analogous ritual, which is seen by some scholars as a form of sympathetic magic. It has been suggested, however, that the term 'sympathetic magic' is a problematic one that does not apply to every instance of magic to which it has been given, and that more useful terms include 'persuasively analogical ritual', 'contagious magic' and 'homeopathic magic'.[77] Both sympathetic and contagious magic work on the principle that what was once conjoined will continue to affect what it was joined with even after separation, or that a representation of the thing-in-itself has an essential link to the thing-in-itself. Persuasively analogous ritual, however, emphasises ritual actions as a means of encouraging future actions through analogical ones, such as piercing the mouth of a figurine so that the tongue of the victim will be bound. In PDM lxi. 79–94, the formula juxtaposes Isis's actions with those of the magician—just as she knotted the flax and in so doing discovered the whereabouts of Set, so the magician knots the flax and discovers the whereabouts of the thief. The persuasively analogous part of the spell can be found in the way in which Isis is said to have knotted the flax: 'tying these forelegs', which Betz notes refers to the forelegs of Set as a bull. Presumably, just as Set was discovered and bound, so the thief that wronged the magician would be discovered and bound, unable to escape detection and, eventually, justice.

Isis Chthonia

The spells of the PGM have long been noted for their association with deities traditionally identified as 'chthonic', such as Persephone, Hekate, Anubis, and Hermes, but Isis is not usually identified in this way by modern researchers and magicians. However, several of the spells in the PGM not only give Isis a dwelling in the world of spirits (which is also perhaps the underworld) but also grant to her the other features of a chthonic deity.

The term 'chthonic' comes from the Greek χθόνιος ('under the earth' or 'in the earth') but is specifically applied to deities of the underworld in magic and religion. However, the classification is not solely based on where a deity dwells: although some chthonic deities, such as Persephone and Hades, are said to live in the underworld, others, such as Hermes and Hekate, have no subterranean abode but instead are granted their chthonic status through the role they play in relation to the dead. Hermes, in his role as psychopomp, was said to guide the souls of the dead to the underworld, and Hekate was presented in the Eleusinian Mysteries as a companion to Persephone, guiding her out of the underworld.

---

77 See Tambiah, S. J., *Form and Meaning of Magical Acts: A Point of View*. In R. Horton and R. Finnegan (eds.), *Modes of Thought: Essays on thinking in Western and non-Western societies*, pp. 199–229.

In PGM XXXVI. 134–60, the slander spell discussed earlier, Isis is caused such torment by unlawful offerings that her cries and convulsions cause the 'daimon world' to be 'smashed to pieces'. These daimons are then sent to torment the target of the spell in turn, being called out from 'beneath the earth' and 'from the depth'. It is clear that in this spell the daimon world is an underworld, possibly quite literally under the earth, yet although it is implied that Isis also dwells in that daimon world, it is not explicitly stated. However, her connection to these daimons from beneath the earth is clearly made, and it can be argued that a dwelling does not need to be literally subterranean for a deity to be classed as chthonic. As Stratton-Kent has identified, in the PGM the 'underworld' is expanded to include the sky, and deities that previously had no underworld role are given one. Stratton-Kent suggests that the reasons for this expansion may have been cultural, 'the pessimism of civilisations conquered by Rome foremost among them',[78] but another possibility should be considered: that the types of magic primarily performed in the PGM handbooks are likely to have been utilised outside of a temple context, separately from a public, religious, and organised sphere, and may therefore represent a more personal approach to a vast universe of gods, spirits, and other entities—ancestors and the dead. Not everybody can expect to experience the beauty of Aphrodite, or the skill of Apollo, and many of the Olympian deities and their like seem far removed from mortal life, but every single person that lives has their dead.

Isis's connection with the dead is mentioned several times in the PGM and utilised to grant the magician the power to call upon the dead and control them. The vessel divination spell of PDM xiv. 1–92 opens with an invocation first to the underworld ('Open to me, O earth! Open to me, O underworld! Open to me, O primeval waters!') and then to the 'gods in heaven, who are exalted', yet the divination occurs only when the diviner speaks with Anubis, the 'master of secrets for those in the Underworld'. Then, it is Isis's name that is used to command Anubis, indicating her indirect power over the dead through Anubis. In another vessel divination spell, PDM xiv. 239–95, Isis is one of the gods that the magician identifies to call the spirits of the dead to service, along with Osiris and Anubis, who are both associated with the underworld and the dead.

Isis's chthonic role as commander of the dead in the PGM is reminiscent of her role as protector and mother of the dead king in the Pyramid Texts and, later, protector and mother of all the dead. She is often represented in the Pyramid Texts

78 Stratton-Kent, J., *Geosophia: The Argo of Magic. Enyclopeadia Goetica, Vol. II*, p. 157.

as giving her milk to the dead king so that he may achieve life among the stars after death ('Raise yourself, O King! You have your water, you have your inundation, you have your milk which is from the breasts of the mother Isis.'),[79] and in her mortuary role she was known as 'Mistress of the Pyramid'.[80] Her funerary role in the preparation of the deceased king is mythically paralleled with the preparation and mourning for the dead Osiris, a role that she shares with her sister Nephthys, and both goddesses are depicted in the Pyramid Texts as being the means, both literal and figurative, by which the deceased ascends to the stars: 'I ascend upon the thighs of Isis, / I climb up upon the thighs of Nephthys'.[81]

It is perhaps this understanding of the destination of the dead being located among the stars that influences the expansion of the 'underworld' in the PGM, the handbooks of which are rich in syncretism and represent not only a coexistence of religions but a mingling of them. In this sense, the Isis Chthonia of the PGM defies the categorisation of the godly realm into chthonic/heavenly, and she is not alone in doing so: the PGM treats several other gods, both Egyptian and Greek, in the same way; even Helios, the Greek god of the sun, is given rulership of the underworld.[82] In their continuation of the much earlier concepts of Isis from the Pyramid Texts, the spells of the PGM show both the Hellenisation and modernisation of ancient ideas (or an influence on invasive Hellenistic ideas by native/earlier ones), demonstrating that the authors/redactors of the PGM not only contributed new material to the presentation of Isis but also continued more ancient traditions that had become less popular and relevant in the late antique period.

What is missing?

Isis as conceiving mother and protector of mortal mothers

As the main demographic of the PGM's various authors/redactors might suggest, the spells in these handbooks were written for the use, predominantly, of men (both as magician and as the magician's client). As a nursing mother, Isis was depicted frequently in statues with the child Horus on her lap suckling at her breast. Medical texts (such as the London Medical Papyrus and the Ebers Papyrus) from ancient Egypt are pseudo-magical when they call for the 'milk of one who has borne a male child', referring specifically to Isis and her son Horus. It was also called 'Isis's milk' and was obtained through a transubstantiation ritual in which human milk was poured into and out of

---

79 *Pyr.* 412: 734.

80 Breasted, J. H., trans., *Ancient Records of Egypt, vol. 1: The First through the Seventeenth Dynasties*, pp. 84–5.

81 *Pyr.* 269: 379.

82 PGM IV. 1596–715.

an anthropomorphic vase of Isis nursing Horus, while speaking a chant about them.[83] In such cures, Isis is shown as a nurturing mother, whose breast milk is the archetype of all human breast milk and can cure all ills. However, as with other aspects of childbirth and conception, spells concerning nursing and the medical conditions associated with it are almost absent from the handbooks in the PGM, with only one spell—PGM VII. 208–9—offering a prescription to cure 'hardening of the breasts'.

There are very few spells in the PGM referring to fertility, whether in the form of preventing conception or aiding it, even though magic to help would-be mothers and to prevent miscarriage and haemorrhaging was performed in Isis's name in ancient Egypt.

Outside of the PGM, Isis was seen as having special care for mothers, as her own divine womb was also at risk of stillbirth, deformed birth and miscarriage:

> It was believed that various threats extended even to childbearing goddesses and their offspring; mythology therefore ascribes to various deities the task of safe-guarding both the personified divine mother, Isis, and her son, Horus. These motifs from the myths about Isis and Horus were in turn used in apotropaic magic, applied at the birth of earthly beings—for example, in the form of numerous amulets.[84]

One such amulet was called the 'knot of Isis', made of red jasper or carnelian. It was designed in the form of a stylized tampon or girdle, which, according to the Coffin Texts, Isis herself used to plug her vagina[85] to protect the unborn Horus, under advice from Ra.[86] Some have interpreted this amulet, also called the 'blood of Isis', as the girdle that Egyptian women wore while menstruating, but both interpretations share the feature of staunching the flow of blood. There is also a carved magical gem, currently residing in the Oriental Institute, that shows Isis, Osiris and Nephthys beneath a womb that has been shut with a key, which has been identified as a gem to prevent miscarriage and haemorrhaging.[87] It is probable that the myth of Isis's son being hunted by Set/Typhon, even while he was still in her womb, gave rise to the role of Set as the causer of miscarriage. Just as Isis's pregnancy was threatened by him, so every pregnant woman was at risk of his interference.[88] Since Isis was seen as particularly protective of pregnant women, there are a great number of spells performed in her name to accelerate

---

83 Laskaris, J., Nursing Mothers in Greek and Roman Medicine. *The American Journal of Archaeology* 112 (3) (Jul., 2008), p. 460.

84 Packer, G. and Mysliwiec, K., *Eros on the Nile*, p. 142.

85 A pillar-shaped tampon was prescribed by another magical text, not found in the PGM, mentioned in Ritner, R. K., A Uterine Amulet in the Oriental Institute Collection. *Journal of Near Eastern Studies*, 43 (3) (Jul., 1984), p. 213.

86 Packer, G. and Mysliwiec, K., *Eros on the Nile*, pp. 142–3.

87 Ritner, R. K., A Uterine Amulet in the Oriental Institute Collection, pp. 209–221.

88 Ibid., p. 215.

childbirth,[89] yet none of them are to be found in the handbooks of the PGM. In fact, only one spell in the collection concerns childbirth directly—PGM CXXIII. a–f—and only one spell offers a solution for what may be a prolapsed uterus—PGM VII. 260–71 ('For the ascent of the uterus'). There is also one entry in the Demotic spells offering a pregnancy test (PDM xiv. 956–60) and a handful of contraceptive charms, spells to stop a woman bleeding, and spells to stop 'liquid in a woman'. The small number of such spells in comparison with the large number of spells concerning divination, love, giving someone 'evil' sleep, and treating fever highlights possible areas for reflection upon the sociological features of the creation of the PGM handbooks. However, it is perhaps a disappointing feature of the PGM that the face of Isis as mother is absent from its magic.

Isis as mistress of the seas

Another aspect of Isis was as a mistress of the seas, goddess of navigation and protector of sailors, to whom the annual Navigium Isis festival was dedicated. As a maritime goddess, she was most often called Isis Pharia ('Isis of Pharos'), Isis Pelagia ('Isis of the sea'), Isis Euploia ('Isis of the fair voyage'), and Isis Soteira ('Isis who saves'). Although Isis was mythically presented as travelling on divine barges in the underworld and on the Nile, along with many other deities, her maritime associations came much later, after the establishment of a firmly Hellenistic Isis in the Graeco-Egyptian and Roman periods and, in particular, after her association with Arsinoë II and Aphrodite in the third century BCE.[90] In fact, the association between Isis and Aphrodite is found in the spells of the PGM, such as in love spells using apples.[91] However, not only is Isis as a maritime goddess entirely absent from the PGM (although there are brief mentions of her being on a divine barge in the underworld), the handbooks that make up the collection include no spells for the success of sea journeys or the safety of sailors. This raises another sociological question about the creators/redactors of these handbooks: why are such concerns absent from their magic? It could be suggested that such concerns were already being addressed by public religion and ritual, such as the Navigium Isis itself, but the fact that the PGM includes initiatory texts and theurgic texts that would not be alien to the mystery religions that could be accessed at the time, medico-magical texts that deal with health issues that would also have been addressed by non-magical means, and dream divination rituals that would serve the same purpose as temple-based dream incubation, suggests that a delineation between public/private and accessible/inaccessible is not necessarily productive in relation to the PGM.

Furthermore, the absence of Isis as mistress of the seas, and indeed of spells concerning journeys on the sea, suggests a feature of the PGM spells that places them in the same tradition as conjure magic and grimoire magic. This form of Isis was not a well-established aspect of the goddess until the Graeco-Egyptian and Roman

---

89 Ibid., p. 217.

90 Bricault, Laurent, *Isis Pelagia: Images, Names and Cults of a Goddess of the Seas*, pp. 12–42.

91 See, for example, PGM CXXII. 1–55.

periods, the periods from which the PGM handbooks come. However, analysis of the compositional patterns of the collections of spells demonstrates that, in many cases, the spells are copied, sometimes several times over, from earlier sources; they are pieced together and misunderstood, with fragments of spells being merged into other spells, reorganised and recreated, and added to over time by different scribes, redactors and authors (as demonstrated by LiDonnici in their analysis of the compositional patterns of PGM IV).[92] It is possible that Isis as mistress of the seas does not feature in the PGM because this aspect of the goddess was not prevalent at the time the earlier versions of the spells were written. Importantly, this reflects the need for us to understand the magic of the PGM not as a monolithic, consistent whole but as several individual handbooks and fragments of handbooks. It reminds us that the spells of the PGM were part of a living tradition even when they came into the form in which they were found by modern historians and that they are just one aspect of the continuation of conjure magic.

CONCLUSION

The faces of Isis presented to us by the magicians of the PGM share in common several features of the Isis we know from mythology and the religious texts of earlier Egypt; in this familiarity we find an Isis whose power and magical knowledge were used to legitimize the magical activities of these magicians and whose main myths offered a cornucopia of motifs that were used for a wide array of spells, from amatory curses and attraction spells to divination, business magic, spells to find thieves, charms to cure snakebites and spells to raise the dead. It might be suggested that the prevalence of emotion attributed to Isis in the PGM shows us an authentic Isis, one who felt the pangs of love and separation, desire and yearning, one who feared, and one who sought help in her time of distress; principally, a goddess who shared the yearnings and sufferings of those mortals who called upon her name and power in magic.

Is the Isis of the PGM the Isis of the Mysteries? The Isis of the New Kingdom Pyramid Texts? The Isis of the Egyptian *Book of the Dead*? The Isis beloved in the Graeco-Egyptian and Roman worlds? No, and yes. Undoubtedly she is recognizable as the beloved Egyptian goddess who guarded the soul of the dead king with her sister, searched for her dead husband, was a passionate and loving wife, and held great magical skill and power; and yet there are nuances to her character touched upon by these spells that either did not survive in myth and mainstream religion or that reflect a contribution to the character of Isis by the scribes and authors of the PGM—in other words, the spells of the PGM can be considered as valid in their representations of Isis as are the narratives found in surviving mythological texts.

For those studying the PGM from a historiographical perspective, a study of Isis in these handbooks highlights several features of the composition of the PGM and the philosophies/theologies that underpin it. For the modern magician and occultist, the ways in which Isis is called upon in the PGM offer an early glimpse of how later

---

92 LiDonnici, L. R., Compositional Patterns in PGM IV (= P.Bibl.Nat.Suppl. gr. no. 574). *The Bulletin of the American Society of Papyrologists* 40 (1/4) (2003), pp. 141–178.

grimoires and conjure magic call upon gods, spirits, and other entities. And for those looking to the PGM for a sociological understanding of its authors, its magicians, and its clients, not only the types of spells for which Isis was invoked but the absence of certain types of spells and aspects of Isis in the PGM offer significant areas of consideration.

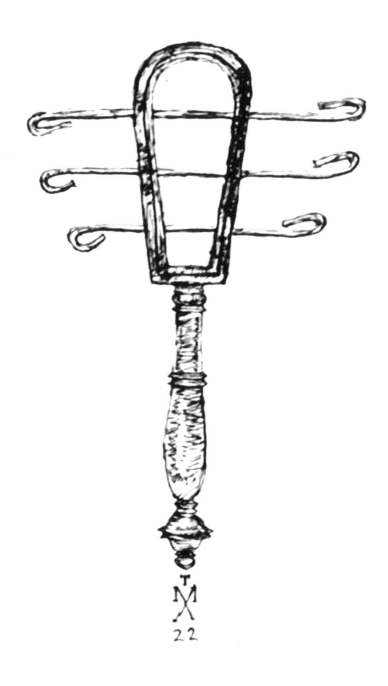

BIBLIOGRAPHY

Alföldi, A., 1938. A Festival of Isis in Rome under the Christian Emperors of the Fourth Century. *The Journal of Roman Studies* 28 (1), pp. 88–90.

Ankarloo, B. and Clark, S., eds., 1999. *Witchcraft and Magic in Europe, vol 2: Ancient Greece and Rome*. Pennsylvania: University of Pennsylvania Press.

Borghouts, J. F., 1978. *Ancient Egyptian Magical Texts*. Leiden: Brill.

Betz, H. D., ed., 1992. *The Greek Magical Papyri in Translation including the demotic spells*. London: University of Chicago Press.

Brashear, W., 1995. The Greek Magical Papyri: an Introduction and Survey; Annotated Bibliography (1928–1994). *Aufsteig und Niedergang der römischen Welt II*, 18.5, 1995, p. 3439.

Breasted, J. H., trans., 2001. *Ancient Records of Egypt, vol. 1: The First through the Seventeenth Dynasties*. Illinois: University of Illinois Press.

Bricault, L., 2020. *Isis Pelagia: Images, Names and Cults of a Goddess of the Seas*. Religions in the Graeco-Roman World, vol. 190. Translated from French by G. H. Renberg. Leiden: Brill.

Daniel, R. W., and Maltomini, F., eds., 1990. *Supplementum Magicum. Vol. I. Abhandlungen der Rheinisch-Westfälischen Akademie der Wissenschaften*. Opladen: Westdeutscher Verlag.

Dunand, F., 1973. *Culte d'Isis dans le Bassin Oriental de la Méditerranée*. Brill: Leiden.

Durham, E., 2016. Metropolitan styling: figurines from London and Colchester. In Hoss, S. and Whitmore, A. (eds.), *Small Finds and Ancient Social Practices in the Northwest Provinces of the Roman Empire*. Oxford: Oxbow Books, pp. 75–97.

Faraone, C. A., 2001. *Ancient Greek Love Magic*. Massachusetts: Harvard University Press.

Faraone, C. A. and Obbink, D., eds., 1997. *Magika Hiera: Ancient Greek Magic and Religion*. Oxford: Oxford University Press.

Faulkner, R. O., trans., 1969. *The Ancient Egyptian Pyramid Texts*. Oxford: Oxford University Press.

Gager, J. G., 1999. *Curse Tablets and Binding Spells from the Ancient World*. Oxford: Oxford University Press.

Heyob, S., 1975. *The Cult of Isis Among Women in the Graeco-Roman World*. Leiden: Brill.

Laskaris, J., 2008. Nursing Mothers in Greek and Roman Medicine. *The American Journal of Archaeology* 112 (3) (Jul., 2008), pp. 459–464.

Lichtheim, M., ed., 2006. *Ancient Egyptian Literature: vols. 1 and 2*. California: University of California Press.

LiDonnici, L. R., 2003. Compositional Patterns in PGM IV (= P.Bibl.Nat.Suppl. gr. no. 574). *The Bulletin of the American Society of Papyrologists* 40 (1/4), pp. 141–178.

LiDonnici, L. R., 2001. Single-Stemmed Wormwood, Pinecones and Myrrh: Expense and Availability of Recipe Ingredients in the Greek Magical Papyri. *Kernos* [online] 14. Available at: <http://journals.openedition.org/kernos/770> [Accessed 27 April 2021].

Lucian, n.d. *Lovers of Lies*. In *The Works of Lucian of Samosata*, translated by H. W. Fowler and F. G. Fowler, 1906. Oxford: Clarendon Press.

Luck, G., ed., 2006. *Arcana Mundi: Magic and the Occult in the Greek and Roman Worlds.* Maryland: John Hopkins University Press.

Meyer, M. W. and Smith, R., eds., 1999. *Ancient Christian Magic: Coptic Texts of Ritual Magic.* New Jersey: Princeton University Press.

Nunn, J. F., 1996. *Ancient Egyptian Medicine.* Oklahoma: University of Oklahoma Press.

Pachoumi, E., 2013. The Erotic and Separation Spells of the Magical Papyri and Defixiones. *Greek, Roman, and Byzantine Studies* 53, pp. 294–325.

Packer, G. and Mysliwiec, K., 2004. *Eros on the Nile.* London: Gerald Duckworth & Co. Ltd.

Plaisance, C. A., 2020. *Evocating the Gods: Divine Evocation in the Graeco-Egyptian Magical Papyri.* London: Avalonia Books.

Pomeroy, S. B., 1994. *Goddesses, Whores, Wives, & Slaves: Women in Classical Antiquity.* London: Pimlico.

Pritchard, J. B., ed., 1969. *Ancient Near Eastern Texts Relating to the Old Testament.* New Jersey: Princeton University Press.

Reeder Williams, E., 1985. Isis Pelagia and a Roman Marble Matrix from the Athenian Agora. *Hesperia* 54 (2) (Apr.–Jun., 1985), pp. 109–119.

Ritner, R. K., 1984. A Uterine Amulet in the Oriental Institute Collection. *Journal of Near Eastern Studies* 43 (3) (Jul., 1984), pp. 209–221.

Schubart, W., 1918. *Einführung in die Papyruskunde.* Berlin: Weidmann.

Skinner, S., 2014. *Techniques of Graeco-Egyptian Magic.* Singapore: Golden Hoard Press.

Spiegelberg, W., 1978. *Demotische Papyrus aus den königlichen Museen ze Berlin.* Berlin: Akademie-Verlag.

Stratton-Kent, J., 2010. *Geosophia: The Argo of Magic. Enyclopeadia Goetica, Vol. II.* London: Scarlet Imprint.

Tambiah, S. J., 1973. Form and Meaning of Magical Acts: A Point of View. In R. Horton and R. Finnegan (eds.), *Modes of Thought: Essays on thinking in Western and non-Western societies.* London: Faber & Faber, pp. 199–229.

Tower Hollis, S., 2000. Goddesses and Sovereignty in Ancient Egypt. In E. Benard and B. Moon (eds.), *Goddesses Who Rule.* New York: Oxford University Press, pp. 215–232.

Von Lieven, A., 2006. Seth ist im Recht, Osiris ist im Unrecht! *Zeitschrift fur agyptische Spracge und Altertumskunde* 133, pp. 141–150.

Witt, R. E., 1997. *Isis in the Ancient World.* Maryland: John Hopkins University Press.

Every Nekuomanteia is a Katabasis:
Ancient Insights for Contemporary Goetic Practice

Kadmus

I. Introduction

DANIEL OGDEN OBSERVES that "...even when evocating ghosts a necromancer could be imagined to be dissolving the boundaries between the lower world and the upper one in such a way that the distinction between the descent of the consulter and the ascent of the ghosts is effaced."[1] In other words, every act of necromancy also involves a process of *katabasis*, or going down into the underworld. If we take this point seriously it immediately suggests that much of the framework and apparatus of necromantic practice can be read against the background of the challenges and dangers associated with underworld journeys such as those presented in Homer's *Odyssey* and Virgil's *Aeneid*. The challenges include gaining access to the underworld to begin with as well as getting safely back, while the dangers include navigating underworld guardians such as Cerberus, Charon, and hordes of hungry or angry spirits—both of the dead and otherwise.

I mention spirits both dead and otherwise because shifting our focus, in considering the nature of necromancy, from the target of our work to the location or place to which our work takes us implies that the necromancer may have much to do with underworldly spirits which never were human, either living or dead—spirits such as Cerberus himself. Much of the work preserved in the Greek Magical Papyri as well as in the various grimoires we might call goetic, is necromantic even, or especially, when it deals with spirits that make no pretense of having been living humans.

Fixating on Ogden's surprisingly simple observation above is part of a larger project, specifically attempting to leverage ancient, mainly pagan, insights for contemporary occult practices. Although it may seem a humble enough project, it involves some strikingly difficult challenges, not the least of which is removing blinders born of inherited post-pagan metaphysical commitments that color nearly all of our contemporary perspectives on magical practice. I hope to make clear how extensively our occult instincts are different from those that would have been seemingly natural to an ancient pagan practitioner and the practical outcomes of this realization.

---

1 Daniel Ogden, *Greek and Roman Necromancy* (Princeton University Press, 2001), p. xxi.

II. Agrippa and the Platonic Inheritance

Contemporary occult practice and theory, like most of it for the last two thousand years, is primarily built on the foundation of Platonic and Aristotelian philosophy which dominated late ancient and medieval thinking. This remains the case even when tweaked by the mechanistic view that dominated early modern science or the subjectivist psychologism that dominates much thinking today. To put the point rather bluntly, occult philosophy is dominated by some version of the theory of correspondences (or sympathies) amongst abstract energies (or powers, or virtues, or emanations, or essences and so on). In either more scientist materialist or contemporary subjectivist variations on occult philosophy we generally just find the substitution of one ontology for another beneath the still dominating view of correspondence amongst these 'energies'. The master text of this occult philosophy is, of course, Cornelius Agrippa's *Three Books of Occult Philosophy* that, in its turn, was the foundational influence on the work of both Johann Weyer and Reginald Scot. Together Agrippa, Weyer, and Scot form the basic configuration of occult philosophy since their time either through overt influence or through the foundation they provided for grimoires that followed from their writings. Even before them, however, the foundational influence that gave rise to Agrippa was at work. The main target against which both Weyer and Scot aimed their work, namely the *Malleus Maleficarum*, derives its own occult philosophy from the same source as Agrippa—Thomas Aquinas's monumental *Summa Theologiae* of roughly two centuries earlier. What Aquinas accomplishes for theology, Agrippa accomplishes for the occult, specifically achieving the utter dominance of an Aristotelian and Platonic philosophy.[2]

It is important to note that actual books of magic such as grimoires and practitioner notebooks, rather than books about magic, tend not to contain involved explorations of occult philosophy. In fact, I will argue, they tend to preserve (if often without understanding) ancient aspects of occult practice without engaging in philosophical explanation of these elements. This results in the use of texts such as Agrippa's to interpret the content of grimoires and practitioner handbooks. Where such books *of* magic do contain overt philosophical reflections, the metaphysics is often a later addition taken from works such as Agrippa's appended to older spirit catalogues and ceremonial mechanics.

The view of magic to which I intend to present an alternative is presented explicitly in the first of Agrippa's three books and is likely to seem very familiar to most of my audience. For this reason I hope I will be forgiven for presenting it a bit schematically and very briefly. First, we have the overall structural element that provides for magic's efficacy, namely correspondence or sympathy:

> Magic... doth instruct us concerning the differing, and agreement of things amongst themselves, whence it produceth its wonderful effects, by uniting the

---

2 I should note here that I repeatedly refer to 'Aristotelian and Platonic philosophy' because, though there are extensive and fascinating differences between the two, these differences are not important for my project. In regards to the work I intend to do, Aristotelianism and the many variations of Platonism are easily equated and their distinctions ignored.

virtues of things through the application of them one to the other, and to their inferior suitable subjects, joining and knitting them together thoroughly by the powers, and virtues of the superior bodies.[3]

All things are defined by the virtues or powers they contain, and these powers, in turn, can be combined and controlled through correspondence with still greater powers and so on. The standard example of this might be something like a stone or herb with marked planetary correspondence which is then used either as a source of that planet's power or, alternatively, controlled via the triggering of the proper planetary force. This picture is extended in the very first words of Agrippa's work by appealing to an idea of three different worlds drawn from Platonic philosophy: "Seeing there is a threefold world, elementary, celestial, and intellectual, and every inferior is governed by its superior, and receiveth the influence of the virtues thereof…".[4] This threefold model is what was at work in my example when the celestial influence of a planet was used either upon or through the corresponding elemental configuration that made up the basic body of the stone. Any given thing will have elemental correspondence, celestial correspondence, and finally intellectual correspondence through which we can understand its nature and powers. Allow me to add one final quotation from Agrippa to fully pull these elements together with their Platonic underpinning:

> The form therefore, and virtue of things comes first from the Ideas, then from the ruling, and governing intelligences, then from the aspects of the heavens disposing, and lastly from the tempers of the elements disposed, answering the influences of the heavens, by which the elements themselves are ordered, or disposed.[5]

The "Ideas" addressed in this passage were originally, in Plato, perfect unchanging non-material entities that provided both the nature and impetus to change for all things in existence. They were the highest divine thing, utterly abstract and non-anthropomorphic. Christianity, in turn, transformed these divine unchanging entities into Ideas in the mind of God in order to avoid the heresy that Plato had proposed in placing the gods beneath the Ideas as their emanation and servants. Still, in Agrippa these divine servants remain in the from of the "Intelligences" to which he appeals. As angels, or planetary intelligences, they remain the conscious and intelligent emanations of the perfect unchanging Ideas, though those Ideas are now housed in the mind of God rather than existing as self-sufficient and eternal independent entities. The key for our purposes, however, is to see clearly this great chain of being and command. Intelligences arise from abstract perfect ideas, these intelligences rule the planets and stars, and these planets and stars rule the elements. Thus you have the super-celestial, celestial, and sub-lunar worlds of the classic medieval theology and metaphysics.

---

3 Cornelius Agrippa, *Three Books of Occult Philosophy* (Lewellyn, 1998), p. 5.

4 Agrippa, *Three Books of Occult Philosophy*, p. 3.

5 Agrippa, *Three Books of Occult Philosophy*, p. 39.

This framework allows me to provide an example of a ritual garment to which I will return later in order to provide a very different explanation and theory, the famous lionskin belt of the *Lemegeton*. In asking why one would find a lionskin belt helpful in working with the 'demons' contained in the *Arte Goetia* section of the *Lemegeton* it is not unusual to find the following answer (though none is given in the text): the lion has both solar and martial correspondences and so serves to grant the energy, power, virtue, etc. of these celestial influences that are particularly useful when dealing with unruly or dangerous sublunary spirits (i.e. demons). Writing the god names from the larger circle on this belt also serves to command and empower the celestial solar-martial aspects of the belt with the greater Intelligences that rule over the Sun and Mars. Thus we have the super-celestial (the god names and those intelligences that obey them) commanding the celestial (the Sun and Mars), and both in turn empower the sublunary (the actual mixed elemental materia of the lion skin) and command the sublunary (the spirits of the *Arte Goetia*). This type of interpretation is so standard, so pat and universal, that even rehearsing it here is likely obvious for my audience. But let me stress that it is necessary to keep examples like this in mind in order to more clearly see the different perspective I hope to offer.

To offer a slightly different, and historically much more weighty, example allow me to glance briefly at the premier magical act of the medieval Christian world—the transubstantiation of the bread and wine during the Catholic Mass into the body and blood of Christ. One reason why early modern mechanistic views of reality, such as those of Descartes, were such a scandal to the Catholic world was because they sought to offer a new cosmology different from the metaphysics offered by Aristotle and Plato, and without the Platonic-Aristotelian metaphysics it was very hard, or perhaps impossible, to explain how the bread and wine might literally become the body and blood of Christ during the Mass. Aristotelian Platonism allows us to understand this transformation, however. As most powerfully codified by Aquinas, the substance of the bread and wine (what we might more easily think of as its essence) is transformed without the accidents of the bread and wine (what we might more easily think of as its sensory characteristics) changing. This ability to conceptualize essential changes (via changes in body, form, or both) without any corresponding change to sensory accidents is a central one to the framework which both Agrippa and Aquinas, as well as the Catholic church both during the medieval period and now, share.[6] Note that a consecrated lionskin belt and a non-consecrated one need not differ in any sensory way, but the 'virtues' of the belt have been accentuated through adding to its already existing correspondence with the 'virtues' of the planets and so on. The substance from which derive its virtues, but not its appearance or smell, has changed.[7] The mystery of substantial change (which exists on a wide spectrum with the full change of the Eucharist in transubstantiation being

6 See Aquinas, *Summa Theologiae*, Question 75.

7 There is a lot we could dig into here concerning different types of substantial change and their origins, for example material or bodily change versus formal change and so on. Agrippa understands form as deriving primarily from the Ideas and Intelligences while matter is Elemental. Occult ritual might *in-form* a given elemental body, changing its substance but not its accidents. But this level of detail in the analysis is likely not necessary.

the most extreme change possible) is at the heart of the mysteries of magic for Agrippa and, arguably, remains so for most contemporary thinkers despite the tendency to try unsuccessfully to fit Platonic 'virtues' into mechanistic or even quantum 'energy' boxes.

Let us take a step back and look at the view I have been attempting to target a bit more generally. The key aspect of the Platonic view is that magic is effected by means of abstract properties, i.e. powers/virtues/energies, for example the virtue of Jupiter, or the power of the element Fire, and so on. The magical potency of a given ritual, action, or instrument derives from its correspondence with these powers and its ability to draw on them and be empowered by them. The lionskin belt can be made magically efficacious because of its natural correspondence with these abstract powers such as Fire, Mars, and the Sun. Indeed, the more abstract a thing is, the more powerful it is according to the basic Platonic principle that all truth and goodness is ultimately immaterial, abstract, and perfect. The more particular and concrete a thing is the further it is from the source of all true power and being.

The one glitch in this system, and indeed it was consistently a glitch in the Platonic system from the beginning, is the uncomfortable status of exalted entities with personality—in other words the Intelligences. Plato and Aristotle alike had little use or need for gods and divinities with anything resembling personality or individuality. Indeed, such characteristics are inherently incompatible with the levels of perfection and divinity one might wish them to occupy. While Aristotle's Unmoved Mover is indeed an intelligence, the full content of its intelligence and personality is an abstract one—it thinks only about itself and its own perfection which consists entirely of this very self-sufficient self-reflection. It has, as indeed only a perfect thing can, no desires or emotions or thoughts as we might recognize them. Pretty quickly, however, the popularizers of Platonism and what would become known as Neoplatonism recognized that the abstract perfections of philosophy were inadequate for capturing the common mind. Instead, people needed anthropomorphic characters to worship and connect with. This provides the ground for the expanding role of intermediary personalities and Intelligences in Platonic systems. This leads to an inconsistent and uneasy compromise in which gods, or angels, or celestial and super-celestial spirits might exist, but they do so as living tensions between purely symbolic representations of abstract forces/Ideas or odd avatars and mouthpieces of those forces and Ideas. Apollo, or an angel of the Sun, are either just ways by means of which the abstract perfection of solar energy might speak and act, or are just symbolic emanations of the more real abstract Idea. Intelligences are a stop-gap measure in Platonism, one that has never comfortably fit the framework. The same goes, just as much, for human individuality and personality. Adopting a Platonic or Neoplatonic view of the journey of the soul after death, ask yourself how much of 'yourself' can really survive the purification and increasing abstraction to which your individuality will be subjected. Keep in mind that within Plato's philosophy desire and emotion are almost entirely bodily, and so are almost completely purged by true purification.[8] Aristotle, likely seeing this, never proposed any type of personal immortality at all. Ultimately the immortality offered by Platonism can never be a personal one, for nothing of your personal characteristics exists on the abstract level of super-celestial perfection. Rather than thinking about a drop of water returning to the great sea, think instead of one atom of oxygen from that drop, purified so as to be indistinguishable from any other atom of oxygen. Nothing characteristic of the original water remains. Despite these challenges the Platonic public maintained a belief in personal survival after death, as indeed most Christian-style Platonists do today.

It is my contention that the entire system of complex correspondences and abstract forces is utterly foreign to oral societies and thus to the oldest strata of magical practice.[9] Elements of these strata have been preserved in occult practice as captured, for example, in aspects of the grimoire tradition either because of complex intellectual descent or because certain practices work even when we don't remember why or how. It is my contention that we have valuable lessons to learn from regaining the forgotten roots of occult practices.

I have offered a version of this argument extensively in my book *True to the Earth: Pagan Political Theology*, so I will only briefly present important details of it here. The logic we are contrasting with, that of Agrippa for example, is one of abstract entities and forces woven together through structures of correspondence (i.e. resemblance, sympathy, emanation, and so on). The logic I am going to offer is what I would call a logic of meaning as captured in myth, history, and personality, all of which can be captured in the idea of narrative. To put it directly and simply, the oral societies which form the oldest level of human civilization as well as the origin point of both religious and magical practices did not have the abstract concepts that provide the heart of the logic of correspondence found in Agrippa and others. In an oral society there would be no concept of the energy, or essence, of Mars for example. Mars the wandering star would have been known, and its nature would be captured in its history of appearing and behaving in given ways at given times. It might end up being connected to a divine personality, Ares for example, with his own history, myths, and narratives capturing his nature. But if you were to ask 'What is the nature of Ares?' or 'What is the nature of Mars?' you would be answered with stories, not an attempt to define the general virtue or force of this thing. To work with Ares or Mars, in an occult ritual for example, would involve finding a way to enter into the history and myth that capture their nature. We make ourselves part of Ares's story. I will discuss this approach more fully later.

---

8 I stress the term 'almost' here because some sort of emotion and desire remains, but it is likely only the experience of love for the divine perfections and the desire to be as like them as possible. In other words, a basic impetus to draw near perfection but nothing else. Dante recognized this point, over a millennium later, when he ended his *Paradiso* with the saints losing all personality and individuality as they utterly dissolve in the divine rose that is the communion of the faithful glorifying God. [Yeah, we get some notions of 'spiritual joy' not being entirely a matter of the sensitive faculties of the soul eventually, but it's a bit shonky exceptionalism honestly...].

9 For a complete development of the distinction between oral and literate world-views and its implications for religion, magic, and metaphysics see Kadmus, *True to the Earth: Pagan Political Theology* (Gods&Radicals Press, 2018).

The idea of 'general energy' or 'general virtue' not only did not exist but would have made no sense in an oral culture. The introduction of writing causes certain fundamental changes to our cultural psychology and what it is possible to say and think. We need, however, to excavate this ancient oral pagan understanding by uncovering aspects of it in texts that are either direct documentation of oral sources or that we might suspect preserve this older worldview. It is not my purpose here to fully develop, present, and argue in favor of the position I have just sketched out since I have already done so in my book. Instead, I wish to follow this insight and apply it through specific historical examples drawn from ancient and early modern sources to necromantic practice. The heart of this new presentation of the ancient understanding of necromancy is captured nicely in the idea that every act of necromancy is, at least partially, one of *katabasis*, i.e. a *going down* into the underworld. I will pursue this project by focusing on several elements of necromantic practice that are mapped in the titles of the following sections.

III. Place

Our central claim that necromancy is katabasis makes it clear that our thesis deals extensively with the issue of place. What, one might ask, is the fundamental place in which necromancy occurs? Our simple answer is, in the Underworld, but ultimately things will not be quite as simple as all that. Let us first consider several important historical depictions of necromancy in order to make clear our basic foundation, and certain challenges to it. In ancient sources, what is the place of necromancy?

Katabasis, going down into the underworld, is the single oldest subject of western poetry as it has been preserved for us. Arguably the first example of western poetry we have is that captured in the epic poem *The Descent of Inanna*. This is overtly a story of a goddess's katabasis, a passage down into the underworld involving a progressive process of purification. This isn't, strictly speaking, necromancy but we should keep it in mind as proof of the unavoidably fundamental nature of katabasis for the history of human thought. Dante's *Inferno* is, of course, a sibling of this genre as well. More useful for our purposes are Odysseus's katabasis in the *Odyssey* and Aeneas's katabasis in the *Aeneid*. These are more useful examples for us since, first, they are examples of humans venturing into the underworld and, second, these journeys are undertaken for the explicit purpose of speaking with the dead and learning from them. Only the examples of Inanna and Odysseus come directly from oral sources, with Aeneas's own journey being heavily modeled on Odysseus's. Mythologically we have, as well, the famous katabaseis of both Orpheus and Heracles, both topics to which we will return later.

Odysseus's katabasis is our privileged example then, so we must ask where it occurs. Interestingly, within the text of the poem preserved for us which was itself just one version of the story as it would have appeared within the oral epic tradition, Odysseus does not engage in a full katabasis. He doesn't, strictly speaking, fully go to the underworld and take a tour. Instead, he goes to the edge of the world, to a liminal space, and from there calls forth the spirits of the dead. In this regard, the main dangers he must face are the hungry ghosts with whom he does not wish to speak. He does not overtly deal with Cerberus, for example, or other underworldly guardians and dangers. He is not, however, in the normal world of everyday life. He travels to the very edge of Oceanus, the vast sea that encircles the world and not the sea on which normal trade and travel occurred. This edge is called 'Persephone's strand and grove', a bit of beach that is perhaps just barely within the realm of the underworld. He is, then, outside the everyday world and on the very edge of the underworld but he does not cross over. As noted, however, this is not the only version of the story that existed and we have other sources that suggest there was an alternative story of Odysseus undergoing a full exploration of the underworld. The most important example of this alternative story is likely the famous painting at Delphi, created by Polygnotus sometime in the mid 5th century B.C.E. and based on a poem that has been lost. This painting showed a full descent into the underworld by Odysseus and encounters with numerous underworldly guardians and dangers including Charon, Cerberus, and lesser-known underworldly monsters such as Eurynomos who devoured the flesh off the bones of the dead and crouched perpetually on vulture skins.[10] Odysseus, then, presents us with two answers to the question of place. Either one practices necromancy in an extra-human space near the underworld, or one fully enters the underworld.

Virgil, in the *Aeneid*, will capture both of these themes, for he has Aeneas travel to a cave mouth that is known to be a gateway into the underworld. The cave matches Odysseus's journey to the edge of Oceanus, but a full katabasis into the underworld follows. It is my suspicion that this blurring of lines is not accidental, but rather an inherent part of the necromantic practice and of the original magical perspective. The underworld and our world are interpenetrating and no great gulf or veil exists between them. Despite this, it can be useful to be in a place closer to the underworld, more fully on or over the uncertain boundary line, in order to better access the dead. A good example of this ambiguity between a liminal space in which necromancy occurs, and a space which is actually part of the underworld and thus appropriate for necromancy, is stressed in Lucan's depiction of necromancy in his *Pharsalia*. In this work, on the eve of battle, Sextus "the unworthy son of Pompey" turns to a Thessalian witch in order to hear an oracle from the dead concerning the outcome of the battle to come. The witch has them acquire one of the bodies of the recent dead and then drags the body into a deep cave where she engages in an extensive ritual. As the spirits begin to appear Lucan makes an observation which, in the Latin, allows for either an interpretation in terms of the location of the witch specifically or in terms of the nature of the place as a whole. Here is a modern translation that stresses the witch's location: "Although the Thessalian witch imposes her will on destiny, it is doubtful whether she actually sees the shades of the underworld because she has dragged them there [i.e. to her cave] or because she has descended [into the underworld] herself."[11] In other words, the witch sees the shades but it is uncertain whether she does so because she has called them to herself or because she

10 This painting no longer exists but its details were carefully captured by Pausanius in his *Description of Greece*.

11 Lucan, *Pharsalia* 6.655–657, Georg Luck trans., in *Arcana Mundi* (Johns Hopkins University Press, 1985).

has somehow entered into the underworld while her audience is present in the cave. In Lucan the line between calling the spirits up, or going down to them, is indecipherable. An older translation of the same text stresses this ambiguity as applying to the place as a whole and not just the witch herself:

> Nay, though the witch had power to call the shades
> Forth from the depths, 'twas doubtful if the cave
> Were not a part of hell.[12]

Lucan's text, then, lays out very nicely a basic idea: that the practice of necromancy was often understood to change the place (either of the practitioner or of the practice) to that of the underworld. So, we might suggest the basic principle that calling to the spirits of the underworld rulers and the dead can bring one to the underworld. We can offer one final example of this type of understanding in Seneca's *Oedipus*. In this text the priest Teiresias brings Creon to a dark grove outside of Thebes that hides a deep pool that is understood to be a liminal gate to the underworld in a way similar to caves. Teiresias does not, however, call spirits to him in this text as much as he calls the underworld itself up and to him:

> The ground trembles, the earth quakes. 'They have heard me!' cries the seer. 'The spells that I have poured out are working! The dark chaos is breaking open'… The whole forest sinks into the ground. The whole grove quivers in horror. The earth gives way and groans deep inside… Suddenly the earth splits and opens up an enormous chasm. I saw with my own eyes the stagnant pools among the shades; with my own eyes I saw the bloodless gods and the night that is truly night.[13]

This example is striking because the witness, Creon, sees the forest change and the underworld rise up around him. He sees the landscape of the underworld, "the night that is truly night", and the bloodless gods. It is clear that the place, while selected because it is already a nice gateway to the underworld, quite literally becomes the underworld in a successful ritual.

We can add to the first principle *that successfully calling to the dead can bring one to the underworld* another one if we consider other common locations for necromantic practice. We have mentioned caves and deep pools, which bring one geographically closer to the underworld, an understanding reflected in the common practice of burying curse tablets addressed to the dead or the underworld gods at such locations, but we should also consider battlefields and burial places. The use of places where people have died violently is well attested in both modern grimoires and the Greek Magical Papyri. One spell from the papyri uses those who have died a violent death in order to work a love

---

12 Lucan, *Pharsalia* 6.655–657, Ridley trans. (Longmans, Green, and Co., 1905).

13 Seneca, *Oedipus* vv. 530–626, Georg Luck trans., in *Arcana Mundi* (Johns Hopkins University Press, 1985).

spell and counsels us to, "...go to where heroes and gladiators and those who have died a violent death were slain."[14] Another excellent example features the priest Teiresias once more, who performs a grand necromantic ritual outside the walls of Thebes in an area called the Martian plain. It was here that Cadmus sowed dragon's teeth which caused warriors to burst from the earth and kill each other:

> Outside, of vast extent, stretches the Martian plain, the field that bore its harvest to Cadmus... the accursed earth breathes mighty tumults at midday and in the lonely night's dim shadows, when the black sons of earth arise to phantom combat... well suited is the ground to Stygian rites, and the soil, rich with living gore, delighted [Teiresias].[15]

We could multiply examples here extensively, but it is clear that there is a powerful tradition that remains preserved in several grimoires, of using ground that has seen battle or violent death as an appropriate location for necromantic ritual. A related common location, also attested to in studies of curse-tablets, is a place of burials. Aeschylus, for example, in *The Persians*, shows a summoning of the spirit of the dead king Darius at the location of his own grave. Grimoires and practitioner handbooks, similarly, often counsel the performance of magic in graveyards and cemeteries, to say nothing of other folk-magical and African diasporic traditions.

The insight for us is not that battlefields and graveyards are good locations to work necromancy, this fact has been consistent throughout history, but rather what it tells us when understood in light of the overarching idea that every necromancy is a katabasis. Our common assumption is that the dead are likely to be closer or still present at the site of their death or burial, perhaps embellishing this idea with something like a sympathetic connection between the ground on which one dies or the body one inhabited to one's spirit in death. However, the idea of katabasis and particularly the first principle that working necromancy changes your place to that of the underworld allows for us to propose a second principle, namely *that the presence of death or the dead makes a place part of the underworld.* This works for the presence of death on the battlefield and the presence of the bodies of the dead in a graveyard, but also overlaps our first principle whereby the presence of the dead in a successful necromantic rite necessarily makes one's surroundings part of the underworld even if only temporarily. We might suggest, then, that both places where death frequently occurs or occurred in great numbers as well as places that house the remains of the dead are always suburbs on the outskirts of the underworld. If this sounds strange, let me stress once more that for most ancient oral worldviews the underworld is part of this world, just as much as the tops of mountains or the sea. There is no metaphysical transcendence or boundary.

14 Hans Dieter Betz, *The Greek Magical Papyri in Translation* (University of Chicago Press, 1992) IV.1394–1396.

15 Statius, *Thebaid*, J.H. Mozley trans. (Harvard University Press, 1928) Book 4, lines 438–444.

Although overt necromantic rituals from the modern period preserved in grimoires and similar texts tend to insist on the use of external spaces such as battlefields and graveyards, in contrast to much other grimoire practice, nonetheless it is also possible to find examples that allow for one to work within a consecrated space not previously connected to the underworld in the various ways I have pointed out. This is also the case in the ancient world, where necromantic procedures could occur in appropriate temple spaces. Indeed, working within one's own temple is likely to be the more common procedure for most contemporary practitioners. One thing that is worth noting is that in the ancient world necromancy performed in temple spaces was usually performed by means of dream incubation. The ancient world saw specific temple spaces dedicated as oracles of the dead in which one would perform a sacrifice and then sleep within the space in order to receive messages in one's sleep. This method fits into our previous principles because sleep plays a similar, even stronger, role to that of a cave, graveyard, etc. because the ancients understood sleep to be a process of crossing over into the underworld. Virgil, for example, notes that there are two gates to the underworld through which both people and dreams can pass. This connection of dreams with the dead is well attested in modern and contemporary practice as well. If one does not intend to engage in dream incubation, however, then it should be noted that necromantic practice in a personal ritual space does suffer from its disconnection from the second principle (*the presence of death or the dead makes a place part of the underworld*) and must rely entirely on the first (*successfully calling to the dead brings one to the underworld*) unless we have done something to address this limitation.[16] Without the assistance of the second principle, necromantic practice is likely to require more assistance from underworld gods, spiritual intermediaries, and so on, but the overall point remains the following: in performing necromancy in a personal space, even one which uses a traditional circle and other similar ritual mechanics generally assumed to concern protection, one is making one's temple part of the underworld and entering into the underworld itself. Successful necromancy, I would assert, cannot be done in a manner that does not open oneself up to the hazards of katabasis, and much of the practices and tools we are now going to move on to discuss are overtly aimed at negotiating these dangers. Far from being a powerful boundary of protection, your circle is more likely to be the space you have (purposefully or not) marked out for the rulers of the underworld to annex—it is the place of your katabasis and not a protection from it.

---

16 Some very interesting and useful ways to address this limitation are presented in Chapter XVII of Scot's *Discovery of Witchcraft* entitled 'An Experiment of the Dead', to which we shall return later.

IV. THE LIONSKIN BELT

It will be possible to be much more precise in the investigations to follow. Thus far our reflections on place have been rather general, but now we can focus on particular examples of ritual methodology and tools in order to fully present the logic of narrative I am proposing. Let us start by focusing on an item I have already discussed, the lionskin belt from the *Arte Goetia* section of the *Lemegeton*. We have already offered a Platonic, or if you like an 'Agrippan', understanding of this belt's properties and powers in terms of its correspondence with various abstract planetary virtues. A very different understanding of such a garment is suggested by Lucian's *Necyomantia*. In this text the main character, Menippus, describes to his friend Philonides a journey he took to the underworld through the assistance of a Chaldean necromancer named Mithrobarzanes. Before venturing into the underworld the necromancer gives Menippus various tools and clothing and informs him to only answer to certain names:

> *Me.* He... gave me the cap, lion's skin, and lyre which you see, telling me if I were asked my name not to say Menippus, but Heracles, Odysseus, or Orpheus.
> *Phi.* What was that for? I see no reason either for the get-up or for the choice of names.
> *Me.* Oh, obvious enough; there is no mystery in that. He thought that as these three had gone down alive to Hades before us, I might easily elude Aeacus's guard by borrowing their appearance, and be passed as an habitue; there is good warrant in the theatre for the efficiency of disguise.[17]

A key part of the operation, then, is a type of invisibility.[18] Specifically, Menippus must pass through the underworld under the guise of Heracles, Odysseus, and Orpheus. The lion skin and lyre correspond to Heracles and Orpheus respectively, and a specific type of cap was traditionally thought to be worn by Odysseus. In the course of the journey the lyre is used to quiet Cerberus and the lion skin convinces Charon the boatman that Menippus is actually Heracles: "Nevertheless, when good Charon saw the lion's skin, taking me for Heracles, he made room, was delighted to give me a passage, and showed us our direction when we got off."[19] The lionskin belt is a potential survival of this ancient practice of garbing oneself in the traditional clothing of others who have ventured to the underworld successfully. Such garb takes its power and meaning from the narrative it is part of, from its place in the history and myth of katabasis. We wear lion skin so that we may be part of the story of Heracles. We find in other grimoires detailed notes about robes, priestly vestures, fake crowns and the like, and I would hazard to suggest that the logic behind many of the specific guidelines for clothing derive from the

---

17 Lucian, *Necyomantia* 8, in *The Works of Lucian of Samosata* (The Clarendon Press, 1905).

18 Both Jake Stratton-Kent and Peter Grey have discussed invisibility work and spirits that teach invisibility in the grimoires as vital parts of underworld journeys. Their discussions form an important inspiration for much of this investigation and a vital addition to it.

19 Lucian, *Necyomantia* 8.

same basis, they are part of our entrance into a given history and mythology—whether that of Heracles or King Solomon or someone else will depend on the text and the details. But the logic here is not that of correspondence but rather of narrative.

This idea is not entirely foreign to contemporary practitioners and theorists but the attempts at rationalization that are applied to it tend, I believe, to miss the point. It is possible to find some contemporaries offering the explanation that, yes, in wearing a robe and fake crown and so on we are engaged in theater meant to convince the spirits that we are King Solomon himself or some other important figure with whom the spirits have agreements and previous encounters. This works, it is either suggested or implied, because the spirits are not good at telling one human from another and have a different sense of time.[20] This interpretation, I would suggest, is too dependent upon early modern materialist philosophies and misses the deeper insights of ancient oral cultures. Specifically, early modern philosophy and the ideas that have descended from it tend to prioritize an atomistic view of identity and the self with an empiricist epistemology focused on the physical senses as the source of all knowledge. Specifically the assumption is that we, and the spirits, are discrete isolated identities and we primarily relate to each other via sensory interaction.

Despite these contemporary suggestions concerning tricking the spirits, or Lucian's similar assumptions, the deeper meaning of these seeming theatrics was likely to be rather different in the ancient world because the concept of selfhood and identity was dramatically different. The fundamental structure of oral composition, and the worldview and metaphysics it gives rise to, is that of echoing. In order to add something new to an epic poem it must be built out of echoed themes, images, or linguistic structures of previous elements. The new is integrated into an epic poem through a process of weaving it out of, and into, what has already been presented. The view of identity in an oral culture is similar. We, and the spirits and gods, are echoes and interpenetrating threads of each other. These echoes run especially into the past, into history, myth, and narrative in general. For example, the underworld journeys of Orpheus or Heracles or Odysseus are themselves echoes of the constant and easy journey of Hermes into the underworld. To provide a concrete example, Orpheus's use of the lyre to tame both Cerberus and even the underworld gods Hades and Persephone echoes Hermes's own use of the lyre to tame Apollo.[21] Later journeys, in turn, are echoes of the earlier ones. Does this mean that the echo gets mistaken for the original, that Cerberus thinks Orpheus is Hermes for example? Certainly not. It is rather that the identities of Hermes and Orpheus both are part of, and dependent upon, the larger reality of the history and story they are a part of. When we don the lion skin and venture a katabasis we are part of Heracles's story, and the repeated echoes of that story persist and rule to some extent our interactions and experiences. The same goes for when we identify ourselves with Solomon, Cyprian, or Faust by, for example, using one of the many books that are named for them. We do not trick spirits into believing we are these individuals because

---

20 Stephen Skinner has suggested on the podcast *Glitch Bottle* that the spirits have poor eyesight but a great sense of smell, for example.

21 For one rendition of the story of Hermes and Apollo see the Homeric *Hymn to Hermes*.

the spirits have an odd sense of time or bad eyesight. Rather, we are indeed them, echoes and ongoing threads of their myth and story, and the spirits themselves are part of the echoes and ripples of those myths and stories as well. The spirits are not fooled, rather they recognize better than we do the reality of the situation, that we are the surviving threads of an ongoing narrative in which we play but a part. I am the stories in which I play a part, as are the spirits.

Ultimately, despite modern epistemic pretensions to the contrary, neither spirits nor ourselves respond to sensation at all. Rather we both navigate a world of meaning. It is rare, if ever, that I simply have an experience of sense data. I do not hear some undefined sound, I hear a car horn or a voice. We do not just smell a scent, we smell the scent *of* something, even something we can not yet identify but which resembles something that is meaningful for us. The meanings that so-called sensations carry, and are experienced in terms of, are historical and narrative meanings. We experience things in terms of the stories we have lived and are living, and fit new experiences into those complex weaves of meanings. Our identity, similarly, is part of this weave and we experience each other, and are experienced in turn, as part of living continuing stories. With these considerations in mind, then, we can suggest a third principle. Specifically, *when we engage in necromancy we step into the ongoing story of humanity's great katabasis, identifying ourselves with those who have descended and returned before us and being recognized as such by the spirits.*

V. On the Blood of Plants and Stones

We are no doubt well familiar with the various collections of plants and stones that form a vital aspect of grimoire work. There are incense blends, herbs used in asperging ritual space, recipes for inks, special woods for wand construction, particular metals and stones for pentacles, and so on. There are extensive investigations possible here, for example the possibility that the woods used for wand construction are generally ones that are hollow inside, similar to those used in ancient technologies as human-powered bellows for smelting bronze, but for now we will focus primarily upon bloodstone in the grimoire tradition and its unlikely connection to ancient plant magic generally.

The use of bloodstone shows up several times in the grimoire tradition, most particularly in a version of the *Grimoirum Verum* and in the *Grand Grimoire*. In the *Grand Grimoire* a bloodstone is recommended as the tool to be used in tracing the triangle of practice. The older and longer Italian version of the *Grimoirum Verum*, the *Clavicula Salomonis de Secretis*, suggests using bloodstone to craft the 'First Character' of the work. There we are given something of the reasoning involved in this recommendation: "It is better still, if you wish, to have it fashioned from green jasper or heliotrope (bloodstone), for those (stones) indeed have the greatest sympathy with <eastern> spirits, of the solar order, which are wiser and better than the others."[22] In other versions of *Verum* we are advised to use emerald or ruby for a similar reason, because they have "…great sympathy

---

22 Joseph Peterson, *Secrets of Solomon* (Twilight Grotto Press, 2018), p. 4.

with the spirits, especially those of the Sun...".[23] I am going to focus exclusively on bloodstone, but we can ask of both these passages whether the obvious interpretation is that which might be provided by Agrippa. Aren't we given overt planetary and directional correspondences here? Both texts even use the term 'sympathy'. If we deprive ourselves of the Aristotelian or Platonic theory how are we to understand the power and meaning of various stones and plants and their relationship to such entities as the Sun?

The answer will be that we understand stones and plants in terms of their history, which often means in terms of the myths they find themselves within. Let us start with bloodstone and build up from there. Bloodstone, you are no doubt aware, is green jasper with drops of red, and has overtly been associated with the Sun since ancient times—thus its alternative name of 'heliotrope' or 'sun-turner'. Bloodstone gets its name from the red drops which appear to be drops of blood, and this in turn represents the most important aspect of its mythology. For the ancient Greeks, the drops of blood were commonly considered to originate from Ouranos when he was castrated by Kronos, his son. Alternatively, sometimes the blood was thought to have been spilled by the Titans during the war in which Zeus overthrew Kronos. The key, either way, is that the bloodstone is thought to carry the divine potency of the gods or ancient giants from which it gained its nature. During the Christian era this same myth was preserved, but the blood became identified with that of Christ.

This connection between bloodstone and the blood of the primordial gods, whether Titans or older, connects it to important mythology surrounding herbs. Where do magical plants get their power if not through planetary correspondence, we have asked. Well, for the ancients, they frequently got their power by growing from the blood of ancient gods. The most famous such example is the mysterious plant *moly*, meaning strong or mighty, which Hermes gives to Odysseus to protect him from the magics of Circe. Ptolemy Hephaestion, in the fragments of his *New History* which survive, identifies the source of this plant's power, and that of the many magical herbs on Circe's island, as the fact that they grew from the blood of slain giants who fought in the war with Kronos. The ash tree had a similar legend about it, identifying it as having grown from the blood of Ouranos. Aconite, on the other hand, was thought to derive its power from having grown from the spittle of Cerberos himself. We could multiply such examples, but the point is that bloodstone and powerful herbs alike derive their power from being born from the body or blood of divinities. We should note, in passing, that the use of a plant like the mysterious *moly* is frequently seen as essential for underworld journeys, whether willing or unwilling. Aeneas, for example, must find a hidden golden herb sacred to Juno of the underworld in order to gain entry,[24] and Persephone's kidnapping by Hades relied upon her first being seduced by the Crocus flower. In using the bloodstone, then, we should see the resemblance to these herbs which served to open the way to the underworld. This glance at the origin of the power of specific stones and plants makes clear a sense of theft involved in this magic. Magic, in the human realm, has largely come about by stealing the power of the gods or taking advantage of power they

23 Jake Stratton-Kent, *The True Grimoire* (Scarlet Imprint, 2010), p. 51.

24 Virgil, *The Aeneid*, Fitzgerald trans. (Vintage Classic Edition, 1990) Book VI, 200–210.

have lost through violence and conflict amongst themselves. This allows for a fourth principle, *necromancy is possible, powered by magical stones and plants, because of the conflicts and inconsistencies in the universe out of which these plants and stones of power have arisen.*

VI. Offices and Agencies

As I mentioned earlier, and should be clear now, my discussion of necromancy has used the term rather broadly. Indeed I have focused on grimoires generally, and what we might identify as goetic ones particularly, when considering early modern and contemporary practice, while my focus on ancient sources has been much more closely focused on what might be considered necromancy proper. However, part of what our equation of necromancy with katabasis directs us to is the realization that necromancy includes interacting with all those entities one would have to face in the underworld. This includes underworld guardians such as Cerberus and Charon, underworld rulers and gods such as Hades and Persephone, but also a host of 'monstrous' entities, the catalogue of which differs from culture to culture. For the Greeks, many of the Titans who resisted Zeus's revolution were imprisoned in the underworld. For the Celts, the land of the Fey and that of the dead were either identified or close neighbors, along with the implication that the old gods had retreated to this underworld as well. There are a host of spirits one must consider in this regard, not the least of which is Cerberus himself who appears in the spirit list of Weyer, the *Livre des Esperitz*, and the *Grand Grimoire*. In Weyer and the *Grand Grimoire* he is identified with Naberus and connected to Nebiros who himself appears in the *Grimorium Verum* and the *Arte Goetia* of the *Lemegeton*.[25] Keeping in mind the importance of the children of Helios in the ancient occult world, specifically Circe, Aeetes, and Aeetes's daughter Medea, it is also worth noting that one of the goetic kings of the four directions—Oriens—was also a title for Helios himself when identified as the rising Sun. Elsewhere we find goetic ritual and spirits mixed in with Faery kings and queens, as in the *Book of Oberon*. My suggestion is that all of these diverse spirits are connected in being located in the underworld, and thus working with all or any of them is going to involve the necromantic katabasis I have been considering here.

This rich mixing of spirit types, bound together through their association with the underworld, is made particularly clear in Chapter XVII of Scot's *Discovery of Witchcraft*.[26] This chapter is also a useful example for us because of the connection it builds between graveyard necromantic work and private temple work. Earlier I had mentioned the need to find some way to connect our private temple space to locations that might already be considered annexes of the underworld, such as graveyards, in order to achieve katabasis, and Scot's ritual does just this. Briefly, it involves going to the place where a given person is buried, summoning forth their spirit into a crystal and commanding them to go forth and contact 'the fairy Sibylia' and bring her to the

---

25 Jake Stratton-Kent, *Pandemonium* (Hadean Press, 2016), pp. 108–109.

26 This particular chapter has been discussed extensively by Al Cummins in the Endnotes blog section of his site www.alexandercummins.com, a discussion that I have found very useful and important.

magician. Why should the dead be efficacious in contacting a fairy queen if not because they occupy the same space, the underworld? Once contact with the dead is achieved, one retires to a private temple space and summons forth the fairy. Here the temple is prepared for underworld katabasis by an earlier katabasis whereby one has already built a connection with the dead, bringing them back, as it were, with you to your temple and thus joining temple space, grave, and underworld.

Another important and striking part about this ritual is the name of the fairy, a name that also shows up in the *Book of Oberon* and other texts. Sibylia is clearly derived from Sybil, the title of the prophetess/priestess who was thought to have access to the underworld in ancient Italy. Indeed, it is the Sibyl who guides Aeneas on his own katabasis. In using the dead to contact the Sibyl, Scot's ritual offers us something of Aeneas's katabasis in reverse. While the overall purpose of the ritual is unstated — in other words why one might wish to speak with Sibylia and what one might do with her once an audience was gained—it is likely she was to act as an intermediary or guide for future workings—all of which would likely be considered necromantic by the standards I have set up here. This need for an intermediary should come as no surprise to us, for it shows up in the traditions of both necromancy and katabasis many times. Circe clearly plays the role of Odysseus's intermediary, teaching him about the need for the katabasis as well as the location and ritual involved. Once the ceremony is underway Odysseus gains a spirit intermediary in the form of the priest and prophet Teiresias who we have met repeatedly in this investigation. A successful necromancer in life, he is now a valuable guide to necromancy and the underworld in death. In the *Tuba Veneris*, or *Trumpet of Venus*, a goetic grimoire attributed to John Dee, we find the patroness and protector of the work identified as the Black Venus—a reference, I would argue, not to the planet as much as to the underworld aspect of the goddess Venus.

In general, then, the goetic grimoire tradition is filled with the *dramatis personae* of traditional katabasis. I hope that I have shown that it is entirely possible to approach goetic work in terms of a necromantic process of katabasis and, further, that we can understand the elements of this type of work in terms of the personal histories of the entities involved without need to appeal to abstract energies, systems of correspondence, and Platonic multiple worlds. Rather, in taking part in this work we enter into ongoing narratives and take our place within them as echoes of those who have gone before us. We continue these stories and are, to a large part, swept up in narratives already flowing along their pre-existing paths. A final principle then might be: *to practice necromancy is to enter into living myth and, as such, to take part in the ongoing life of those who have died.*

BIBLIOGRAPHY

Agrippa, Cornelius, *Three Books of Occult Philosophy* (Lewellyn, 1998)

Betz, Hans Dieter, *The Greek Magical Papyri in Translation* (University of Chicago Press, 1992)

Lucian, *Necyomantia* 8, in *The Works of Lucian of Samosata* (The Clarendon Press, 1905)

Lucan, *Pharsalia* 6.655–657, Georg Luck trans., in *Arcana Mundi* (Johns Hopkins University Press, 1985)

Lucan, *Pharsalia* 6.655–657, Ridley trans., (Longmans, Green, and Co., 1905)

Ogden, Daniel, *Greek and Roman Necromancy* (Princeton University Press, 2001)

Peterson, Joseph, *Secrets of Solomon* (Twilight Grotto Press, 2018)

Seneca, *Oedipus* vv. 530–626, Georg Luck trans., *Arcana Mundi* (Johns Hopkins University Press, 1985).

Statius, *Thebaid*, J.H. Mozley trans. (Harvard University Press, 1928)

Stratton-Kent, Jake, *Pandemonium* (Hadean Press, 2016)

Stratton-Kent, Jake, *The True Grimoire* (Scarlet Imprint, 2010)

Virgil, *The Aeneid*, Fitzgerald trans. (Vintage Classic Edition, 1990)

CORVID CODEX
CROWS, MAGPIES AND RAVENS IN THE GRIMOIRES AND BRITISH AND IRISH FOLKLORE

DAVID RANKINE

Plumage of the Forgotten Dead

I listen to the magpies talking
As I wander around the graveyard
Their calls pulling me to untended graves
'Over here' they chatter, perched on the stone
So I approach reverently
Here stranger, here is alcohol and tobacco
Here are two silver coins should you need them
Your name is not forgotten
I speak it onto the winds to take it around the world
Saluting the magpies again for their guidance.[1]

THE CORVID FAMILY has long been known as one of the most, if not the most, intelligent of the bird families (their ability to use tools and recognize faces are good examples of this). Combining this intelligence with their striking appearance, and the association between flight and spirits, makes the connection between corvids and the grimoires eminently unsurprising. The corvids tend to be carrion eaters, and in the past were often seen at battlefields, further adding to their connection with the spirit world.

I have always had an affection and affinity for the corvids, and since the 1980s one of the deities I have worked with the most is the Irish Battle Goddess, the Morrigan, who is particularly associated with the crow and raven. Indeed, my fifth book, *The Guises of the Morrigan* (Avalonia, 2005), was written as a devotional act to Her. Literature about the Morrigan actually provides us with a direct equation of crows and demons from the seventeenth century. In Trinity H.3.18 we read: "Gudomain, i.e. hooded crows or women from the sid; lying wolves, that is, the false demons, the morrigna ... they are not demons of hell but demons of the air."[2]

The group names for corvids reflect how they have often been viewed through a malefic lens. The most common names are a conspiracy or unkindness of ravens, a murder of crows, and a mischief or parliament of magpies.

---

1 Written in a graveyard after making offerings, 27.02.22.

2 The Morrigan assumed both wolf and crow/raven forms. The plural form of Morrigan is Morrigna, and she had a triple form that she sometimes appeared in.

When tracing the corvid spirits through the grimoires, they are presented in dated order of the first known manuscript copy. All of the grimoires containing corvid-form spirits are in the *Goetia* stream, i.e. those which fed in to the *Goetia*, thus BML MS Plut. 89 sup. 38 (1494), *Pseudomonarchia Daemonum* (1563), *Book of the Offices of Spirits* (1583), and *Goetia* (1641). It is interesting to observe that although *Livre des Esperitz* (mid C16) contains a number of spirits which subsequently appear in the *Goetia*, none of the spirit descriptions mention corvids.

Who is stronger than hope? Death.
Who is stronger than the will? Death.
Stronger than love? Death.
Stronger than life? Death.
But who is stronger than death?
Me, evidently.
Pass, Crow. [3]

---

3 From *Examination at the Womb-Door* in *Crow*, Ted Hughes, 1970.

CORVIDS IN THE MEDICI LIBRARY

The spirit catalogue in BML MS Plut. 89 sup. 38 (reproduced in *Necromancy in the Medici Library*) is one of the precursors of the *Goetia*, though not all the spirits found therein are present in the latter work. There are three crow forms, being Furfur, Malapas (Malphas), and Yudifliges, and two raven forms, Gorson (Gusoin), and Andras. Of these all subsequently appear in the *Goetia* apart from Yudifliges.

It is interesting to see that Furfur is described as appearing in the likeness of a crow, but later in the *Goetia* (spirit 34) his appearance is as "a great and mighty earl appearing in the form of a hart with a fiery tail". The fiery tail is retained but the animal form changes, perhaps indicating the constancy of the fiery tail as part of his true form. This also raises the question of why so many spirits should choose to appear in corvid form, perhaps indicating a sympathy worthy of further exploration. Gorson, later Gusoin (spirit 11) in the *Goetia*, also changes form between these grimoires. In the *Goetia* he is described as having the form of a Xenophilus.

> *Gorsor*, or *Gorson*, a strong duke, appears in the likeness of a man, his head like that of a night raven. He marvelously grants one the Pythian art. He causes people to gather before the exorcist as though he himself were the provisioner of punishments; they are foreigners, since all murderers are dragged off to the furthest places to be tortured. Of the order of Virtues he was the worst, and he has twelve legions under him.

> *Andras*, or *Vandras*, a great marquis, appears in an angelic form, his head like that of a great night raven: riding upon a great and mighty wolf, carrying a great and very sharp sword; from him arise quarrels and discords, and he knows well how to sow these, such as between two brothers, or between a leader and follower. And he has thirty legions under him.

> *Furfur*, a great count, appears in the likeness of a crow, its tail like fire; he is deceitful in all things unless sent into an angled figure, but once he is there he assumes an angelic form, speaking in a harsh voice; and he is a commander of arms among men, and delivers women. He renders people invisible. He teaches astronomy among all the mechanical arts. He gives understanding of how lightning, flashes, and thunder are produced in those places where they are supposed to be made. He knows best how to answer concerning secret matters, and has twenty-five legions under him.

> *Alphas*, or *Malapas*, a great president, appears in the likeness of a crow, but assuming a human form he speaks with a harsh voice. He marvelously builds houses and towers, and quickly grants a meeting with the greatest artificers; likewise he causes the exorcist to destroy houses, and to shatter towers. He gives very good familiars for destruction. He eagerly receives sacrifices and burnt offerings, and he tricks people into harming themselves. He has twenty legions under him.

Yudifliges, a strong duke, appear in the likeness of a crow; and appearing in a human form when, proceeding before his master preceptor, he is order to, he causes all who see him to hear a symphony of trumpets. And he also carries every kind of instrument he teaches one to play; he is a very good servant. He has nineteen legions under his dominion.

CORVIDS IN THE FALSE MONARCHY

Johann Weyer's 1563 work *Pseudomonarchia Daemonum* is now well established as one of the precursors to the *Goetia*, sharing most of its spirits (sixty eight in common). Of the sixty-nine described spirits, as with the *Goetia* six are seen to have a corvid form. It is the same split of three each of raven and crow. With some there is a question as to whether crow or raven was meant depending on translation.

Amon, or *Aamon*, is a great and mighty marquis, and cometh abroad in the likeness of a wolf, having a serpent tail, spitting out and breathing flames of fire; when he putteth on the shape of a man, he sheweth out dogs teeth, and a great head like to a mighty raven; he is the strongest prince of all other, and understandeth of all things past and to come, he procureth favour, and reconcileth both friends and foes, and ruleth forty legions of devils.

Andras is a great marquis, and is seen in an angels shape with a head like a black night raven, riding upon a black and a very strong wolf, flourishing with a sharp sword in his hand, he can kill the master, the servant, and all assistants, he is author of discords, and ruleth thirty legions.

Stolas is a great prince, appearing in the form of a night raven, before the exorcist, he taketh the image and shape of a man, and teacheth astronomy, absolutely understanding the virtues of herbs and precious stones; there are under him twenty-six legions.

Naberius, alias Cerberus, is a valiant marquis, shewing himself in the form of a crow, when he speaketh with a hoarse voice: he maketh a man amiable and cunning in all arts, and especially in rhetoric, he procureth the loss of prelacies and dignities: nineteen legions hear and obey him.

Malphas is a great president, he is seen like a crow, but being clothed with human image, speaketh with a hoarse voice, be buildeth houses and high towers wonderfully, and quickly bringeth artificers together, he throweth down also the enemies edifications, he helpeth to good familiars, he receiveth sacrifices willingly, but he deceiveth all the sacrificers, there obey him forty legions.

Raum, or *Raim* is a great earl, he is seen as a crow, but when he putteth on humane shape, at the commandment of the exorcist, he stealeth wonderfully out of the kings house, and carrieth it whether he is assigned, he destroyeth cities, and hath great despite unto dignities, he knoweth things present, past, and to come, and reconcileth friends and foes, he was of the order of thrones, and governeth thirty legions.

CORVIDS IN THE BOOK OF OFFICES

Although the first currently known copy of the *Book of the Offices of Spirits* is found in Folger Vb.26 (*Book of Oberon*) dating 1583-86, it is likely that it is at least several decades older, possibly predating works like *Pseudomonarchia Daemonum*. One of the spirits, Hooab, is described as a black bird, which although not specifically a corvid, is included here for completion, as it could be a corvid. There are five raven forms, Kayne, Mallapas (Malphas),[4] Bason (one of the three heads), Mistalas and Zayme. Although never given as a named spirit form, magpie is described in the text as being one of the shapes familiar to the spirits of Mercury.

> *Kayne*, a duke; and appeareth like a raven, and after to take the form of a man, and a counselor to steal, and doth carry treasures from kings' houses, and will leave it there as the master will, and he giveth favour both of friends and enemies, and hath under him twenty legions.

> The sixth is called *Mallapas*; he maketh castles and towers. He can subvert and overthrow all manner of buildings and edifices. He appeareth in likeness of a raven, nevertheless he may appear by constraint like a man. His speech is hoarse.

> The second is called *Bason*; he maketh one invisible and wise, and will answer to all questions. He appeareth with three heads, one like a dog, one like a man, and one like a raven. He rideth upon a wild bear, and beareth upon his fist a goshawk, and out of his mouth proceedeth a flame of fire, and he speaks hoarsely.

> The fifth is called *Mistalas*; he, receiving man's shape. He hath power to teach and instruct one in witchcraft and necromancy, and knoweth the virtues of herbs, stones, and trees, and appeareth like a night raven.

> The twelfth is called *Zayme*; he can bring money from any place he will, or is assigned unto him, and to carry the same to any appointed place. He can in a moment show the building or situation of any plot, city, or castle, and can procure dignity and honour, and cometh like a raven.

---

4 Mallapas, later Malphas, switches from raven here to crow later in the *Goetia*.

Hooab, a prince, a great governor; he appeareth like a black bird, yet when he taketh the shape of a man, then he is a leader of women, and he maketh them to burn in the love of men, and if he be commanded, he maketh them to be turned into another shape, while that the men and they may come together, and he hath under him twenty-six legions.

CORVIDS IN THE GOETIA

There are six spirits in the spirit catalogue[5] of the *Goetia* who have corvid forms, three crow and three raven. That six of the seventy-two spirits should have corvid forms is a significant number, suggesting the connection between these birds and spirits was clearly established. The raven forms are of Amon, Stolas and Andras; and the crows are Naberius, Malphas and Raum. The spirit descriptions follow, note the similarity to earlier descriptions showing a great deal of consistency:

The Seventh Spirit is *Amon* he is a Marquis great in power and most strong, he at first appeareth like a wolf with a serpents tail vomiting out of his mouth flames of fire, sometimes appears like a Raven with Dogs teeth in his head; He telleth all things past present and to come, and procureth love; And reconcileth Controversies between friends & foes and governeth forty Legions of spirits, his Seal is to be worn &c.

The six and thirtieth spirit is *Stolus* [Stolas] he is a great and powerful Prince appearing in the shape of a mighty raven at first before the Exorcist, but after he taketh the Image of a man &c. He teacheth the art of Astronomy, and the virtue of herbs and precious stones, he governeth 26 Legions of spirits his Seal is this.

The sixty third Spirit is *Andras* he is a great Marquis appearing in the form of an Angel with a head like a black night Raven riding upon a strong black wolf, with a sharp bright sword flourishing in his hands, his office is to sow discords, if the Exorcist have not a care he will kill him and his followers, he governeth 30 Legions of spirits, and this is his Seal which is worn as a Lamen.

The twenty fourth Spirit is *Naberius* he is a most valiant Marquis and appeareth in the form of a black Crow fluttering about the circle, and when he speaks it is with a hoarse voice, he maketh men cunning in all arts and sciences but especially the art of Rhetoric he restoreth lost dignities and honours, and governeth nineteen Legions. His Seal is this to be worn.

---

5 The term spirit catalogue refers to a spirit list where descriptions of the spirits are included, distinguishing it from a list of names.

The 39th Spirit is *Malphas*[6] he appeareth in form at first like a Crow but after he will put on human shape at the request of the Exorcist and speaks with a hoarse voice, he is a mighty President & powerful he can build houses & high Towers, and he can bring quickly artificers together from all places of the world. He can destroy the Enemies desires or thoughts and what they have done, he gives good familiars and if you make any sacrifices to him he will receive it kindly and willingly but he will deceive him that doth it. He governeth 40 Legions of Spirits, his Seal is this.

The fortieth Spirit is *Raum* he is a great Earl and appeareth at first in the form of a Crow, but after at the command of the Exorcist he putteth on human shape, his office is to steal treasure out of King's houses and to Carry it where he is commanded and to destroy Cities and the dignities of men, and to tell all things past present and to come and to tell what is and what will be, and to cause love to be between friends and foes, he was of the order of Thrones, and he governeth thirty Legions of Spirits. His Seal is this which wear.

In 2002, following a working with Malphas, I returned home one day to find a baby crow on the doorstep of my home in Chiswick, London. It had clearly fallen out of the nest, and appeared to have something stuck in its throat – so literally a crow with a hoarse voice! My partner of the time and I reared the crow, teaching it to fly, and when it was ready we released it. It nested in our window box for a week, and then rejoined its family which lived in a tree in the street. One of my fondest memories of that time was the crow following me down the street, and when I was standing on the platform of the local underground station (which was above ground), coming and landing on my shoulder, regularly freaking out the other people on the platform. I like to think that looking after the crow and ensuring its survival was part of the exchange between Malphas and me, he having fulfilled the request made of him in full measure.

---

6 There is some similarity between both the name and the description of the previous spirit Halphas. It is possible that in some earlier recension these two spirits were one and the same.

Spirit (Corvid Form)	Necromancy in the Medici Library	Pseudomo-narchia Dae-monum	Book of Offices of Spirits	Goetia
Amon		✓		✓
Andras	✓	✓		✓
Bason			✓	
Furfur	✓			
Gorson / Gusoin	✓			
Kayne			✓	
Malapas / Malphas / Mallapas	✓	✓	✓	✓
Mistalas			✓	
Naberius / Cerberus		✓		✓
Raum / Raim		✓		
Stolas / Stolus		✓		✓
Yudifliges	✓			
Zayme			✓	

CORVID BLOOD, BRAINS AND BODY PARTS

With all the corvid spirit forms, it is unsurprising to find that corvid parts are used as materia magica in a number of grimoires. The range of body parts and their attributions is significant.

Crow blood is used in dream oracle inks in the PGM (*VII:222-249, VIII:64-110*), and in a charm for games (*A Collection of Magical Secrets*). With its Mercurial associations, it is unsurprising that magpie blood is used as an ingredient in Mercurial incenses (*Key of Solomon, Three Books of Occult Philosophy, Grimoire of Arthur Gauntlet, The Magus, Sworn and Secret Grimoire*). Raven blood is heavily used in the *Picatrix*,[7] essentially malefically, being used in the Bead of Al-Istamatis; in incense for spreading hostility and separation; in a talisman to remove desire; and in a potion to cause fatal sickness. Raven blood is one of the bloods used in a charm to have conference with familiar spirits or see spirits of the

---

7 Interestingly, the *Picatrix* contains as much animal body part use as pretty much all the other grimoires put together.

air found in the *Book of Oberon* and the *Grimoire of Arthur Gauntlet* (as is raven fat and raven feathers). Raven blood is also used as an ink in the *Book of the Mightiest Spirits*, for writing the spirit sigil on black virgin paper. The least surprising use of raven blood is in the *Petit Albert*, in a charm to prevent birds eating crops.

Continuing the negative association, raven gizzard and gallbladder are both used in a talisman to set a king against somebody in the *Picatrix*. In this work the head of a raven is used in a charm to cause hallucinations and delusions. The raven's tongue is used in a charm to tongue-tie a malicious person, and the head is used as a sacrifice to Ashbeel, the spirit king of Saturn.

All the corvid brain use is in incenses, perhaps acting as a binding agent as well as for its symbolic value. As with blood, magpie brain was used in Mercury incense, in the *Complete Book of Magical Science*. The *Secret Grimoire of Turiel* uses magpie brain for the incense of the Olympic Spirit of Jupiter, Bethor. Crow brain is used as an ingredient only in Martial incenses, not surprising with the association between crows and ravens and the carrion of battlefields. This use is seen in the *Hygromanteia*, *Key of Solomon*, and *Grimoire of Arthur Gauntlet*. It is also seen with raven brain in the *Complete Book of Magic Science* and *Sworn and Secret Grimoire*. Raven brain was also used in Saturnian incense in the *Picatrix*.

Crow feathers are used in the *Key of Solomon* for writing with and in the operation of the divinatory phial of Uriel. There is an interesting caveat in the text about how crow feathers cannot be used for working with the dead. The *Petit Albert* uses a raven feather in a charm to be fortunate in games of skill and chance.

A bizarre charm in the *Discoverie of Witchcraft* to remove genital bewitchment uses crow gall and magpie (eaten) as ingredients. Other uses of crow parts include the heart in a charm to prevent sleep in *Three Books of Occult Philosophy*, the bird in a talisman to protect from poison and evil effects in the *Picatrix*, and crow egg in a pudenda love spell in the PGM (XXXVI:283-294).

Corvid Goddesses

The Morrigan (Great Queen) often appeared as a talking crow in Irish myths, giving warnings. She whispered warnings of the imminent raid in the ear of the Brown Bull of Ulster (in the *Táin Bo Cúailnge*, or Cattle Raid of Cooley, C11 CE), and as a talking crow in *Aidedd Chon Culainn* (the Violent Death of Cu Chulainn, C12 CE) and *Táin Bo Regamna* (Cattle Raid of Regamna, C12 CE).

As well as the Morrigan, the Badb (or Badbh/Badbdh), whose name means crow or raven, was another Irish corvid goddess. The Badb was not a single goddess, but rather a group, often seen on the battlefield feasting on carrion. The Badb appeared as a hideous black crow-like hag on the threshold and cursed King Connaire in *Togail Bruidne Da Derga* (Da Derga's Hostel, C12 CE). They were often referred to as Badbh Catha, or Battle Crow, and the love of carrion was emphasized in the *Bruiden da Chocae* (The Destruction of Da Choca's Hostel, C15 CE):

The red-mouth Badb will cry around the house. For bodies it will be solicitous. Pale Badbs shall shriek, Badbs will be over the breasts of men

The early 13th century French tale *Huon of Bordeaux*, which describes Oberon as the child of Morgan LeFay and Julius Caesar, also refers to the Badb as "the Badb of battle, who is around the battle with scourges in her hand, inducing the hosts to conflict". The Irish corvid goddesses, as battle goddesses, were keen to encourage conflict at any opportunity, at times acting in ways that would cause conflicts centuries later (e.g. the stealing of the bulls in the *Tain* setting up the eventual slaughter around the death of the hero Cú Chulainn).

Another battle goddess Nemain (meaning Frenzy, Panic, or Venomous), best known for her dreadful shrieks and exhortations to battle, was also equated to Badb in later texts like Michael O'Clery's *Glossary* (1643): "Nemain, i.e. the Badb of battle, or a hooded crow."

The other battle goddess associated with crows was Macha (meaning Pasture, Field, or Plain). "Macha, that is a crow, or it is one of the three Morrigna, ... that is Macha and Badb and Morrigan". The first part of this quote is from *Cormac's Glossary* (C9-12 CE); it is repeated with the rest of the line in Trinity H.3.18.

Corvid Rhymes & Calls

The magpie rhyme is well known, at least up to seven. However there are versions which extend to thirteen. Although probably much older, it was first recorded in a simple four line version in 1780 by John Brand in *Observations on Popular Antiquities*.

One for sorrow, Two for joy, Three for a girl, Four for a boy, Five for silver, Six for gold, Seven for a secret, never to be told, Eight for a wish, Nine for a kiss, Ten a surprise you should be careful not to miss, Eleven for health, Twelve for wealth, Thirteen beware it's the devil himself.

The last line ties in with a custom found in many parts of England, that of saluting magpies when you see them. As a child in Lincolnshire I asked a local farmer why people did this, and was told "Magpies are the devil's bird, we salute them as a mark of respect to not annoy him!" I assumed this was a local custom, but have asked people from other counties around England, and found this seems to be a fairly universal practice and belief. Regional variations include doffing your hat, and spitting three times over your shoulder. The magpie as the devil's bird is also seen in Scotland, where it was believed the magpie had a drop of the devil's blood in its tongue. In the Middle Ages there was a belief that the magpie was the only bird that did not cry when Jesus was on the cross, hence it being seen as a bird of ill omen.

Although not as well known, there is also a similar rhyme for the number of ravens seen:

One for bad news, Two for mirth, Three is a wedding, Four is a birth, Five is for riches, Six is a thief, Seven a journey, Eight is for grief, Nine is a secret, Ten is for sorrow, Eleven is for love, Twelve joy for tomorrow.

The Middle Irish codex, Trinity H.3.17, details divination by the sound ravens make. The outcomes are very specific to the culture of the time, however they present an interesting example of divination by bird call:

If the raven call from above an enclosed bed in the mist of the house, it is a distinguished grey-haired guest or clerics that are coming to you, but there is a difference between them. If it be a lay-cleric the raven says 'bacach'; if it be a man in orders it says 'gradh' and twice in the day it calls. If it be warrior guests or satirists that are coming, it is 'gracc' it calls, or 'grob', and it calls in the quarters behind you, and it is from there the guests are coming. If it calls 'gracc gracc' the warriors to whom it calls are oppressed. If women are coming it calls long. If it calls from the north-east end of the house, robbers are about to steal the horses. If it calls from the house door, strangers or soldiers are coming. If it calls from above the door, satirists or guests from a king's retinue are coming. If it calls from above the goodman's bed, the place where his weapons will be, and he going on a journey, he will not come back safe, but if not, he will come back sound. If it is the woman who is about to die, it is from the pillow it calls. If it calls from the foot of the man's bed his son or brother or his son-in-law will come to the house. If it call from the edge of the storehouse where the food is kept, there will be increase of food from the quarter it calls, that is flesh-meat or first milking of kine. If its face be between the storehouse and the fire, agreeable guests are coming to the house. If it be near the woman of the house, where her seat is, the guests are for her, namely, a son-in-law or a friend. If it call from the south of the storehouse, fosterage or guests from afar are coming to the house. If it speaks with a small voice, that is 'err err' or 'ur ur', sickness will fall on someone in the house, or on some of the cattle. If wolves are coming amongst the house, or on some of the cattle. If wolves are coming amongst the sheep, it is from the sheep-fold it calls, or from over against the good women, and what it says is 'carna, carna' [flesh, flesh], 'grob, grob, coin, coin' [wolves, wolves]. If it calls from the rooftree of the house when people are eating, they throw away that food. If it call from a high tree, then it is death-tidings of a young lord. If it calls from a stone it is death-tidings of an aithech. If it go with thee on a journey in front of you, and if it be joyful, your journey will prosper and fresh meat will be given to you. IF you come left-hand-wise and it calls before you, he is a doomed man on whom it calls thus, or it is the sounding of someone of the company. If it be before you when going to an assembly, there will be an uprising therein. If it be left-hand-wise it has come, someone is slain in that uprising. If it calls from the corner where the horses are, robbers are about to attack them. If it then turn on its back and says 'grob grob', some of the horses will be stolen and they will not be recovered.

CORVID FOLKLORE

The best known piece of raven folklore in England is probably the ravens in the Tower of London. It is said that if the ravens ever leave the tower then England will fall. This has led to the mistaken claim that the ravens living in the Tower have their wings clipped to prevent them leaving – they do not. Of course the living oracular head of the giant Bran (whose name meant crow or raven) was said to be buried under the Tower facing across the English Channel towards Europe, and he was associated with ravens, so we may be seeing the conflation of two myths here.

The banshee, or bean-sidhe, was a foreteller of doom who existed in different forms around the British Isles and Ireland, and who could assume the form of a raven or crow.

The Scottish tale of Diarmuid and Grianne includes doom-telling corvids, a raven pecking a hare's corpse and a crow on a boulder, both of whom warn Diarmuid not to hunt the venomous boar which will be his doom. He ignores them and kills the boar, but is poisoned and dies after the fight.

There was a belief that raven's flesh was poisonous, which may have contributed to the Scottish charm for killing a person by shaking a bridle at them whilst reciting *"raven's flesh and crane's flesh come out of thy way"*.[8] A very different piece of Scottish raven folklore comes from the Hebrides, where giving a child their first drink from a raven skull was said to give the gifts of prophecy and wisdom (this may have been influenced by the Norse ravens of Odhinn, Huginn and Muninn).

A variant of the seventeenth century Scottish witch Isobel Gowdie's famous hare chant replaces the hare with the crow, thus: "I shall go into a crow with sorrow and sighing and blackest throw, and I shall go in the Devil's name until I come home again." This assumption of the spirit form of the crow draws attention to the crow as both familiar and spirit animal.

"Deep into that darkness peering, long I stood there wondering, fearing, Doubting, dreaming dreams no mortal ever dared to dream before"[9]

---

8 Cramond, 1900.

9 *The Raven*, Edgar Allan Poe, 1845.

BIBLIOGRAPHY

Best, R.I. (1916) *Prognostications from the Raven and the Wren*, in Ériu 8:120-126

Boudet, Jean-Patrice (2003) *Les who's who démonologiques de la Renaissance et leurs ancêtres médiévaux*, in Médiévales 44

Cramond, W. (1900) *The Church of Alves*. Scotland: Elgin

Harms, Daniel & Clark, James R. & Peterson, Joseph H. (2016) *The Book of Oberon*. Woodbury: Llewellyn

Hughes, Ted (1970) *Crow: From the Life and Songs of the Crow*. London: Faber & Faber

Jennings, Pete (2017) *A Cacophony of Corvids*. Halstead: Gruff Books

Johnson, Brian (2020) *Necromancy in the Medici Library*. North Yorkshire: Hadean Press

Peterson, Joseph H. (2001) *The Lesser Key of Solomon: Lemegeton Clavicula Salomonis*. Maine, Weiser Books

Rankine, David & d'Este, Sorita (2005) *The Guises of the Morrigan: Irish Goddess of Sex & Battle*. London: Avalonia

Rankine, David & d'Este, Sorita (2007) *The Isles of the Many Gods: An A-Z of the Pagan Gods & Goddesses worshipped in Ancient Britain during the first millenium through to the Middle Ages*. London: Avalonia

Skinner, Stephen & Rankine, David (2007) *The Goetia of Dr Rudd*. Volume 3 Sourceworks of Ceremonial Magic, Singapore: Golden Hoard Press

Stratton-Kent, Jake (2016) *Pandemonium: A Discordant Concordance of Diverse Spirit Catalogues*. West Yorkshire, Hadean Press

A Sable Passage
Black Light and the Magic of the Starry Road

J.M. Hamade

Following the work of Henry Corbin and the Sufic understanding of 'The Black Light', this essay seeks to both elucidate and enliven practices of astrological magic using the conceptual framework therein; an extension of the magic of place amidst the theatre of the night sky. Whereas astrology often places a marked emphasis upon particular celestial bodies, especially within the context of magic, this essay will attempt to look at the magical potential of 'place' and 'station'. In particular, the essay will focus on the Milky Way as a realm of luminous darkness, a starry road, within the purview of astrology and its magics.

To formulate a conception of darkness without the absence of light is nothing less than a challenge. Similarly, in describing concepts of luminosity, we tend to lean into these same polarizing tendencies. The exclusivity of these inclinations seems to be built not only within the language itself, but ever so deeply entwined among our very thought processes.

Acknowledging the limitations of this framework, we can begin to see the gradient between these two polarities as something not exactly discrete. It is this emerging twilight between the two where our journey begins; a path both dark as well as luminous; *a noctilucence.*

+

Perhaps the most well known elucidation of 'black light' as a mystical concept comes from the work of French scholar Henry Corbin. Writing primarily on the philosophical works of great Persianate thinkers such as Shahāb ad-Dīn Suhrawardī and his Illuminationist school, the teachings of Corbin heavily emphasize the play of lights as mystical guides.

Corbin's *The Man of Light in Iranian Sufism* walks the reader through an oneiric journey likened to a pathway of varying luminosities. Signatures of light, or lack thereof, function as signs on the mystical path denoting place. These places are not necessarily geographic, although they may correspond or find familiarity with such. In this way we find a primary distinction between the 'darkness of matter', symbolized by a deep well or a blackened furnace, and the 'light without matter', or 'the darkness above'. According to the philosophies of Suhrawardī and Najm Kobrā, particles of light (the initiates themselves) may be liberated from this well or lower darkness through the spark of *dhikr*, or the Sufic concept of God's remembrance. It is through the fire of the *dhikr* that this light particle begins to rise into the axial dimension and move into the space of 'light without matter', wherein 'the darkness above is the blackness of the stratosphere, of stellar space, of the black sky.' This same distinction is referenced in the work of the philosopher Avicenna as the difference between the 'darkness at the approaches to the *pole* (the northern-axial dimension, immortality)' and that which reigns in the 'far west'; the latter associated with absorptive darkness which restricts light, as well as the *barzakh*, or the barrier between life and death.

Though the spiritual terrain varies from writer to writer, the stage preceding or representing finality corresponds to the 'seventh valley' or the 'black light'. Najm Rāzī relates this seventh light to the attribute of 'Majesty', or obliteration in the divine which 'attacks, invades, annihilates, then annihilates annihilation.' Though it is not stated, we would be remiss in neglecting to compare this sphere with that of the black planet Saturn. Similarly associated with the cold-dry climes of the northern region, Saturn is also cross-culturally symbolized by the color black. Considered the final frontier on the Platonic soul's journey back to the heavenly realms, it is the seventh sphere of Saturn in which this spark faces divine annihilation before reaching the majesty beyond. In this way we may observe two faces of Saturn, one as representative of the chthonic force capable of trapping light (contingent being), and the other as that which is 'darkness without matter (necessary being)', that final stage of ecstatic annihilation on the mystic's journey. We see these same two faces of Saturn within the planet's paired zodiacal rulership of Capricorn and Aquarius, the former representative of the absorptive power of earthen darkness and the latter as the non-material power of airy darkness or the night sky.

+

Somewhere between these two faces of enfolding and revelatory darkness do we find our familiar classical planets as embodied signatures of light. Their luminosity, their color and their movements in the night sky act as manifested qualities of the world in which we live, as well as aspects of our inner being. The reddish hues of Mars; blood, aggression, strife, passion. The radiance of Venus; one's love and ability to shine, to connect. Yet what of the night sky itself? What of the stage upon which these lights of revelation play?

Mallorie Vaudoise's essay 'Dark Matter' points out the necessary astrological preference for the luminous bodies themselves; that is, in opposition to the dark vault in which they are set. In regard to views on darkness in the Western astrological tradition, 'there is the ecliptic, the path traced by the sun through the cosmos. The ecliptic itself is dark and thus, in a sense, unknowable. Like physical dark matter we understand it by the proxy of visible objects. There are also the houses, an alternate and complementary way of dividing space relative to the earth.'

Though it may seem obvious, the demarcation of space within the various astrological traditions is not something to be taken for granted. Referencing the *Picatrix*, Vaudoise points out that even these abstract divisions of space lacking a stellar body may be used with magical efficacy. This is a critical observation. Not only must we consider the latent potential within these darkened spaces, but to compound this, it is astounding to observe the sheer volume in comparison to that which is marked or defined, as 'physicists hypothesize that dark matter and dark energy constitute 95% of the materialist Universe.' In this respect, questions emerge in regard to accessing the magical potential therein. In other words, how might we determine what is viable or not?

Astrological traditions have varied in their logic of spatial division. Take the lunar mansions as an example. Though much of the lore around the lunar mansions has emerged from their associated asterisms, variations remain in terms of spatial divisions and how they are determined. The oldest and most intact system of lunar mansions is that of the Vedic Nakshatras. Still using the symbolism and deities of their associated stars, the houses themselves are based upon a division of the ecliptic into 27 (sometimes 28 if you include *Abhijat*) even segments. This standardized division of a circle is kept intact using sidereal coordinates which link the beginning of said circle to either a particular asterism or point in space (called the *ayanamsa*). The Nakshatras stand in contrast to two other popular forms of lunar mansion systems, the Chinese and the Arabic. The Arabic lunar mansion schema found in both the *Picatrix* and Agrippa's *Three Books of Occult Philosophy* takes on an immensely syncretic quality, as many of its defining features remain linked to the world of star lore with space defined by tropical (or solar) coordinates. Disparities in form have neither dissuaded nor impeded these cultures in deriving magical and divinatory efficacy within their respective conceptual structures.

Returning to the Sufic conception of this darkened space, we may surmise that the presence of matter as we understand it is not necessary in the achievement of this or that revelation. This 'annihilation' is one which destroys material bodies and visible objects. The so-called second face of Saturn, or that which acts as material barrier, must be overcome to achieve the realization of suprasensory efficacy. Countless cultures possessing idiosyncratic means of empty spatial division are testament to this.

That said, there are two primary objections that must be raised. First and foremost, without the use of so-called material markers, how are we to determine much of anything? Does this not lead to a kind of relativistic tail-spin wherein all things become possible? Secondly, would this approach not take a monumental shift in perspective to achieve something we might call coherent?

In response to the first objection, the realization of non-material efficacy does not presuppose the discarding of material signatures. The Sufic philosophy of light reminds us that there are stages of varying hues between these two faces of darkness. These same glowing colors exist as fundamental components of any given process of realization. It must also be emphasized that realizations as such rarely if ever function in a linear fashion. Just as many are familiar with the interplay of stellar bodies within their own natal horoscopes, so too do these luminosities move about in collision, separation, and plenitudes of wayward circlings along the path. To discard the visible signs would be to emphasize the extremes; instead we must use the visible signs as a means of accessing the invisible power of which they are but one manifestation. Lights among lights. As it is described, they are our sign-posts for the road on which we stand. To utilize the signs is not to damn the road.

Regarding the second question, there is no doubt of the necessity of paradigmatic shifting. Interestingly enough, upon further examination, a large swathe of astrological magic already relies upon abstract coordinates with very little relation to physical space itself. We have outlined the ambiguity among divisions of the lunar mansions, yet even within our familiar solar zodiac we find this same notion. The boundaries of the 12 signs do not align even in the slightest with the 360° division of the ecliptic. Putting aside the differences in tropical and sidereal coordinates, a planet's placement in both a sign and a house is based upon an abstraction of our own creation — not to mention the rather large mediation through computers in much contemporary astrology. Though we remain focused on the visible bodies themselves, it would be inaccurate to say that many of the techniques found in astrological magic, both historical and current, do not already rely upon abstract divisions of space.

The foundation as such rests upon that space referred to as 'darkness without matter'. Traditionally, this realm was thought to be the underworld, or that which is invisible. This domain is often situated in 'the below', or sometimes within the very darkness itself. What are the implications of this magical efficacy existing and grounded upon this elusive, often non-material place? To this point, what of the notion that astrology is a magical and divinatory art based in that which is *outside and up there*? Mythologically, both the path of the Sun (the ecliptic) as well as the Milky Way were likened to roads wherein the soul would travel to the underworld. Due to the influence of the Greeks and Egyptians, many are familiar with this solar path and its underworld journey. Lesser known is that other starry path, the Milky Way. This will be the focus of the remainder of our journey.

✛

As we have noted, like the ecliptic, the Milky Way has often been considered a road to the underworld. Where do these cosmologies intersect with one another? Or better yet, how might we begin to frame the Milky Way within our more familiar astrological schemas? The crossing points of the Milky Way with the ecliptic (or the Milky Way as the galactic equator or plane, distinct from the celestial equator) are of vital import here. The tropical coordinates of these points correspond to 27° Sagittarius as galactic center and 27° Gemini as galactic anti-center. These ancient cross-roads have long been considered points of powerful movement. Among the Neoplatonic traditions these points were considered to be the 'Gate of the Gods' and the 'Gate of Men', respectively, wherein the souls passed outside and back into this world through the solstitial points of Capricorn and Cancer.

Modern astronomy has only recently begun to confirm the nature of these points in surprisingly similar language to that of the ancients. The celestial marker for galactic center, or the entrance to the Milky Way road, corresponds to a supermassive black hole situated at the center of our galaxy. Returning to the concept of the 'black light', this particular black hole, as well as the phenomenon in general, represent a physical manifestation of this same mystical concept. Even more so, the notion of *sol niger*, or the black sun, is pronounced here as a body of shining darkness.

In Marlan Stanton's *The Black Sun: The Alchemy and Art of Darkness*, the symbolism of the black sun is likened to the luminary of alchemical *nigredo*, or the notorious stage of blackening wherein the seeker is confronted with all manner of trial concerning death, struggle and all-consuming sorrow. Stanton relates *sol niger* to the shadow of Carl Jung's often-perceived holism, 'The Self', wherein the luminous darkness signals our profoundest 'Anti-Self', in a manner not unlike Christ and Anti-Christ. Similarly we find the likeness of the Milky Way as well as its cross-road points along the Sun's path. Due to the lack of *our* star's light upon this road, we may say that it belongs to all things which are not familiar, i.e. 'the self'. The so-called 'anti-self', or the radiant star of shadowy no-things, becomes that of the galactic center. This 'sun of the sun' is the true gravitational or axial point within our galaxy. Just like the stage of alchemical *nigredo*, no work may begin without it. In this way it is ontologically prior, the dark mother who births and destroys all things which are familiar. 'Annihilation of annihilation'.

The lunar nodes, also known as Rahu and Ketu in the Vedic tradition, mimic the effects of these cross points. In this respect, they are of a similar nature to the phenomenon of black holes, 'radiant darkness', or shadow planets as they are often called. Observing the points of nodal exaltation — 3° Gemini for the exalted north node, Rahu, and 3° Sagittarius for the exalted south node, Ketu — we find an intriguing connection: a few hundred years ago these degrees would have aligned to the ecliptical sidereal degrees of the Milky Way cross-roads. Additionally, the north node is often likened to Saturn, whose angel dwells in the corresponding lunar mansion (sidereal to tropical), while the south node was likened to Mars whose angel does the same.

In the Islamic tradition, the angelic personae of these locations are sometimes determined through the use of Arabic letters. In the original Abjad sequence, the 28 letters of the alphabet correspond to each of the 28 lunar mansions, wherein particular letters stand out as representational. In this way, the first chapter of the Quran, *al-Fatiha*, uses 21 of these letters while lacking the other 7. These 7 letters which have been left out correspond to the 7 lights or planetary bodies previously discussed. It is also interesting to note the qualities of the Arabic lunar mansions that occupy the tropical coordinates of these crossroads. *Al-Dhira*, mansion #7, is ruled by the angel Kasfiel (ز) who is considered the angel of Saturn. The Andalusian mystic Ibn Arabi likened this mansion to 'The Throne', *al-Arsh*, and to the force which englobes or encircles all things. *Al-Balda*, mansion #21, is ruled by the angel Samsamiel (ش) who is considered to be the angel of Mars. Ibn Arabi terms this mansion 'The Death-Giver', likening it to the Earth itself. Note the repetition of the numbers 7 and 21, as well as the exaltations of the nodes stated above.

The Vedic Nakshatras maintain a similar symbolism. The sidereal locations of the Milky Way cross-roads roughly align with *Ardra* (late Gemini), ruled by the storm deity Rudra-Shiva and Rahu in the Vimshottari Dasha, and *Mula* (late Sagittarius), ruled by Niritti-Kali and Ketu in the dasha system. Rudra and Niritti were seen as consorts, Shiva and Kali, and both associated with destruction of illusion and extreme forms of yogic practice. Once more, 'annihilation of annihilation'. Curiously, the name *Mula* refers to a root. Sharing the qualities of Kali in her most destructive aspects, this portion of the sky fits quite nicely with the discoveries of contemporary astronomy, not only as the root of our galaxy itself but also as the location of a supermassive black hole.

Greco-Egyptian decan gods and daemonic attributions often vary. For our purposes, the Ostanes list of 36 decans attributes Praxidice to the third decan of Gemini, while the third decan of Sagittarius is ruled by Ananke. Praxidice is frequently likened to a form of Persephone representing the 'practice of justice', but often in its harsher forms; presumably, as Underworld Queen, this entails the taking of life. Ananke alongside her consort Cronos (the embodiment of Time, not precisely Saturn) act as principal archaic manifestations, solely preceded by Chaos itself. She is often depicted seated upon a throne with a pole standing behind her. This is quite appropriate for the deity who rules the portion of the sky closest to galactic center. To compound all of this, both decans are traditionally Saturn-ruled. With the imagery in these decans often portraying people on the verge of sacrifice before the solstice, we see once more a strong theme of approaching death. Though this may be viewed primarily through the lens of solar cycles, the Milky Way crossing points should not be ignored in their symbolic contribution as places of entrance and exit regarding death. Their rulership by the planet Saturn as gatekeeper reaffirms this notion.

+

Where might we begin a practical approach within these rich and potential-laden locales? First and foremost, the paradigmatic shift of perspective must be kept at the forefront in following this road. Not only must we remember to approach these paths continually through the use of sign posts, but we must emphasize the nature of the road beneath our feet. In this respect, what might be interpreted as an open freedom to divide the heavens at our personal whim, is more akin to recognizing natural boundaries and paying attention to the signs along the way. We must not mistake the potency of darkness for the arbitrary.

The Milky Way and the cross-roads therein mark a new potential among Western traditions of astrology; an underutilized division of space, yet one which has its precedent in cross-cultural observations of the sky. Due to the shadowy nature of these places, once more we can begin to find new inroads using techniques and signs already known to us.

The cross-roads between the ecliptic and the Milky Way become our two primary points of emphasis. The point aligned to late Sagittarius (or early Sagittarius if you are using sidereal coordinates) resonates deeply as a place of dissolution. As the 'Gate of the Gods', souls were thought to exit existence in this part of the sky as they entered into the underworld. As this location corresponds to galactic center, one might utilize ritual timing or astrological elections around great endings in totality; if one is feeling bold, perhaps timing the beginning of an underworld journey through dream and visionary work. The second point aligned to late Gemini (again, early Gemini in sidereal) shares similar associations with death yet also with the birthing process. As the importance of twin symbolism is prominent, the 'other half' is often seen to be slain here. This locale speaks to 'the hunt' and the deliberate destruction of particulars as opposed to oneself or things in their entirety. As the 'Gate of Men', this region of the sky has long been associated with birth and creativity. Staying to the present theme, one must choose the necessary sacrifice or offering to ensure this birth is well supported by the means of mutual exchange.

Planetary, decanic, and lunar mansion rulerships have been listed above as other potential means of accessing the points in question. If it is not the evocation of the entities themselves, astrological elections, transits, and talisman construction are all possibilities around timing near or in relation to these places. This begs the question: are there other possibilities beyond the intersections with our familiar ecliptic? In this respect we may acknowledge the presence of countless stars who share the sky alongside the Milky Way. The presence of well known constellations like Orion, Sagittarius, and Scorpio, many of whose stories explicitly interact with that of the Milky Way, may hold revelations of how one might explore these often uncharted abodes.

In conclusion, and perhaps of great importance, are the possibilities of access which do not necessarily rely on well established and familiar modalities. Though we have become quite complacent with tables of correspondence, precise computer-generated ritual timing, and the like, we must remember that the emphasis here is not solely upon that which is 'visible'; this includes established patterns for accessing the power of celestial intelligences. Beginning upon the foundations laid out thus far, we may hopefully avoid the pitfalls of arbitrary action and solipsistic approach. Every night we turn our eyes toward new possibilities, reflected in glimmers of luminous darkness. The veil of night, a theatre for our creativity and dream. Each star, a new potential.

BIBLIOGRAPHY

Burckhardt, Titus, *Mystical Astrology According to Ibn ʿArabi*, Fons Vitae, 2001.

Corbin, Henry, *The Man of Light in Iranian Sufism*, translated by Nancy Pearson, Omega Publications, 1994.

Hazel, Elizabeth, *Little Book of Fixed Stars*, Kozmic Kitchen Press, 2020.

Johnson, Kenneth, *Mansions of the Moon: The Lost Zodiac of the Goddess*, Archive Press, 2002.

Stanten, Marlan, *The Black Sun: The Alchemy and Art of Darkness*, Texas A&M University Press, 2005.

Stratton-Kent, Jake, *The Testament of Cyprian the Mage Vol. 1*, Scarlet Imprint, 2014.

Vaudoise, Mallorie, 'Dark Matter', in *The Celestial Art: Essays on Astrological Magic*, ed. Austin Coppock and Daniel A. Schulke, Three Hands Press, 2018.

Warnock, Christopher & Greer, John Michael, *The Illustrated Picatrix*, Renaissance Astrology, 2015.

LODGED AMONG THE GRAVES
TOWARDS A PRACTICAL SYLLABUS OF EARLY MODERN NECROMANCY

ALEXANDER CUMMINS

A BLACK SCHOOL CURRICULUM

IN 1656, the unusually Catholic antiquarian and legal scholar Thomas Blout published his *Glossographia*, a 'dictionary interpreting the hard words of whatsoever language, now used in our refined English tongue'. Containing around eleven thousand unusual words, it was the most substantial contribution to the field of technical lexicography at the time, offering not only definitions but (for arguably the first time) etymologies of both obscure designations and expert terms of art.

Or at least it *was* the most substantial dictionary, until Edward Phillips—a nephew of John Milton—published his *The New World of Words* but two short years later in 1658. While almost double the size of Blout's work and committed to publishing common as well as extraordinary words, it was widely held that many of these entries were plagiarised wholesale from the *Glossographia*. Perhaps none held such a notion as fervently as Blout himself. The resultant lexicographers' arms race of amendments and edits to their respective works by the two men lasted years, and of course included bitter denunciations of one another's works. Blout lamented cholerically,

> Must this then be suffered? A Gentleman for his divertissement writes a Book, and this Book happens to be acceptable to the World, and sell; a Bookseller, not interested in the Copy, instantly employs some Mercenary to jumble up another like Book out of this, with some Alterations and Additions, and give it a new Title; and the first Author's out-done, and his Publisher half undone....[1]

In response Philips pointed an accusatory finger back at Blout and declared his works 'barbarous and illegally compounded'. So why do we begin an essay on early modern necromancy with this relation of the acrid vitriol of seventeenth-century dictionary writers? Because it is from these very *barbarous* words and embitterances that we come to read Blout's entry for 'necromancer' in his 1661 edition of the *Glossographia*:

---

1 Thomas Blout, *A World of Errors Discovered in the New World of Words* (London, 1676), To The Reader.

Necromancer (*necromantes*) he that practises that wicked Art, a Master of the Black Art, one that seeks to the dead; or consults with Satan in the shape of a dead man. The Hebrews describe him thus; he made himself hungry, and then lodged among the Graves, that the dead might come to him in a dream, and make known to him that which he asked, &c. Others there were that clad themselves with cloathes for that purpose, and spoke certain words, burned Incense, and slept by themselves, that such a dead person might come and talk with them in a dream.[2]

From this colourfully black description, thoroughly efficacious points concerning the study and practice of necromancy can be constelled into a very serviceable black school syllabus. Such a necromancy would by necessity include an understanding and contextualisation of the wider catacombs of the term *nigromancy*: a dark wingspan under which the corpse components and blood magic of traditional necromancy could be considered. Likewise, considering necromantic practices under the umbr(ell)a of nigromancy, as we shall explore, finds them set as grave bedfellows alongside the devils of demonology.

Beyond such endeavours to categorise necromancy and its related deeds—both those with and those without names—a set of very practical techniques are presented in our syllabus. Hunger is emphasised as operationally important, highlighting various practices of fasting, as well as humoural dimensions of diet, and other foodways, not to mention having the right guts for the work. Graveyards are similarly foregrounded, bringing to mind an appreciation and observation of the protocols and etiquettes of the land of the dead. Particularities concerning appropriate dress are emphasised, beyond the sartorial and into the ritualistic and operatively sorcerous. Breath (and, perhaps by extension, the lack thereof) is doubly stressed in the attention paid to both magical speech acts and suffumigation: both means of charging the medium of the airs that swirl in inspiration and enspiritment. Finally, the importance of dreaming is especially signified several times, emphasising that this seems the most common modality by which encounters between the living and the dead can be conjured and cohered.

My inclinations of both study and practice are to seek counsel from the shades of the cunning dead, and as such our sources will be heavily drawn from the texts found upon their shelves, in the bottom of locked trunks, and occasionally chained and hanging from the rafters of barns. The *Fourth Book of Occult Philosophy*—occasionally referred to as 'Agrippa's Teaching negromancy'—is of particular utility, as are the working-books of cunning-folk and the historical accounts of their practices.

Thus stands our goetic curriculum, plucked from the embitterances of lexicographers: a nigromancy that dances with both devils and the deceased, tutoring us to correctly comport ourselves in sustenance, solitude, garb, scent, and speech in pursuit of the boneyard *trivium* of sleep, dream, and spirit.

---

2 Thomas Blout, *Glossographia or, A dictionary interpreting all such hard words of whatsoever language now used in our refined English tongue with etymologies, definitions and historical observations on the same: also the terms of divinity, law, physick, mathematicks and other arts and sciences explicated* (London, 1661).

THE BLACK ART

Formulating our syllabus of practical necromancy requires an understanding of the context of nigromancy, that old black magic, what we might most easily consider the *denigrated* forms of practice deemed variously illicit, impious, immoral, and dangerous. Such concentration upon labelling theory and what others deem evil—upon what is summoned by the mid-air sigils traced by the pointed fingers of frothing dogmatists and demagogues—might seem somewhat alarmist. But we should bear in mind that such approaches, far from simply allowing enemies to define us, are remarkably traditional. Here's *Onkel* Heinrich doing just that, in one of those *Three Books of Occult Philosophy* more securely attributed to him than is the *Fourth*:

> Now the parts of Ceremonial Magick are Goetia and Theurgia; Goetia is unfortunate, by the commerces of unclean spirits made up of the rites of wicked curiosities, unlawfull charms, and deprecations, and is abandoned and execrated by all laws. Of this kinde are those which we now adayes call Necromancers, and Witches… These therefore are they which call upon the souls of the dead…[3]

To practice this early modern conjugation of nigromancy is not simply to summon the dead in some form. It is to operate in a moral universe, and either obey or deny the so-called 'natural' moral authorities that seek to control you. Watch out for appeals to such a naturalism, they will occur again in demonological discussion later.

This is not to say the *Three Books of Occult Philosophy* lack technical analysis of our black art. Agrippa presents two flavours of black magic, defined by their central principle of operative action: compelling and worshipping. The first is considered the lesser of the two evils, for some nigromancers did 'endeavour to call and compell evil spirits, adjured by a certain power, especially of divine names'. This emphasis upon compulsion and adjuration highlights that while such black magicians traffic with wicked spirits, they at least do so at arm's length, and with the names of God upon their lips; 'for seeing every creature fears, and reverenceth the name of him who made it, no marvel, if Goetians, Infidels, Pagans, Jews, Saracens, and men of every prophane sect and society do bind Divels by invocating the divine name.' As a personal note, I am rather fond of the sort of Black Rainbow Coalition herein described, disparate creeds united by a commonality of being othered. The necropolis is cosmopolitan, the land of the dead requires no singular passport for emigration, and in the face of theological monopoly and religious or moral totalitarianism, those called outsiders will—one way or another—all hang together.

Agrippa's second and far worse form of the 'Geotick' art can be characterised by the worship of these devilish spirits, for 'there are some that are most impiously wicked indeed, that submit themselves to Divels, sacrifice to, and adore them, and thereby become guilty of Idolatry, and the basest abasement'. Such acts are not merely base,

---

3 Agrippa, *Three Books of Occult Philosophy* (London, 1651), III: 'Of Goetia Necromancy', p. 572.

unclean, or un-Christian, they are *crimes* against God and the natural laws. Moreover, 'to which crimes if the former are not obnoxious, yet they expose themselves to manifest dangers.'[4] Heresy and blasphemy are not only evil, they are dangerous. Of course, dangers of trafficking with wicked spirits are often acknowledged from within nigromantic traditions too. I know no sane practicing goetic magician who would disagree that this whole black magic business is indeed potentially a profoundly dangerous path. We would all do well to remember that and act accordingly and responsibly.

In terms of exactly what such diabolical submission, adoration, and sacrifice actually looked like, we can turn to the *Three Books*' illegitimate sister. The *Fourth Book of Occult Philosophy* puts forth further reflections on how necromancy and witchcraft interact in this tenebrously nigromantic spiritwork. For the purposes of our emergent curriculum, I refer to the early modern adoption and conventions of the term 'goetia': John Smith's *Christian Religion's Appeal* of 1675 declares 'Goetia is an art to constrain the dead by invocation',[5] and good old Blout defines '*Goetie* (goetia)... the Black Art; Divellish Magick or Witchcraft'.[6]

But what of early modern analysis of the term? The *Fourth Book*'s comparison between 'goes' and 'magus' is worthy of consideration: 'many men there are, that abhor the very name and word *Magus*, because of *Simon Magus*, who being indeed not *Magus*, but *Goes*, that is, familiar with evil Spirits, usurping that title...'[7] We have a sharp and concise description of one who practices goetia as one who is 'familiar with evil Spirits'.[8] Again, being able to understand the virtue and potency of both technical criteria and moral biases—our own as well as ones espoused by those at whom we point our accusatory fingers—is an essential dimension of not losing our way in the blackening and potentially embittering darkness.

Furthermore the *Fourth Book* begins to adumbrate functional details of this diabolic turn in necromantic study and practice. Most significantly, it presents that 'Necromancy and Witchcraft, and such Arts... are effected by combination with the devil, and whereof he is a party.'[9] Here we meet our demons. Not only does this diabolical 'combination' define such practitioners as doing the Devil's work, for 'these Witches and Necromancers are also called *Malefici* or *venefici*, sorcerers or poisoners; of which name witches are rightly called', but their own works are facilitated by devilish intervention and empowerment— for they perform black magic 'without the Art of [natural] Magicke' and thus 'do indeed use the helpe of the devill himselfe to do mischiefe'.[10] So far so demonological, yet two points are worthy of particular note here. Firstly, the centrality of spiritwork: nigromancers work *with* spirits to perform their nigromancy, requiring the

---

4 Agrippa, *Three Books*, 'Of Goetia...', p. 572–73.

5 John Smith, *Christian Religion's Appeal From the Groundless Prejudices of the Sceptick* (London, 1675).

6 Thomas Blout, *Glossographia* (London, 1661).

7 *Fourth Book of Occult Philosophy*, trans. Robert Turner (London, 1655: 1665), Preface.

8 Ibid.

9 Ibid.

10 Ibid.

inhuman potencies and wisdoms of spirits to conduct their craft efficaciously. Secondly, they break or exist outside of the realms and laws of even natural magic.

They also do so in expressly necromantic manners, 'practising to mix the powder of dead bodies with other things by the help of the devil prepared'.[11] All is dusts and ashes, not only returned to dust but conjured from it. More fundamentally, the assistances of familiar spirits and patron powers are not immaterial, no mere psychism or astral abstraction. They are present and cohered at the skeleton-crushing pestle-point, and teach from the dancing tongues of flame that blacken and dry flesh. Bone and breath, dancing together, through and from each other. Such powders make their way into numerous early modern 'loving-cups', yet also are used 'at other times to make pictures of wax, clay, or otherwise (as it were *sacramentaliter*) to effect those things which the devil by other means bringeth to pass.'[12] As I have related in a previous work, such construction of wax images and their use as sacrifice substitutions is not an uncommon feature of the so-called Baconian grimoires.[13] Effigies and offerings, poppets and placations, *Agnus Dei* and sacrificial lambs, oh my.

SEEKS TO THE DEAD...

The *Fourth Book* is the most likely contender for representing the sort of treatises actually owned by arrested cunning-folk and referred to in trial records as 'Agrippa's Teaching negromancy'.[14] This again is no mere fearful projection. The collection of texts titled the *Fourth Book of Occult Philosophy* does indeed include vital and eminently practical necromancy. Crucially, it finds the points of intersectionality between two oft separated fields of our black art: 'true' necromancy—that is, the use of the material components of the dead—and sciomancy, divination by the very *shades* of the dead. Consideration of the immortal soul is not merely a resort of the guilty or penitent, but of the practicing necromancer:

> Souls do still love their relinquished Bodies after death, as it were a certain affinity alluring them; such as are the Souls of noxious men, which have violently relinquished their Bodies, and Souls wanting a due burial, which do still wander in a liquid and turbulent Spirits about their dead carcasses...[15]

---

11 Ibid.

12 Ibid. *Sacramentaliter* meaning, in short, 'sacramentally'. Sacramentality is a detailed theological concept, but—in broadest brushstrokes—refers to a ritual action, ceremony, or object regarded as a means of receiving sanctifying grace.

13 For more on (pseudo-)Baconian grimoires and wax images, see Alexander Cummins, 'In the Manner of Saint Cyprian': A Cyprianic Black Magic of Early Modern English Grimoires, in *Cypriana: Old World*, ed. by Alexander Cummins, Jesse Hathaway Diaz, & Jennifer Zahrt (Revelore Press, 2017), p. 83–116.

14 Jon Butler, 'Magic, Astrology, and the Early American Religious Heritage, 1600-1760', *The American Historical Review* 84, 2 (1979), p. 333.

15 *Fourth Book*, p. 66–67.

While it is not in the purview of this article to stray too far into the older deadlands of ancient Greek necromancy, there is certainly a consistent—dare we say, revenant—attitude surviving into the early modern period, that the violently killed (*biaiothanatoi*) and those denied proper funerary rites (*ataphoi*) are among the most active ghosts. The noxiousness of such spirits is in some ways environmental, yet nevertheless returns us to a further reasoning behind the danger and harm of necromancy—these are not *nice* spirits. They are often spirits that may have known great violences, pains, and sorrows; and they may bring with them their own shades, skeletons, and demons.

More importantly in terms of occult practicalities, the relationship between corpse and shade is considered operatively in terms of the allurement, habit, and turbulence of spirits in and as a radiating medium. Such spirits are not considered to be entirely and individually imprisoned by their earthly remains. Death is especially porous, and these shades drift and coagulate and rush and crash like waves, 'liquid and turbulent'. The liquidity of these spirits is worth expressly foregrounding here, as the currents in and around their carcasses...

for these Souls by the known meanes by which heretofore they were conjoyned to their Bodies, *by the like vapors, liquors, and savours*, are easily drawn unto them. From hence it is, that the Souls of the dead are not to be called up without blood, or by the application of some part of their relict Body.[16]

This significance of 'vapors' and 'savours'—a sympathetic mimesis of the activity of the dead—gives us our first indication of the particularly necromantic importance of fumigation, another part of our black school curriculum addressed in more depth below. Such wraithly liquidity is not limited to actual liquids, and the vast medium of breath and spirit too roils and curls and dissipates with the dead. Fundamentally the coherence of spirit and breath in liquid form is understood as blood. Speaking most practically of the magical efficacy and potency of blood, occult philosopher and geomancer Robert Fludd relates a fundamental unity of being in terms of occult sympathy: 'that all mankind is made of one blood onely: and therefore this vnion of symphoniacall or sympatheticall harmony, is not easily to bee limited'.[17] Such a profoundly sanguine harmony—a living, pulsing, nurturing emblem and instantiation of *sympathia* poured forth into the future—is not even limited by death it seems. Thus, in lieu of corpse components of the specific specter, employing the one blood that all humanity is said to share in order to stir the deceased seems conceived—beyond simply 'feeding' shades—as the most enlivening, catalysing, and cohering libation. And one that certainly brings the most attentions when shed in a place of the dead...

---

16 *Fourth Book*, p. 67. Emphasis added.

17 Robert Fludd, *Doctor Fludds Answer unto M. Foster or, The Squeezing of Parson Fosters Sponge, ordained by him for the wiping away of the Weapon-Salve* (London, 1631), p. 128.

...or Satan in the Shape of a Dead Man

Fludd's communion of blood was of course also understood as a bad old principle of inversion. And what Black Mass would be complete without an appearance from the Devil Hisself? The small-s-satanism of early modern nigromancy in general is easy to parse: black magic is bad magic and the Devil has the best tunes. The diabolism of necromancy specifically requires a little more context: cosmologically, in terms of concepts of (un)natural magic; and theologically and politically, in terms of the Protestant Reformation. Let's begin with natural magic:

> The raising of the dead: Yea and the healing of diseases, that by no natural meanes of any creature can be cured, and a great many more, such like set down in the scripture: the which cannot be wrought but onely by the finger of God: and therefore not by any diuilish meanes or sorcery: Albeit the diuell may sometimes counterfeit the same. Yet his legerdemaine is heere sooner espied, then in any other kind of miracles, by reason that he wanteth the ground of naturall causes to support it.[18]

In other words, necromancy doesn't just break the laws of man, but the laws of God and nature. It usurps Christian God's monopoly on victory over death, and that's not a protection racket the Church was willing to just give up. Therefore it proclaimed necromancy must be a lie. The closest the Devil can come is to fake it, to forge counterfeit ghosts out of his demonic retinue. We may think of the demon in a Helen-of-Troy suit in Marlowe's *Faustus*. Understandably, however, being told an apparition of your dearly departed is in fact just a demon wearing a Grandpa mask has a tendency to upset people somewhat. So from whence did this wider rejection of ghosts come?

The short—although not necessarily simple—answer comes in the form of the Protestant Reformation's rejection of 'the Romish Doctrine concerning Purgatory'. What almost certainly begins as a technical repudiation of the Catholic Church's policy concerning indulgences—those dispensations originally put into practice in the edict of *Unigenitus* in 1323 as a straightforward means of fundraising for St Peter's by charging the bereaved admission and administrative fees for their loved ones to get past the pearly gates—spiraled into a top-down ideological abolition of the most populated areas of the afterlife.

The Swiss reformist pastor Ludwig Lavater, and his work *Of Ghosts and Spirites Walking By Nyght* (1572), is generally singled out by historians as a particularly strong influence and example of this Protestant denial of any place for the dead beyond Heaven, Hell, or 'resting'—supine and utterly out of contact—in their graves. He puts forward several important points. Most significantly he posits that souls could not return before Judgment Day. Thus he marsh-gaslights ghost sightings as hoaxes, optical illusions, the reports of the insane or confused. After all, to argue that the dead could

---

18 James Mason, *The Anatomie of Sorcerie VVherein the wicked impietie of charmers, inchanters, and such like, is discouered and confuted* (London, 1612), p. 16.

return was to contradict The Almighty's power. He also admits another explanation for ghost sightings: devils (or indeed *the* Devil) in the shape of those who were in fact passed on and resting until the trumpets of Judgment. This of course only further extended the domain of the diabolic to a variety of traditions delineating what people thought happened when you died, and how they felt about encounters between the mortal and the eschatologically othered.

The effects of this new doctrinal abolition of Purgatory—and the freshly stoked suspicion that the dead might be devils in disguise—upon folk eschatologies were profound and various. In her excellent *The Fate of the Dead* Theo Brown outlines four key consequences. Firstly, and most obviously, it produced 'a dreariness in orthodox religion', pointing to how even the skeptic John Seldon was moved to remark that 'there never was a merry world since the fairies left dancing and the parson left conjuring.' Secondly, it produced 'the most virulent upsurge in millennial cults', as Protestant radical commitment to self-interpretation of Scripture bumped up against an utterly dualistic world of Heaven and Hell and nothing in between. Thirdly, all this produced a condition of considerable psychic distress and paranoia:

> ...for ordinary folk a state of enormous bewilderment... there was a dread of the erstwhile holy, but now there was also an obsessional terror of Judgment even worse than that of the pre-Reformation period. In a cosmos devoid of the kindly prayers of Our Lady and the saints, and of the mitigating organization of requiems and Purgatory, the extremes of Heaven and Hell now stood out as an unrelenting dichotomy in black-and-white moralistic terms. Such exaggerated horror is impossible to bear if it is not countered by an equal sense of the love of God, but this in a popular, moralistic religion is grimly lacking.[19]

Finally, Brown brings us back around to Old Scratch, and a significant shift from folksier Devils outwitted by countless folk heroes, to a far more powerful and dangerous figure, clad in the colours of our Art no less, as 'the most dramatic expression of this misery was the arrival of a reinforced Devil, no longer the horned and hoofed buffoon which could be dispersed by the sign of the cross, but the sinister, prosaic Man in Black who invaded Jacobean society.'[20] It was this Man in Black who looms large over the suspicions of spirit identification both implicitly in the background of the operations of countless conjurors—from Dee to Napier—and who is explicitly foregrounded in the grave work of those who sought to the dead.

To a necromancer, all history is necromantic, of course. Oriented with some historical and historiographical context—interrogating the tellers as well as the stories and the spirits stirring through them—we may better and more concisely consider the

---

19 Theo Brown, *The Fate of the Dead: A Study in Folk Eschatology in the West Country after the Reformation* (Folklore Society, 1979), p. 18.

20 Ibid.

techniques of our syllabus: hunger, graveyards, dreaming and its discernment, clothing, speaking, and smoking. Let us begin with hunger, for even a skeleton army marches on its stomach.

HUNGRY

When we examine ritual hunger, it is perhaps easiest to consider the purification taboos of preparatory fasting. The corpus of pre-modern European grimoiric magic typically includes requirements of three-, seven-, nine-, or occasionally forty-day periods of ascetic practice, which heavily lean on ritual purity—often forsaking strong drink as well as swearing, and impious company along with sex, base thoughts, and of course rich foods and drinks. Regulating consumption was a further sacrificial component of asceticism. So the *Heptameron*, a textual basis from which much of later grimoiric material is drawn, instructs 'the Master therefore ought to be purified with fasting, chastity, and abstinency from all luxury the space of three whole days before the day of the operation.'[21] One should bear in mind that *luxuria* does not simply refer to excess or otherwise treating yourself, but to *sin* specifically...

Consulting another of the cunning-folks' favourite texts—and one of the first to make available a range of grimoiric material in vulgate English to a broad and, yes, hungry audience—Reginald Scot's *Discovery of Witchcraft* points out nigromantic fasting also has specifically antinomian or at least inversional significances. Ungodly, even diabolic, foodways are included in a range of sacrilegious activities of the witches: 'not fasting on fridayes, and their fasting on sundays, their spitting at the time of elevation, their refusal of Holy-water, their despising of superstitious Crosses, &c. which are all good steps to true Christianity...'.[22] In typically rigorous detail Scot even describes a specific rite attached to such nigromantic fasting, once again included by our trusting author to warn sensible Christians against such practices, but most certainly acquired and studied by folk for the purposes of putting it to use. It is a rite that includes spitting, and also alludes to further suffumigation practices:

A Charm to be said each morning by a Witch fasting, or at least before she go abroad
> *The fire bites, the fire bites, the fire bites; Hogs-turd over it, Hogs-turd over it, Hogs-turd over it; The Father with thee, the Son with me, the Holy-ghost between us both to be: ter.*

Then spit over one shoulder, and then over the other, and then three times right forward.[23]

---

21 *Fourth Book* , p. 77.

22 Reginald Scot, *Discoverie of Witchcraft* (London, 1584: 1665), p. 33.

23 Scot, *Discoverie*, p. 138.

Deeper study into specifically necromantic diet—especially the occult philosophical and magically operative significance of hunger, deprivation, melancholy, and bitterness—must await further research. However, as a final brief note on necromantic foodways, it should be borne in mind that neither ritual purity nor self-consciously sacrilegious diabolism seem to be quite the meaning conveyed in our root definition and description of the Bloutian ways of necromancy. Both modalities are essential contexts for this work, clearly, but the necromancer does not seem to simply make themself pure by religiously-observant fasting nor satanically empowered by being at odds with usual Christian observances; rather, they simply make themself *hungry*. This implies to me far more about the work of the night at hand—and, centrally, a far more practical function for the incubation of dreams—rather than a whole period leading up to the operation.

Haunting Graves

One of the striking themes of Blout's description remains the sheer practicality of its notae-cum-instructions. If we were in any doubt about the down-to-(grave-)earth pragmatism of our working definition, the necromantic terroir of the graveside and the graveyard are heavily emphasised as the very lodgings of such work and such workers. For a start,

> those who are desirous to raise up any Souls of the dead, they ought to do it in those places, wherein these kinde of Souls are most known to be conversant; or for some alliance alluring those souls into their forsaken body; or for some kinde of affection in times past, impressed in them in their life, drawing the said Souls to certain places, things, or persons; or for the forcible nature of some place fitted and prepared for to purge or punish these souls. Which places for the most part are to be known by the experience of visions, nightly incursions, and apparitions, and such-like prodigies seen. Therefore the places most fitting for these things, are Church-yards. And better then them, are those places wherein there is the execution of criminal judgements. And better then these, are those places, in which of late yeers there have been some publick slaughters of men. Furthermore, that place is better then these, where some dead carkass, that came by violent death, is not yet expiated, nor ritely buried, and was lately buried; for the expiation of those places, is also a holy Rite duly to be adhibited to the burial of the bodies, and oftentimes prohibiteth the souls to come unto their bodies, and expelleth them far off unto the places of judgement.[24]

A range of options of relative strengths is presented. Churchyards are excellent, but better yet are execution sites which also *just so happen* to be sites commonly recommended for goetic operations involving other unclean spirits too. Literal murder scenes, especially before the appropriate holy rites chase away usefully turbulent shades, present especially

---

24 *Fourth Book*, p. 67.

potent—which is to say, dangerous—areas for necromancing. Potters' fields and other unconsecrated sites of burial also form uniquely volatile necromantic sites.

Of course, working in churchyards or graveyards more generally requires understanding and observation of particular protocols of action and etiquette. The land of the dead is not without its politics or economics, including taxation and the policing of such tithes and offerings. It behooves us as responsible workers to be aware of such authorities—both of mortals and of ruling spirits—and to comport ourselves either respectfully or invisibly, perhaps preferably both. If you do not know how to properly enter and exit a cemetery, churchyard, graveyard, or potter's field—and, crucially, if you do not know the differences between these places—you are almost certainly not ready to work in one. Be prepared.

Once appropriate protocols of respect, protection, and authorisation have been learned and employed, these various Saturnine boneyards offer a range of *materia* with which one can begin and continue to work with 'the graves' beyond the physical sites of such places of interment. These might include dirts, dusts, and powders compounded from harvested flora and fauna; pieces of funerary equipment, tools, and offerings; and of course the quotidian relics of the dead themselves, often jostled to the surface by burrowing beasts, ants, and weather. It can be amazing what one finds just lying about.

While detailed study of the formulae and rites of utilising such *materia* is again a little beyond this paper's intentions to merely outline our syllabus, I would like to include some brief discussion of two workings: the first, to heal and exorcise, an incredibly useful practice for the working necromancer; and the second to derive incredibly practical (not to mention lucrative) information from a skull. The first is an operation performed under the explicit auspices of Saint Cyprian, found in a 'Cyprianus' of the Swedish Black Art Books tradition, as analysed by the late Dr. Thomas K. Johnson. It involves a long, long prayer of exorcism and healing to be incanted while giving the patient a very particularly prepared bath:

> …then he should go, or another in his stead, to a church yard and ask for permission to take three bones and put them towards the fire, until they become warm, and then throw them into the water and put the bones in the same place, that you took them from, and wash the sick one in the water and recite [the exhortation of Cyprian] then with God's help it will get better.[25]

There are many notable aspects of this 'churchyard bone soup for the soul'. One of the things I find particularly significant about this rite is that occult virtue is imbued *into* the cleansing bath, rather than simply transferring the sickness or malady into the bones or the grave to be taken away as they are re-buried. Instead:

> In terms of protocol, permissions are sought and blessings received from the dead of the churchyard to perform the healing. In terms of operation,

25 MS 13 NM 41.652; cited in Thomas K. Johnson, *Svartkonstböcker: A Compendium of Swedish Black Art Book Tradition* (Revelore Press, 2019), p. 399.

the bones are heated and their virtue is transferred to the water itself. It is a transference *from* the dead of sacred ground not *to* them.[26]

Another bone-borrowing working included in Dr. Johnson's *Svartkonstböcker* collection highlights nuanced aspects of the 'permissions' sought. In a relatively straightforward operation 'to win at the lottery', one is instructed to 'go to the churchyard and borrow a human skull'. The borrowing is addressed initially to the owner of the skull—'*that I may borrow your head for three nights,*' along with promising '*I shall bring back at the same time and place.*' But along with seeking permission comes commandment: '*And I order you my brother or sister in Christendom, that upon the third night to come and tell me what numbers will come up in the Royal Number Lottery (such and such a date, such and such a position).*' So a polite albeit bold request is swiftly followed by imperative demand that the spirit of this person deliver particular information. The means of this delivery look distinctly pertinent to dream incubation:

> Then, take the skull and put it under the head piece of your bed and the third night the dead one will come and will want his or her head back. Then you say to the corpse: *Tell me first the numbers that I order you, then you shall have your head brought back.* Then he will say all five numbers, and then you have to have a piece of board on top of the blanket and a piece of chalk, and as quickly as the corpse says the numbers then write them up. But no light can be lit, and then the dead one will leave, and after that you take back the head to its place again.[27]

Even though the ghost has been 'asked' if you can borrow their head, it certainly doesn't sound like they have consented. At the very least, they seem to be experiencing a palpable lender's remorse. While neither of these Swedish workings explicitly name a more senior authority of the churchyard to whom one might be asking for license to work our black arts, what I think is important to bear in mind in 'lodging among graves' more generally is that permission to work in or from a churchyard or place of graves is not limited to speaking with the individual spirits whose bones you may wish to employ. The Lord and Lady of the cemetery—along with their relevant ministers—should definitely be saluted, honoured, and propitiated to allow the work to happen.

DREAM INCUBATION

Speaking of retiring to bed with a skull under your own naturally leads us to consider the role of dreaming in our necromancy. The *Fourth Book* begins by pointing out that dreaming is itself a natural phenomenon, that can be attended and modified to

26 Alexander Cummins, 'The Black Art Books of Cyprian, Pt. II: A Svartkonstbok Exhortation', http://www.alexandercummins.com/blog/blackartbooks2, last accessed 26/12/19.

27 MS 6 KU 11120 Svartkonstbok Slimminge Socken, Vemmenhögs Härad, Skåne, 1853; cited in Johnson, *Svartkonstböcker*, p. 292.

our purposes depending upon humoural regulations and catalysts—for 'natural things, and their commixtures, do also belong unto us, and are conducing to receive Oracles from any spirit by a dream: which are either Perfumes, Unctions, and Meats or Drinks'.[28] While our Bloutian description specifies *burning* incense, it seems remiss not to point out that perfuming the air remains of central import. Moreover, diet—as perhaps the best known and most discussed 'non-natural principle' of humoural regulation, along of course with *sleep*—here is highlighted as absolutely essential. We may stir our dreaming receptivity through our choices of food and drink, or indeed, lack thereof.

As already discussed, making oneself hungry has been foregrounded as an operatively important necromantic practice. Hunger brings forth its own *melancholia*, and the black bilious humour is especially attractive to unclean spirits. We shall arise to stalk further the applications of melancholy below.

For now let us also consider what magical work we might do to shepherd the dream-flocks of our counted sheep and indeed to pull the wool of the wake-world from our eyes. The *Fourth Book* continues:

> But he that is willing always and readily to receive the Oracles of a Dream, let him make unto himself a Ring of the Sun or of Saturn for this purpose. There is also an Image to be made, of excellent efficacie and power to work this effect; which being put under his head when he goeth to sleep, doth effectually give true dreams of what thing soever the minde hath before determined or consulted on. The Tables of Numbers do likewise confer to receive an Oracle, being duly formed under their own Constellations.[29]

Once more, the place of objects for directing or improving dream-work is firmly secured beneath the sleeping head of the dreamer. Once more, 'images' are of central importance. Moreover, planetary magic is explicitly employed: and, far from the typical modern associations of the Moon ruling over dream, the dying-and-reborn Sun and melancholic Saturn are both specified as especially efficacious for this endeavour. I cannot help but consider the illuminating sight that sovereign Sol bestows, and the retentive virtues of imprisoning Saturn, as both incredibly useful for perceiving and remembering the oracles of dream. Not to mention these two planets' own relations to katabasis and the ways of the dead.

---

28 *Fourth Book*, p. 60.

29 *Fourth Book*, p. 60.

Nor are such appeals to planetary virtues through the 'Tables of Numbers' especially unusual or exotic in the context of early modern European magic. Number squares or *kamea* are employed in a variety of works, from 'high ceremonial' altar-work, to talismans carried on one's person, to burial under disliked pubs as curse tablets.[30] Nor should their specific mention in a passage concerning the use of planetary images be considered in any way 'tagged on'. We are perhaps more familiar with astrological image magic demonstrating and utilising a heraldry of associated mythological persons, poses, flora and fauna: say, of an image of Venus as 'a little maide with her hair spread abroad, cloathed in long and white garments, holding a Laurell[,] Apple, or flowers in her right hand, in her left a Combe'.[31] But number squares too are—in at least an idealist sense— also representational, also images of sorts. As Agrippa himself analyses, 'tables of the planets, endowed with many, and very *great virtues* of the heavens, in as much as they *represent that divine order* of celestial numbers, impressed upon celestials by the Ideas of the Divine Mind, by means of the Soul of the World, and the *sweet harmony* of those *celestial rays*, signifying according to the proportion of *effigies*, supercelestial intelligencies'.[32] As I have argued, kamea operate on a different but interrelated level of representational complexity from typical images of the planets, and 'both directly represented and abstractly signified celestial forces; forces which could be utilised for concrete sublunary ends... as precise mathematical models of the parts of the cosmos...'.[33] A model is an image, after all; and the modelled may be managed and manipulated, magically.

Planetary tables of numbers are also not the only means of planetary dream magic. The document called Wellcome MS 4669 includes a concise grimoire of just such planetary dream incubation. Its preparatory work specifies actions that should by now be beginning to look very familiar to us. The operator is instructed to 'fast during that day and only to eat at the permitted hour...'.[34] Categorically, we have confirmation that fasting or making oneself hungry for dream-work can be a matter of simply observing restrictions on consumption for the day of working only. 'Permitted hours' brings to mind—amongst other timing concerns—planetary hours, and further highlights cultivation of astrological virtue in dietary humoural regulation for magical workings. The operation is to be conducted at night and alone. Indeed, in keeping with the solitary nature of working expressed in our root description, the dreamer 'will enter alone into his chamber, which must be kept very clean, and into which, no person may

---

30 W. Paley Baildon, 'Sixteenth Century Leaden Charm (obverse and reverse) found at Lincoln's Inn', *Proceedings of the Society of Antiquarians of* London, Second Series, 18, (1901), p. 146, *passim*.

31 Agrippa, *Three Books*, p. 387.

32 Agrippa, *Three Books*, p. 318. Emphasis added.

33 Alexander Cummins, 'Textual Evidence for the Material History of Amulets in Seventeenth-Century England', in Ronald Hutton (ed.), *Physical Evidence for Ritual Acts, Sorcery and Witchcraft in Christian Britain: A Feeling for Magic* (Palgrave Macmillan, 2015), p. 176.

34 *A Collection of Magical Secrets Taken from Peter de Abano, Cornelius Agrippa and from other Famous Occult Philosophers*, ed. by David Rankine, Paul Harry Barron & Stephen Skinner (Avalonia, 2009), p. 123.

enter during that day.'[35] Suffumigations are once more essential, and the dream-worker 'should have a censer in his hand' and 'cense the whole room and the other rooms'.[36] The operator then undresses and kneels before an *image*—in this case, 'an image of God'—with a blessed candle in their right hand, and recites prayers; that is, of course, 'certain words'. Moreover, one should have framed and executed a talismanic sigil:

> ...have the Sign of the Living God all ready and prepared, drawn on blessed paper, written with new and blessed ink and with a blessed feather pen from a Dove.... After this, you should place the Sign of the Angel of the Day, as you can see below, and under the last Sign, you should write the item you wish to have.... When you have done this, you should get up off your knees, holding the Signs we have mentioned in your hand and you should extinguish the candle and then place the Signs under your bed head and go to sleep quietly.... When you are in your bed, you should devoutly recite your usual everyday prayers and at the end, you should add the prayer of the Angel of the Day, as you will see in due course and it is important for you to have learned it by heart, while always making sure that you have chosen the days ruled by the Angel, whose mission corresponds to our request.[37]

An extinguished candle cannot hold back the spirits that come in the night, nor would we want it to do so. The operative place of dreaming sigils as with talismanic rings or borrowed skulls is under one's bed head. A particular prayer to the planetary angel of that day is intoned. Finally, the importance of specifying the appropriate planetary virtues and spirits is confirmed. Any of these planetary *angeloi* may be of help—our 'mission' is not simply 'to have a magic dream', but to divine specific information and understandings to be transmitted, aptly suited to the potencies and powers of the principalities so invoked.

A necromantic tool of dream incubation (which I encountered while collecting my own *notae* of practice) further emphasises the role and utility of magical rings. Perusing the Colmer Treasure collection housed at the Met Cloisters in the Bronx, I came across a beautiful onyx ring with this appended explanatory context:

> A lapidary in Hebrew from about 1290, drawing on Marbodius of Rennes' widely circulated 'On Stones' (*De lapidus…*), asserts that wearing an onyx ring can affect dreams: "And if he who wears it on his finger or hung around his neck wants to talk to his dead friend at night, he talks to him in his sleep; and in the morning he remembers what the dead needs."…[38]

---

35 *Magical Secrets*, p. 124.

36 Ibid.

37 *Magical Secrets*, p. 125.

38 Entry on onyx ring, from the Colmer Treasure (second half 13th–early 14th century; gold, onyx; on loan from Musée de Cluny—Musée National du Moyen Âge, Paris).

This particular ring, along with bearing an onyx stone, was inscribed 'AVDI, VIDI': 'I hear, I see'. It is especially significant to me that the lapidary cited specifies it for communing with the shade of a deceased *friend*. Moreover, the ring does not simply call the spirit; it specifically improves recall of the encounter with said spirit, and particularly the dream recall of details concerning what the dead need. This is not simply a tool for marshalling, binding, and forcing work from ghosts. It is an intimate tool for bridging the veil and ensuring our beloved friends who have passed have what they *need*...

GATES OF HORN AND IVORY

It is hardly a stretch or hard sell to emphasise dream-work in magic, even in necromantic magic. Yet if we are to take such oracles seriously as an integral part of our practice—as many of us do—it also behooves us to have a means of confirming what we dream and, crucially, whether our interpretation of such a dream is accurate, and if our proceeding actions are effective. It has been a point of considerable weight since antiquity that not all dreams are of import, and moreover not all apparently significant dreams are even to be believed. We should bear in mind the words of patient and no-less-crafty Penelope:

> Stranger, dreams verily are baffling and unclear of meaning, and in no wise do they find fulfillment in all things for men. For two are the gates of shadowy dreams, and one is fashioned of *horn* and one of *ivory*. Those dreams that pass through the gate of sawn *ivory deceive* men, bringing words that find no *fulfillment*. But those that come forth through the gate of polished *horn bring* true issues *to pass*, when any mortal sees them.[39]

And so—beyond the talismanic employment of such *materia magica* of course—how might we distinguish those dreams that come to us from gates of horn from those of ivory? The grimoires and handbooks utilised by early modern cunning-folk offer us a simple solution: geomancy.[40] Many early modern geomantic manuals consider that one can confirm the validity—that is, veracity or falsity—of the messages received in dream. In terms of specific technique, a shield chart is cast to query *Iter*, The Ninth House. The figure that is found there will reveal the bona fides of the dream. Those figures considered *stable*, that is, those that can be read as 'downward pointing', such as Acquisitio and Caput Draconis, are firmly on Team Horn. Those 'upward pointing' *mobile* figures, such

---

39 Penelope, in *Odyssey*, Bk. 19, l. 560–569. Here, of course, two plays on words are being employed: the 'ivory' (ἐλέφας) is used to invoke 'deceive' (ἐλεφαίρομαι), and 'horn' (κέρας) to invoke 'fulfillment' (κραίνω).

40 Butler, 'Magic, Astrology', p. 333. For more on the use of geomancy by cunning-folk, see Jim Baker, *The Cunning-Man's Handbook: The Practice of English Folk Magic 1550-1900* (Avalonia, 2013), p. 161-195.

as Puer and Cauda Draconis, are Team Ivory.[41] Modern geomancer John Michael Greer further suggests that 'if a stable figure in the ninth house passes to another house, this points toward the aspect of the querent's life to which the dream relates.'[42] If one is searching for a dream concerning a magical operation one is attempting, or indeed if one is trying to ensure that one's impression of an oneiric encounter with the dead is accurate, the other house is going to be *Mors*, the Eighth House: both House of the Dead and of the Nigromancy Which You Do.

John Heydon, whose geomancy handbook was owned by seventeenth-century cunning-folk on both sides of the Atlantic, also details a further employment of geomancy in dream analysis. Not only can a geomantic shield tell you if a recalled dream is 'true', it can also assist 'if a man hath dreamed a Dream, and he hath forgot what it is'.[43] That is, it can inform the reconstruction of a dream otherwise lost to waking in the blinking bleary light of tomorrow-come-today! Such a technique should be of paramount interest and import to anyone hoping to improve their dream-work.

As a final brief note on the efficacy of geomancy in confirming dream, we should bear in mind that such an approach weaves together several modalities of work. At its core, of course, it is a non-computational divinatory engagement with Spirit in the dreaming itself, in the dance of Dream at turns both mellifluous and turbulent, blossoming and soul-revealing, diagnostic, and (to return to our point, at least potentially) oracular. But this trance journey is merely the opening and consecrating of the Gate of Horn: we rely on the agency of particular spirits to reveal information through that engagement. Furthermore, in employing geomancy for confirmation and further analyses we wield a reliable computational means of verification to ensure accuracy of recall and interpretation, as well as of the spirits' messages themselves, and indeed the soundness of remedial or other proceeding activity. The pragmatic reasons for setting a shield or other concretely sortilegious methods for confirming a dream should be obvious to anyone who has professionally divined for strangers. Dream is intimately personal, and some folks are occasionally very unwilling to detach themselves from their tight grip on a bad take. The fall of dice or cards or sticks or coins or shells or bones should give a definitive answer, void of personal feelings one way or the other.

It is utterly crucial that spirit-work not descend into unchecked nebulous feeling or unexamined externalisation of egoic impulses. That you dreamed of being made powerful might be a testimony of your own ambitions and/or perceived inferiorities, or it might be a sign you have indeed been chosen. We owe it to ourselves, and certainly our clients, to check. Our spirits and the works we do with them are too valuable for us not to make best informed endeavour to *swear together* accurately and keen-sighted.

---

41 See John Heydon, *Theomagia, or the Temple of Wisdom* (London, 1664), Book II, Chapter IX, 'Of the ninth House': on Acquisitio, 'his dreams will generally prove true', p. 66; on Caput Draconis, 'his Dreams, Revelations, and Visions (to speak like an Enthusiast) will for the most part prove true and certain', p. 67; on Puer, 'his dream will be frivolous and false', p. 66; on Cauda Draconis, 'his dreams will be idle and deceitful', p. 69.

42 John Michael Greer, *Art and Practice of Geomancy: Divination, Magic, and Earth Wisdom of the Renaissance* (Weiser, 2009), p. 164.

43 Heydon, *Theomagia*, III, p. 107.

To conclude this brief foray into the techniques and tools of dream incubation that should form valuable content in our black school curriculum, we can examine an example of useful magical information derived from dream. The endeavours of Humphrey Gilbert and John Davies that form the content of the *Excellent Booke of the Arte of Magicke* and its attendant scrying record of their *Visions*, conducted over the course 1567, begin with an initiating prayer that was delivered in dream, 'revealed by King Solomon, Anno Domini 1567, on the 20 February circa 9–10 AM':

O God of Angels, God of Archangels, God of Patriarchs, God of Prophets, God of us sinners; O Lord be my help, that this my work may proceed in good time, to thy glory O God; and to learning, and not anything else, that I would this day have. O my God be in my tongue, that I may glorify thee in all works. Amen.'

Let no evil spirit enter my mind O God, not anything else but all to thy glory O God; for learning is all my desire, Lord thou knowest even as it was to thy servant Solomon. O Lord send me some of his good hidden work, that has not been revealed to any man. then for that cause I desire thee O God to send it to me, that in these our last days it may be known. Amen Amen, Lord, Amen.[44]

The goals of this entreaty are clearly laid out: bring us the knowledge of exactly how to perform magic, and let us not be fooled by evil spirits. The twofold intent here implies an understanding of how such information will be come by: by transmission from spirits. The repeated appeal that one's endeavours be holy and sanctified by God is a further bulwark against deception or impious conduct. The magic is likewise doubly 'Solomonic': it is asked that God reveal (and/or license spirits to bring) the as-yet-unknown 'good hidden works' of Solomon; and indeed the means of making this request, the very terms of the prayer before us, are said to have been already delivered by the shade of King Solomon himself! This is magic conducted not only in a form that might imply a mythological lineage, 'Solomonic' meaning merely a particular style of magic, but literally under the express tutelage of this dead grimoire magician and king. If such immediate tutelary transmission—and, indeed, transmitted authority[45]—were not enough, this dream also seems to have included a set of simple but mysterious sigils recorded by the dreamer, which in later scrying experiments formed an integral part of receiving further good hidden works....[46] Such are but one set of possibilities of necromantic dream incubation.

---

44 Additional MS 36674, f. 47r.

45 The divesting of Solomon's actual authority is specified later in the text explicitly when it is noted that 'Salomon said that H. G: & Jo. should rule' the spirits that arrive to lend advice and with which they will work magic (Additional MS 36674, f. 59r).

46 For more on this, see *An Excellent Booke of the Arte of Magicke*, ed. by Phil Legard & Alexander Cummins (Scarlet Imprint, 2020).

CLOATHES FOR THAT PURPOSE

It will perhaps not surprise grimoire magicians that special garments are singled out by Blout as an operatively functional component of a necromancer's practice. Most pre-modern European handbooks of spirit conjuration specifically require one to don priestly vestments. To again take our lead from the *Heptameron*, there is talk of 'a Vesture' and being 'clothed with pure garments' which must be 'rightly and duly consecrated and prepared'.[47] More specifically, 'let it be a Priests Garment, if it can be: but if it cannot be had, let it be of linen, and clean.'[48] Already there are options: ideally, the robes of a priest, but at the very least a particular material and a state of cleanliness are required. Other examples of clerical garb abound in various grimoires and accounts of such operations: the astrologer William Lilly—one of the most famous astrologers of seventeenth-century England in fact—speaks of his master John Evans summoning an angel of Mars wearing his surplice (a linen vestment typically worn over a cassock by clergy and choristers) for instance:

> Evans applies himself to the invocation of the angel Salmon, of the nature of Mars, reads his Litany in the *Common-Prayer-Book* every day, at select hours, wears his surplice, lives orderly all that time; at the fortnight's end Salmon appeared...[49]

If such a reasoning were not clear enough, wearing priestly attire is at least in part about ritual purity—indeed, part of living in an 'orderly' manner, as Lilly puts it, before a ritual or conjuration as well as during such work. There is rarely in my experience any significant gloss that purports such hieratic raiment is about disguise or pretending to actually be a priest. Spirits worth working with are not that stupid.

We have another, very different, set of rather specific instructions for proper ritual attire from the *Excellent Booke of the Arte of Magicke*. Not only are these instructions given for working with the shades of the dead, the specifications are given *by* dead magicians. Some echo familiar themes, as when Adam—First Man, First Father, and First Magician—advises to 'goe cleane in apparell'.[50] Just because our spirits may be unclean, does not mean we should. Others are more specific, less priestly, and far more colour-coded to operations of the Black Art: as when the shade of Roger Bacon instructs 'Jo[hn]. yor skryer, especially in ap[pare]l & cloke of black clothe continually; & your selfe [i.e. H.G.] also except when you ride.' Moreover, such reliance on black garb is mirrored by Gilbert and Davies's early scrying experiments which offer them a vision on February 24th 1567 of '[HG] being apparelled in a black robe, & cape cloak, with a payer of black silk netherstocks gartered with black, gathered close above the knee;

---

47 *Fourth Book*, p. 77.

48 *Fourth Book*, p. 75.

49 Lilly, *History*, p. 57.

50 Additional MS 36674, f. 60r.

having a velvet cap, & a black feather.'[51] As I have remarked before, 'necromancers' sartorial proclivities are not merely stylish: they may be to some degree necessary for their operations.'[52]

I have in fact spoken at length about the importance of black clothes in works of Saturnine magics in an anthology on astrological magic.[53] To summarise: in most astrological correspondences, 'dyers of black cloth' are Saturnine, and the *Picatrix* specifies 'the black cloak of a doctor' to be operatively useful apparel for operations of the Greater Malefic who rules time, death, the grave, and the wraithly spirits of such.[54] Connections with doctoring bring us to Ficino's consideration of scholarship as an inherently melancholic endeavour,[55] and here we may stake further the importance of weaponising *melancholia* in goetic practice. In short, melancholy 'doth induce, also to entice evil spirits... so great also they say the power of melancholy is of, that by its force, Celestiall spirits also are sometimes drawn'.[56] Wearing black imbues us with the virtues (and vices) of the black bilious humour, which absolutely include attracting spirits to us via the 'gravity of the grave'.[57] Black clothes are not the only wardrobe options for cohering and deploying melancholic virtues however. One might well bear in mind that 'a cloth that was about a dead corpse hath received from thence the property of sadness, and melancholy'.[58] To be clear, this is not a result of the clothing of the departed being necessarily haunted by the ghost of the deceased. Rather, such grave melancholic properties are soaked into the fabric by sheer proximity to the remains of

51 Additional MS 36674, f. 59r.

52 Legard and Cummins, *An Excellent Booke of the Arte of Magicke*, p. 196.

53 Alexander Cummins, 'The Azured Vault: Astrological Magic in Seventeenth-century England', in *The Celestial Art,* ed. Austin Coppock and Daniel Schulke (Three Hands Press, 2018), p. 221–222.

54 William Lilly, *Christian Astrology* (London, 1647), p. 59; *Picatrix*, ed. John Michael Greer & Christopher Warnock (Adocentyn Press, 2010), III.7, p. 159.

55 Marsilio Ficino, *Three Books on Life*, trans. Carol Kaske & John R. Clark (Tempe, 1998), I.II–X:111–137.

56 Agrippa, *Three Books*, p. 133.

57 Cummins, 'Azured Vault', p. 222.

58 Agrippa, *Three Books*, p. 50.

someone who has died; or perhaps more succinctly, by proximity to death itself. Death has a weight all its own, a contagion of necromantic virtue and application. An act — especially a violent one—has a ghost of its own.

CERTAIN WORDS

Blout's apparent coyness about the necromancer's use of 'certain words' is especially interesting coming from a lexicographer. As we have already identified, the use of divine names was common currency even for works of black magic, although diabolic names and appeals to infernal hierarchies and their superiors are obviously also potent. Conjurations contain *historiolae*—appeals to mythic precedent in ritual action—as well as *voces magicae*, the passwords, natural Adamic languages, and word-spirits of the naturally magical cosmos. As we have seen, workers have derived their words direct from spiritual sources by dream, scrying, or personal conversation with spirits. Such words are empowered by breath, the vehemence and prosody of speech, the affectivity and ritual myth-weaving of poetry spoken in the cadences and meters of kairotic time.

But overwhelmingly, one way or another, early modern nigromancy relied on 'books of darkness'. Agrippa fleshes out this tenebrous sobriquet for the corpus of a nigromantic library with an extensive bibliographic litany of authors alleged to have written such black books.[59] Injunctions to the Four Regents of the cardinal directions frequently included commands to deliver magical books—and crucially *the understanding* of such books!—as well as consecrate tomes to be more magically effective.[60] Books of the offices of spirits form a central component of early modern goetic conjuration. Possession and utilisation of books of calls was itself necessary for various other endeavours of conjuration, the *Excellent Booke* insisting somewhat openly that 'the master must also have one or two good books to call by'.[61] There are a wealth of bibliographic options arrayed before the prospective necromancer for fulfilment of these criteria of our syllabus of study. Good divination as always should be a guide to the efficacy of the texts and their deployment.

However, if we read Blout's description of 'certain words' as not only *particular* words, but *words delivered with certainty*, we may well find ourselves reminded of the Instructions of Cyprian, patron of grimoire magicians and nigromancers. These 'Instructions of Cyprian' are laid out in Sloane MS 3851, and were published by David Rankine, in recognition of the seventeenth-century cunning-man who compiled this working-book, as *The Grimoire of Arthur Gauntlet*. They run as follows:

---

59 '…Zabulus, who was given to unlawful Arts, then Barnabas a certain Cyprian… Adam, Abel, Enoch, Abraham, and Solomon, also Paul, Honorius, Cyprianus, Albertus, Thomas, Hierome, and of a certain man of York, whose toys Alphonsus King of Castile, Robert an Englishman, Bacon, Apponius… Raziel, and Raphael the angels of Adam and Tobias.' (Agrippa, *Three Books*, p. 695).

60 For instance, Folger Vb26, f. 73–74; cited in *The Book of Oberon*, ed. Daniel Harms, James R. Clark, & Joseph H. Peterson (Llewellyn, 2015), p. 192–195.

61 Additional MS 36674, f. 47v.

1. The Master must have a firm faith And doubt not in his work for he that Doubteth to obtain his petition Prayeth with his Mouth Not with his heart
2. He must be secret And betray not the secrets of his Art but to his fellows and to them of his counsel
3. He must be strong minded severe and not fearful.
4. He must be clean in conscience Penitent for his sins never willing to return to them again so far forth as God shall give him grace.
5. He must know the reigning of the Planets And the times meet to work.
6. He must lack none of his Instruments He must speak all things plainly and distinctly He must make his Circle in a clean Air and One time.[62]

All of these six instructions are worthy of extended meditation and consideration. But most immediately pertinent to our reading of the importance of certainty as an operative element of prosodic necromantic conduct are the 'firm faith' and absence of doubt—not only in God but in oneself—as well as the importance of being 'strong minded' and even 'severe'. The injunction to be not fearful is equally not simply conjuror's machismo, but rather seems a further acknowledgement that the karcist must have control of their own racing passions within their area of influence as much as they do the forces without. Given the porous nature of early modern passions, and especially the literally contagious affectivity of nightmares and fearful imaginings, mastering one's fears is not only about steadying a shaking hand that holds the hazel wand; it is always wise not to feed the trolling energies and entities that accompany those spirits stirred by such black arts.

SUFFUMIGATIONS

Throughout this article, we have discussed the *whys* of suffumigations: stirring the air as a medium of Spirit; spicing and cooling the gyring of ghosts; lacing ourselves, our shady working companions, and the work itself with air-borne contagions of affect and direction; and all manner of manipulations of the vicissitudes of the winds of life and death. In considering how both scent and speech are carried upon the airs, and 'the truly vivifying link between incense and incantation is, of course, the breath',[63] we must acknowledge that fumigation also empowers the magician, for 'suffumigations also, or perfumings, that are proper to the stars, are of great force for the opportune receiving of celestial gifts under the rays of the stars, in as much as they do strongly work upon the Air, and breath', meaning the operator, being 'affected with the qualities of inferiors, or celestials… quickly penetrating our breast, and vitals, doth wonderfully reduce us to the like qualities.'[64] But we have scarcely specified the actual *whats* of suffumigation. To rectify this, I have assembled three types of options.

---

62 Sloane MS 3851, f. 1–2; cited in *Grimoire of Arthur Gauntlet: A 17th century London Cunning-man's book of charms, conjurations and prayers*, ed. David Rankine (Avalonia, 2011), p. 39–40.

63 Cummins, 'Azured Vault', p. 209.

64 Agrippa, *Three Books*, p. 129.

The first approach is the most explicitly necromantic, and comes to us from the *Fourth Book* once again: 'in the raising up of these shadows, we are to perfume with new Blood, with the Bones of the dead, and with Flesh, Egges, Milk, Honey and Oil, and such-like things, which do attribute to the Souls a meanes apt to receive their Bodies.'[65] The one 'harmonicall' blood that unites and enlivens all humanity is once more applied, as are the relics of the dead in a further unification of sciomantic and true-necromantic application. The other ingredients have great weight and depths of occult virtue to them: milk and eggs both express explicitly life-giving properties, of course; honey and oil share qualities of incorruptibility as well as combination and co-mingling. I thoroughly recommend the application of further study towards these mysteries of *materia* before experimenting.

The second approach is based in wider dream incubation practices beyond those occurring among the graves of the departed. For the planetary dream-work of MS Wellcome 4669, we are recommended to burn 'white [frank]incense, some mastic, some wood of aloes and others scents'.[66] Such a recipe bears a striking resemblance to the circle-consecrating incense of the *Grimorium Verum*.[67] This resemblance itself recalls historian Sophie Page's observation concerning the endeavours of ritual magic to bring spirits down to earth and/or bring operators across to the world(s) of spirits; or, as I would rather, to consecrate and quicken liminal *momenta* where both can occur. Both a magic circle and a ritual of dream incubation are a 'connecting bridge' across this cosmological gap between practitioner and spirits; as Page remarks, 'as a special space into which spirits could descend, it was *the spirit's equivalent to human dreaming*, a fragile and ambiguous context for communication that was not firmly attached to Heaven or Earth.'[68] Returning us to oneiromancy from a different but equally important facet of the necromancy at hand, this equivalence itself is well worthy of considerable further analysis and investigation.

The broadest approach to fumigation might be that offered by the *Excellent Booke*, which notes merely that one should have stock of and employ 'great plenty of sweet powders, and perfumes.'[69] No particularities are described, beyond having a plurality at one's disposal. Many different entities appear in the workings of the *Excellent Booke*—

---

65 *Fourth Book*, p. 67.

66 *Magical Secrets*, p. 124.

67 The *Grimorium Verum* instructs 'when you have made your circle, and before entering inside, it is necessary to fumigate it with musk amber, lignum aloes, and frankincense.' (Joseph H. Peterson, ed. & trans., *Grimorium Verum: A Handbook of Black Magic*, CreateSpace Independent Publishing Platform, 2007, p. 37).

68 Sophie Page, 'Speaking with Spirits in Medieval Magic Texts', in *Conversations with Angels: Essays Towards a History of Spiritual Communication, 1100-1700*, ed. by Joan Raymond (Palgrave Macmillan: New York, 2011), p. 130. Emphasis added. Page goes on to point out the use of *materia* and incantation are also part of this goal of conjunction: 'Many magic texts, especially those deriving from the Arabic tradition, worked on the basis of constructing such strong correspondences between Heaven and Earth at a particular moment that all the elements of the operation—star, herb, stone, spirit, word, character and intention—united in a congruence that surpassed the metaphysical separation of the conversing beings.' (Ibid.).

69 Additional MS 36674, f. 47r.

from the ghosts of Evangelists and dead magicians to popular angels of the European grimoire traditions; from the senior demonic regents of the cardinal directions to the shades of Biblical persons such as Job; and from the very Lord of the Dead and keeper of the dry bones to a shifting, living host of elemental, terrestrial, and aerial spirits. The breadth and sheer lack of specificity detailed in this adumbration of 'sweet powders and perfumes' might well be seen to facilitate this openness to myriad types of spirits.

Yet even in this broadest of criteria we have two pertinent details. There must be 'great plenty' of such incensing. We should not skimp. Abundant smoke must whorl and drift and galvanise. Secondly, the sweetnesses of such fumigations should once more remind us that we seek the most helpful and efficacious working strategies, for even in nigromantic operations, 'Good Spirits are delighted and allured by sweet Perfumes, as rich Gums, Frankincense, &c. Salt, &c. which was the reason that the Priests of the Gentiles, and also the Christians used them in their Temples, and Sacrifices: And on the contrary, Evil Spirits are pleased and allured and called up by Suffumigations of Henbane, &c. stinking Smells, &c. which the Witches do use in their Conjuration.'[70] Even—or perhaps more aptly, *especially*—when stirring the tempestuous spirits of the graves, the use of sweet 'savours' seems to be favoured.

Lest the lack of individually named ingredients in this last approach suggest a lack of importance in suffumigations, I feel it would be remiss to not include this cautionary tale from William Lilly on the dangers of skipping such a crucial step in one's spirit-work. He recounts a tale of his magical teacher Evans, who

> ...was desired by the Lord Bothwell and Sir Kenelm Digby to show them a spirit. He promised so to do: the time came, and they were all in the body of the circle, when lo, upon a sudden, after some time of invocation, Evans was taken from out the room, and carried into the field near Battersea Causeway, close to the Thames. Next morning a countryman going by to his labour, and espying a man in black cloaths, came unto him and awaked him, and asked him how he came there? Evans by this understood his condition, enquired where he was, how far from London, and in what parish he was; which when he understood, he told the labourer he had been late at Battersea the night before, and by chance was left there by his friends. Sir Kenelm Digby and the Lord Bothwell went home without any harm.... I enquired upon what account the spirit carried him away: who said, he had not, at the time of invocation, made any suffumigation, at which the spirits were vexed.[71]

For those still unconvinced of the importance of incensing, or complaining of its impracticality in the high winds and low darks of a midnight graveyard, consider yourself warned.

And for those *still* looking for a specific necromantic formulary, I direct your attention to the *Compendium magiae innaturalis nigrae* (c. 1533). Stephen Gordon describes

---

70 John Aubrey, *Miscellanies* (London, 1696), p. 136–7.

71 William Lilly, *History of his Life and Time, from the year 1602 to 1681* (London, 1715), p. 58.

this 'pamphlet, as a distilled reinvention' of a necromantic experiment attributed to Michael Scot, the thirteenth-century translator and alleged nigromancer, which moreover 'reflects a type of streamlined commercial grimoire that flourished among the lay populaces of early modern Europe.'[72] Amongst its instructions,

> the longer *Compendium* texts all contain references to a suffumigation of *semen papaveris nigri, herbam cicutam, coriandrum, apium,* [*et*] *crocum* (black poppy seed, hemlock, coriander, celery, and saffron). The author of the urtext must surely have consulted Agrippa in the formulation of his own experiment. Not only did he choose the correct herbs to make spirits appear (what Agrippa terms *herbas spirituum*), but even the phrase "of each a like quantity" (*aequis ponderibus*) is repeated in the unabridged *Compendium* manuscripts (e.g. Rylands 105: *et hec in aequali pondere*).[73]

Interestingly, some copies of the *Compendium* streamlined further, insisting only upon 'a suffumigation comprising celery seeds, black cumin, and saffron.' As Gordon notes, 'as a "quick-fix" conjuration devoid of the type of ritual extravagance expected by the scholarly elites, the ingredients were certainly less exotic (and much less potent) than the poppy seeds and hemlock used in the longer texts.'[74] I foreground this work and this formula as it seems one particularly open to adjustments. May your experiments be as informed and airy as they may.

Why Necromancy

Having assessed our *whats* and our *hows* for these notes towards a necromantic syllabus, I would like to leave you with a last consideration of *why*. Why necromancy?

> And Salomon said that H. G: & Jo. should rule him; and also Job said to Jo.'s hearing: "Trust no spirit visible or invisible, *but the spirit of dead men. For they love man more then the others do*."[75]

The surface meaning is plain and excellent advice: spirits are not all to be trusted. Demonology is built on tales of not only the arrogance but the *gullibility* of conjurors. Don't be a mark about this. But I suggest this message can be read as more than simply paranoia about the agendas and motivations of spirits. I believe it can remind us of an important lesson. Necromancy does not have to be about the external trappings of spooky persona, shadowy vestments, or the grandiosely impenetrable gobbledygook characteristic of style-over-substance Darque Fluff peddlers schilling spelling mistakes

---

72 Stephen Gordon, 'Necromancy for the Masses? A Printed Version of the *Compendium magiae innaturalis nigrae*', *Magic, Ritual, and Witchcraft* 13, 3 (Winter, 2018), p. 340.

73 Gordon, p. 353

74 Gordon, p. 350; citing Owen Davies, *Grimoires*, p. 54.

75 Additional MS 36674, f. 59r. Emphasis added.

bound in bat scrotum. Having just stated that, it should also certainly not be about high-horsing or otherwise scoring points over strangers on the internet. It does not have to be fundamentally about bitterness, though perhaps bitterness can on the right nights still be bridled by tightly held reins to good endeavour. And, as Maria Bamford characteristically bleak-cheerfully entreats: 'if you stay alive for no reason at all, please do it for spite.'

What the advice from Job's shade suggests is that necromancy at least has been—and I maintain *is* in part still—about Love: Empedoclean cosmic *sympathia*. It is this Love that can teach soul-rending lessons of melancholy and sanguinity alike. It is this Love that can transcend the boundaries of life and death, time and space, dream and reality. It is Love that can stir the humourally oceanic feeling of that kairotic sensation of eternity. It is Love that can teach both boundaries and their dissolution in the grand co-mingling of the Great Ocean of the Dead.

And it is love—for our work, for our spirits, for our kin, for our selves—that can aid and guide in our katabatic return to ourselves with the rising sun after a hard and hungry night's toil among the smoke and spectres.

BIBLIOGRAPHY

British Library MS Additional 36674

Heinrich Cornelius Agrippa, *Three Books of Occult Philosophy* (London, 1651)

An Excellent Booke of the Arte of Magicke, ed. by Phil Legard & Alexander Cummins (Scarlet Imprint, 2020)

John Aubrey, *Miscellanies* (London, 1696)

W. Paley Baildon, 'Sixteenth Century Leaden Charm (obverse and reverse) found at Lincoln's Inn', *Proceedings of the Society of Antiquarians of* London, Second Series, 18, (1901)

Jim Baker, *The Cunning-Man's Handbook: The Practice of English Folk Magic 1550-1900* (Avalonia, 2013)

Thomas Blout, *A World of Errors Discovered in the New World of Words* (London, 1676)

Thomas Blout, *Glossographia or, A dictionary interpreting all such hard words of whatsoever language now used in our refined English tongue with etymologies, definitions and historical observations on the same: also the terms of divinity, law, physick, mathematicks and other arts and sciences explicated* (London, 1661)

The Book of Oberon, ed. Daniel Harms, James R. Clark, & Joseph H. Peterson (Llewellyn, 2015)

Theo Brown, *The Fate of the Dead: A Study in Folk Eschatology in the West Country after the Reformation* (Folklore Society, 1979)

Jon Butler, 'Magic, Astrology, and the Early American Religious Heritage, 1600-1760', *The American Historical Review* 84, 2 (1979)

A Collection of Magical Secrets Taken from Peter de Abano, Cornelius Agrippa and from other Famous Occult Philosophers, ed. by David Rankine, Paul Harry Barron & Stephen Skinner (Avalonia, 2009)

Alexander Cummins, 'The Azured Vault: Astrological Magic in Seventeenth-century England', in *The Celestial Art*, ed. Austin Coppock and Daniel Schulke (Three Hands Press, 2018)

Alexander Cummins, 'The Black Art Books of Cyprian, Pt. II: A Svartkonstbok Exhortation', http://www.alexandercummins.com/blog/blackartbooks2, last accessed 26/12/19

Alexander Cummins, 'In the Manner of Saint Cyprian': A Cyprianic Black Magic of Early Modern English Grimoires, in *Cypriana: Old World*, ed. by Alexander Cummins, Jesse Hathaway Diaz, & Jennifer Zahrt (Revelore Press, 2017)

Alexander Cummins, 'Textual Evidence for the Material History of Amulets in Seventeenth-Century England', in Ronald Hutton (ed.), *Physical Evidence for Ritual Acts, Sorcery and Witchcraft in Christian Britain: A Feeling for Magic* (Palgrave Macmillan, 2015)

Marsilio Ficino, *Three Books on Life*, trans. Carol Kaske & John R. Clark (Tempe, 1998)

Robert Fludd, *Doctor Fludds Answer unto M. Foster or, The Squeezing of Parson Fosters Sponge, ordained by him for the wiping away of the Weapon-Salve* (London, 1631)

Fourth Book of Occult Philosophy, trans. Robert Turner (London, 1655: 1665)

Stephen Gordon, 'Necromancy for the Masses? A Printed Version of the *Compendium magiae innaturalis nigrae*', *Magic, Ritual, and Witchcraft* 13, 3 (Winter, 2018)

John Michael Greer, *Art and Practice of Geomancy: Divination, Magic, and Earth Wisdom of the Renaissance* (Weiser, 2009)

Grimoire of Arthur Gauntlet: A 17th century London Cunning-man's book of charms, conjurations and prayers, ed. David Rankine (Avalonia, 2011)

John Heydon, *Theomagia, or the Temple of Wisdom* (London, 1664)

Thomas K. Johnson, *Svartkonstböcker: A Compendium of Swedish Black Art Book Tradition* (Revelore Press, 2019)

William Lilly, *Christian Astrology* (London, 1647)

William Lilly, *History of his Life and Time, from the year 1602 to 1681* (London, 1715)

James Mason, *The Anatomie of Sorcerie VVherein the wicked impietie of charmers, inchanters, and such like, is discouered and confuted* (London, 1612)

Sophie Page, 'Speaking with Spirits in Medieval Magic Texts', in *Conversations with Angels: Essays Towards a History of Spiritual Communication, 1100-1700*, ed. by Joan Raymond (Palgrave Macmillan: New York, 2011)

Joseph H. Peterson, ed. & trans., *Grimorium Verum: A Handbook of Black Magic*, (CreateSpace Independent Publishing Platform, 2007)

Picatrix, ed. John Michael Greer & Christopher Warnock (Adocentyn Press, 2010)

Reginald Scot, *Discoverie of Witchcraft* (London, 1584: 1665)

John Smith, *Christian Religion's Appeal From the Groundless Prejudices of the Sceptick* (London, 1675)

ADVERTISEMENTS

GUIDES TO THE UNDERWORLD
Hadean's collection of pamphlets for the discerning reader.
WWW.HADEANPRESS.COM

THE OCCULT CONSULTANCY
.Rootwork and conjure services. .spiritual and magical supplies.
.readings. .consultations.
WWW.THEOCCULTCONSULTANCY.COM

Midian Books
Rare, secondhand and selected new books on occult subjects.

www.midianbooks.co.uk

AYNBATH

Read anything for free and subscribe at:
www.aynbath.com

Finely bound journals and grimoires

Archival clamshell boxes

Rebinding services

Bindery & Book Arts
Est. 2013
McCall Co.

IG: @mccall_company
mccallcobindery.com

I am Adam Darkly, a Professional Sorcerer & Card Reader, a practicing Alchemist & Animist. Everyday I help clients all over the world shift their fortunes, repair a relationship or charm a lover, expand their fortunes & open their roads to success, and more. I have over 12 years of experience working in Folk Magic & Sorcery.

I employ many tricks of the trade when I work for clients. This includes lamp & candle magic, the formulating of cleansing baths or holy anointing oils, petitioning Gods & spirits, travelling in spirit to a location to gather info on a target, communing with my spirits & the Dead to seek their counsel, and more.

Devil's Conjure is the living embodiment of the Devil, of my own treading of the Serpent Road, a manifestation of my destiny, a vehicle for my own gifts, and the birthing of products ensouled by the pneuma of many Hags & Devils, Fae & Dead into this world.

Every oil & amulet is a vessel of the many spirits who lend their power to these creations. Every bath, incense, ritual powder, a formulation of momentum, of formidable power, for victory & glory, or lust & domination.

Devil's Conjure is the very crossroads between this world and all others, a force of liberation & revolution, of healing & sovereignty. And day by day, IT grows, stretching forth into the world, its roots deep in the heavens and hells.
You can book Ritual Magic & Divination, or shop my wicked offerings at Devilsconjure.ecwid.com!

Lightning Source UK Ltd.
Milton Keynes UK
UKHW052205011122
411463UK00005B/46